BILATERAL DIPLOMACY

Words of Appreciation

'The book is the fruit not only of the author's long and varied diplomatic experience but also of his teaching in Malta and, most recently, on a Commonwealth assignment at the Ministry of Foreign Affairs in Windhoek, Namibia.

The first part of the book deals with the purposes of bilateral diplomacy and has some emphasis on commerce, finance and aid. The second deals with institutions: the MFA, embassies and consulates, joint commissions and other groups, and bilateral summits. And the third covers methods: diplomatic reports, cross-cultural sensitivity, diplomatic signalling, negotiating, and performance enhancement. In the long conclusion, the author pulls together the threads of his theme. This is that the resident embassy is more important than ever, not least because so many "home-based actors" are now involved in bilateral relationships that only the embassy is in a position even to approximate to a grasp of the complete picture. Not surprisingly, he concludes, we are witnessing a "renaissance" of bilateral diplomacy.

Kishan Rana's insistence on the importance of bilateral diplomacy is not only compelling because of the force and elegance of his reasoning but also because he is no dinosaur striving to conjure up a lost world. On the contrary, his book oozes the language of modernity and has no hesitation in claiming that diplomats have much to learn from "business management methodology". As a teaching book, the style and presentation are also very good. It is lucid and economical, points are generally enumerated, examples are often amusing, and chapters are rounded off with a list of questions to stir student thinking. It has a good index. . . . It conveys the author's enormous enthusiasm for his subject.

. . . . I recommend it most warmly.'

Professor GR Berridge, Professor Emeritus, University of Leicester, http://www.grberridge.co.uk/

'Although obviously based on the author's personal experience, the discussion ranges over the experience of many countries and is free of any special pleading or national bias. The chapter on performance includes a discussion on the German as well as the American inspection system, French ambassadors' instructions, U.S. "Mission Program Plans", British experimentation with corporate techniques, and Singapore's "cutting-edge administrative concepts".

It would indeed be useful . . . for orientation background for political appointees to the State Department (Department appointments as well as ambassadors) and the interested general public. It would also benefit media contacts, many of which obviously do not believe that knowledge of diplomacy theory and practice is a requirement for writing about those subjects.'

Ambassador Edward Marks, *Foreign Service Journal*, September 2002

BILATERAL DIPLOMACY

Kishan S. Rana

Manas Publications
New Delhi - 110002 (INDIA)

MANAS PUBLICATIONS
(Publishers, Distributors, Importers & Exporters)
4402/5-A, Ansari Road (Opp. HDFC Bank)
Darya Ganj, New Delhi - 110 002 (India)
Phones: Off.: 011-23260783, 23265523,
Res.: 011-23842660
E-mail: manaspublications@gmail.com
manaspub6@gmail.com
www.manaspublications.in

New Impression 2016

ISBN 978-81-7049-154-5 (13 digits)
81-7049-154-1 (10 digits)

Rs. 450/-

Designed at
Manas Publications

Printed in India at
R.K. Printers, Delhi
and published by Mrs Suman Lata for
Manas Publications, 4402/5-A,
Ansari Road (Opp HDFC Bank),
Darya Ganj, New Delhi - 110002 (INDIA)

For Mimi

Contents

PART III METHODS

Acknowledgements

My first thanks go to Jovan Kurbalija, with whom a fortuitous meeting in March 2000 has led to friendship, and my involvement in the activities of the DiploFoundation. He and distinguished diplomacy teacher, Professor Dietrich Kaeppler of Geneva, have strongly encouraged the writing of this material. I am also indebted to Professor Geoff Berridge, eminent diplomacy historian and diplomacy guru, who as an academic has placed a strong focus on practice-oriented scholarship, and done much to bridge the chasm between the theorist and the practitioner. My thanks also go to Aldo Matteucci, formerly Deputy Secretary General of EFTA, and now colleague and collaborator at the DiploFoundation. I am also grateful to Ambassador Kamal Bakshi for his generous help.

Deep thanks also to Priya Rana, stern critic and copy editor, wno has spent many hours revising the text and suggesting changes. And special gratitude to my wife Mimi for bearing the brunt of the author's moods, and offering the stability and calm that one often takes for granted. I dedicate the book to them and to the rest of the Rana family, Ajit, Deepika, Suneira, and Karnavir, our little Tembo.

November 23, 2001

Introduction

Why Bilateral Relations?

This collection of lectures began as material prepared for a post-graduate diploma program run by the DiploFoundation of the Mediterranean Academy of Diplomatic Studies, Malta, where in January 2001, Jovan Kurbalija, directing the program, asked me to handle a module on building bilateral relations. At the same time, during my 6-month Commonwealth assignment at the Ministry of Foreign Affairs in Windhoek, Namibia, a training program for desk officers was organized there with the support of the DiploFoundation, and the same module was utilized, with some adaptation.

The experience from these activities has reinforced my impression, based on a 35-year career in the Indian Foreign Service, that both in the operation of foreign ministries and in diplomacy training, bilateral relationship building is taken for granted. Professional diplomats tend to view it as a set of techniques and skills that are assimilated without narration, and expect that new entrants routinely learn these from their mentors, the ambassadors and the senior diplomats with whom they work at missions abroad and in foreign ministries. Admittedly, apprenticeship is the best learning method in this profession. As Michael Oakeshott pointed out in a seminal work long back, diplomacy belongs to the category of practical knowledge, and 'it exists only in practice '.[1] Oakeshott also affirmed that 'the only way to acquire it (this knowledge) is by apprenticeship to a master'. But the pedagogic diplomacy training tradition of 40 years in many countries, and the operation of 55 foreign service training institutes either run directly by diplomatic services or on behalf of foreign ministries, challenges that viewpoint. Countries such as France, Singapore, UK, and US provide little or no initial training to new recruits but apply them directly to work, either in the foreign ministry or in embassies abroad. In contrast Austria, China, Germany, India, South Africa and a host of others run structured entry training programs of around a year in duration. And all countries run extensive mid-career training programs, or send diplomats to attend courses run by foreign institutions.

There are standard methods that need to be set out in descriptive form, and learnt in training programs. These create a frame of reference, within which the individual diplomat's accumulation of personal observation and experience becomes easier.

The audience targeted by this book includes students of diplomacy at academic institutions who are interested in practical issues, and particularly young diplomats who are under training, or at the early phase of their careers. Perhaps the bilateral relationship methodology that is set out here will find a stronger echo among those who have worked on at least one assignment in an embassy abroad, and/or have experience in the operation of foreign ministries. I believe the book fills a gap that exists in the teaching materials used in diplomatic training academies.

The book may also be of interest to observers of international relations, as a practical guide to relation building among states. It may offer a dose of realism to those more accustomed to the theory and analysis of great events, to consider the operational setting of the profession in real environments.

THE CONTEXT

What is likely to be the defining characteristic in the way countries conduct relations with one another in the 21st century? Will the diplomatic process of the next several decades resemble all that we have witnessed since the end of World War II, during what may be the called the post-colonial era and the Cold War years, or will it be something quite different?

Let us consider the evidence before us. The world is characterized by deep disquiet in the months immediately following the terrorist attacks of September 11, 2001 on New York and Washington DC, which has forced every state to reassess its domestic and external vulnerability. In time, we may come to regard the world as it was before this date as an age of innocence. These events have created an unprecedented global coalition against terrorism, and the first war of the 21st century. We also witness many other intertwined and complex factors that affect the way states deal with one another. From a practitioner's perspective, the following elements are relevant as we try and assess the shape of diplomacy in the years ahead.

First, the international system of nation-states is with us for now and is unlikely to change. Decolonization took the number of UN member-states from 50 at San Francisco in 1945 to over 160, and the 1990 breakup of the Soviet Union and the upheavals in former Yugoslavia have raised the number to 190. Barring the unforeseen splintering of other states, we may expect the number to remain stable. The European Union, as an unparalleled process of political engineering, is unlikely to abolish the concept of member-state sovereignty, even while the process of integration and outward expansion into East and Southern Europe continues over this decade. Even while notions of a 'federation' are debated, it seems destined for now to remain a 'Europe of States' as the majority view seems to insist. Diplomatic dealings between autonomous states will thus remain for the foreseeable future as the first—but far from exclusive—component of the international relations system. One scholar has wryly noted: 'Diplomats are embedded in the world of sovereign-territorial states.'[2] But as evidence shows, there is considerable learning ahead for them, to take on board the multiple non-state dimensions that have gained ground.

Second, the post-Cold War world order remains in flux. Unipolarity, with domination by the US as the sole superpower, has acquired a new assertive edge in the aftermath of the September 11 terrorism. Awesome power to exert military force in any corner of the world faces the paradox of vulnerability in the homeland, against amorphous adversaries who do not fit the pattern of the international state system and do not play by the rules at all. In our globalized, 'wired' and super-efficient world of interdependence, it was axiomatic that technology was supreme and unlimited prosperity was assured for the winners of globalization. But powerful countries find themselves woefully ill-equipped against the formless terrorist operating on the fringes, fueled only by visceral hatred. Will the global anti-terrorism coalition and its first successes in Afghanistan, at the end of November 2001, represent the definitive emergence of a single unified alliance structure? Or will the trend evidenced since 1991 of economics-driven poly-centrism, and incipient multi-polarity return, with the European Union, Russia, Japan, China—and India—sometimes pulling in their own directions?

In such an unpredictable international situation, questions outnumber the answers. Each state seeks to maximize its international options, building networks of friends and cooperation partners in its neighborhood, region and with major and medium powers located afar. Pluri-directional diplomacy is one option that each state pursues as a high priority, to insulate itself from uncertainty and potential insecurity. Economic interest, and the need for export markets reinforces this trend. It means among other things a strong push for bilateral diplomacy, and based on this, intense networking among states working to establish coalitions and interest groups. We are also sure to see a clustering process among states that is issue-determined, shifting as events develop. This too makes for a stronger emphasis on building affinities with states that share similar interests.

Third, multilateral diplomacy through the UN and other international organizations now becomes even more urgent than before. Regional structures too look more attractive than ever, as a means of leveraging assets, and providing an influence-multiplier platform. Take the situation in Africa, after decades of marginalization, and the fear of becoming a victim of globalization. In mid-2001 the continental organization OAU has made a leap of faith towards the advanced concept of an 'African Union'. Outside observers may view this as premature, but their political decision to overlook the many existing intercine conflicts, and work for this dream, is driven by the same urge to find strength in unity, and carve a larger place on the global stage. We may anticipate thus an accentuation of multilateral diplomacy.

As a decade earlier, in the aftermath of the successful UN-led coalition of the Gulf War, there had been a push for international 'peace making' as a means of preventing conflict, and after the current phase of the war on terrorism we may expect a like demand to emerge. But the zeal of the moment will surely pass, and a reluctance to take on engagements in distant lands, on issues unrelated to one's own national interests must re-emerge. With this one may expect a reassertion of inherently divergent self-interests of different states, and a gradual whittling down of the existing war coalition.

Fourth, within virtually all countries, international affairs attract greater domestic attention and participation. It is a truism that a state's external profile is a function of domestic capacity and performance, and this has always been the case. But now there are new elements. The entry of new subjects in the inter-state dialogue means that virtually every agency of the government is engaged in external contacts. The partition between domestic and external affairs has largely evaporated. Public opinion is deeply concerned with foreign issues that are perceived as vital to national interests. Organizations of civil society of many different shades are enmeshed in foreign affairs, forcing foreign ministries to practice internal diplomacy and outreach—which in turn calls for new mindsets of inclusiveness and transparency. Diplomacy systems traditionally accustomed to isolation from public accountability, save in the formal settings of parliament or measured information doses for the media, are forced to learn public outreach skills. In India we see this in the passions that WTO issues arouse, the level of public engagement in the proceedings of the Doha Ministerial Conference of mid-November 2001, and the inclusion of non-governmental stakeholders in the official delegation to that trade conference. Governments also find that in areas such as economic diplomacy they must sometimes bargain with foreign private firms to secure their interests. An example is a company such as Standard & Poor, whose 'country rating' index determines interest rates that a country has to pay for external commercial borrowing, as also that country's attractiveness for portfolio investments from abroad.

Of course, the influence of internal public opinion is uneven among states. Having to answer to domestic critics is irritating for governments, but it is an aspect of a democratization process that touches also states that are not practicing democracies. It takes the shape of emergence of 'foreign affairs communities', investigative journalism, and feedback from the media into policy. Networking among non-state participants across the globe, aided by Internet communications, helps this process.

Fifth, continuous transformation in information technology and communications affects the way states deal with one another, especially when these changes interconnect with other factors. For example, 'hypertext' as an application of Internet has been around for some years. The twin pressure of disruptive demonstrations by combative NGOs led by anti-globalization zealots (as witnessed at the WTO meetings of Seattle in December 1999, and the G-8 Summit in Genoa in July 2001), and reluctance by many to travel abroad excessively owing to the dangers of terrorism, has forced change. International agencies like the World Bank are shifting a part of conference negotiations to 'distance' hypertext-based dialogue via the Internet.

Generally diplomatic systems have been slow to adapt to new methods (with notable exceptions like Australia, Canada and some European states). Perhaps that is beginning to change. It may well be that some diplomatic functions will evolve with technology. Service tasks, like visa issue, and the handling of routine commercial, tourism or general queries that do not require direct local contact, actually resemble the 'back-office' work of corporations and could be shifted to home capitals, or even farmed out to service-providers. But as detailed later, technology and instant communication have added to the work and value of embassies, not diminished them.

Sixth, linked with the above, some other diplomatic tasks may also change. An experienced German diplomat has written: 'Most of the negotiation functions that once devolved upon the ambassador have disappeared. But at the same time the tasks of presentation and interpretation have grown, to an equal or even larger extent.'[3] Corporate methods are now being applied to public service and diplomacy is not an exception. We could see other changes, like a reduced 'representational' role for embassies and for ambassadors (perhaps even the giving up of prestigious and expensive official residences and some of the other outwardly ostentatious paraphernalia), and a tighter focus on country marketing. What is unlikely to be reduced is the need for outreach and promotion to the many constituencies in the countries of assignment that is possible only through personal relationship building. Politics remains the foundation of inter-state ties. With this caveat, economics will be an even bigger driver of day-to-day work, together with a multitude of new subjects. In handling these, the diplomat as a generalist-multi-specialist will be needed as the communicator, bridge-builder, and the one responsible for finding interconnections, and creating leverages that have to be used to project state interests.

Seventh, the embassy has become the co-manager of bilateral relationships. There is simply no agency of government—not even the 'country director' or equivalent at the foreign ministry—that has a better overview of the totality of relations in any foreign capital. Modern communication makes is easy to treat the ambassador and his team as stakeholders for continual consultation at every stage of the policy development process.

In sum, we are at the cusp of a renaissance of bilateral diplomacy, not at the cost of multilateral and regional focus, but as a vital activity in its own right in the pursuit of state interests. It is also the indispensable building block for these wider forms of the craft.

There are two major hypotheses that this book advances, the strengthening of the need for bilateral diplomacy, and this new responsibility of the resident embassy. These are the threads that run through this collection of lectures. May I venture to submit that how well this is recognized and accepted by foreign ministries will determine in part the success of their diplomacy?

GOOD GOVERNANCE

Former Canadian diplomat and editor of a fine collection of essays on foreign ministries in developing and emerging countries, Justin Robertson, has highlighted an oft-overlooked point about diplomacy[4]—that externally funded technical aid projects have seldom covered the foreign ministry and the diplomatic system as a legitimate object for capacity-enhancement and institution-building. He has written: 'Development administration in concept and practice has tended to bypass the foreign ministry.' Yet, the notion should not be difficult to accept that a good system of foreign policy management and projection of external interests is as much a 'public good' as any other service provided by governments. In fact donor countries' multilateral institutions should have a self-interest in this arena, since it relates directly to cooperation between states. It could well be that a misplaced sense of reticence, or sensitivity, has led donors to treat the foreign ministry as an agency where offers of external aid are inappropriate. Developing countries have also been inhibited in articulating demand for foreign assistance to improve efficiency. While bilateral aid in this sector has an obvious disadvantage (i.e. giving another country undue access to the foreign policy process), there are multilateral funding and technical aid sources that can be used to advantage.[5]

Sensitivity apart, diplomacy is an arena where the playing field can be easily leveled, to produce a substantial advantage for developing countries. If the nations of the South negotiate better, and protect their external interests more efficiently, they have something to gain. And if foreign ministries can learn the ways they enhance their relevance in the entire governmental system, better integrating external and domestic work, and adding better value for the other ministries, the country as a whole is the immediate beneficiary. This can easily be done, provided the diplomatic apparatus shifts to a mindset that is focused not on the privileges of foreign service and the monopoly of the foreign ministry as the 'gatekeeper' to external contacts, but as a service provider to other government and non-official agencies. One begins by accepting that they are all partners in external affairs, and that the foreign ministry is not a monopolist! These are some concrete aspects of the issue that are examined in this book.

Another dimension is performance enhancement for the foreign ministry (MFA) and its subsidiary agencies, led by the embassy. Brian Hocking is the author of a definitive study on foreign ministries.[6] But even this major study leaves out a comparison of MFAs in the ways they perform, and the steps they actually undertake as deliberate performance enhancement measures. A preliminary approach to this complex issue is provided in the penultimate chapter in this book. It is not easy to collate the relevant information, and the methods are under continuous evolution. There are surely some omissions as well. Nevertheless it is interesting to trace the different methods that countries are deploying to tackle this common issue.

The data gathered reinforces the wider conclusion that diplomatic systems seldom engage in deliberate emulation, or even study the methods used by others. In any other business such activity would be called 'bench-marking', and undertaken routinely. One major exception are the EU states that have recently included foreign ministry administration and systems within the ambit of regular dialogue that is carried out between specialists in different fields. The result is that a process of mutual observation and learning is taking place, where some good ideas from the French and the British, for instance, are percolating to other EU members. It is one small indicator of the breadth of the EU's unification effort. Another country that has used bench-marking is Australia, where a close examination of methods used in several other foreign ministries was carried out by the combined Ministry of External Affairs and Foreign Trade one year back.

NICHE DIPLOMACY

Alan K. Henrikson's article 'Diplomacy and Small States'[7] is a brilliant survey of the methods open to small states to carve out a distinctive role for themselves in the international state system. The issue has also figured in another study focused on middle powers, edited by Andrew F. Cooper, *Niche Diplomacy: Middle Powers After the Cold War* (Macmillan, London, 1998). The approach in both these studies has been to identify methods and activity areas where the international system offers the best prospects for small or middle states to project their own identity and pursue national interests in a dynamic manner. Cooper has noted that in the post-Cold War era middle powers 'have enhanced maneuver space to widen the repertoire of activity'. They are able to better play both the role of catalysts (generating political activity aimed at a particular issue) and that of facilitators (planning and hosting meetings, and setting priorities).

This subject goes beyond the immediate field of building

bilateral relationships, though once states have identified their niche, they are able to target those bilateral partners that are appropriate to that niche, and carry forward one's interests in that chosen sector. For instance, if marine resources are a vital resource for one's country and the law of the seas is the chosen focus area, it becomes essential to develop close ties with those states that have the expertise and/or long-term interest, by virtue of their geographic situation, experience or long-term interest in that sector (e.g. Jamaica, Malta, and Singapore). I fully endorse the contention of the specialists who recommend niche diplomacy, that more states should consider such options.

NOTES

1. Michael Oakeshott, *Rationalism in Politics* (Methuen, London, 1962).
2. Richard Falk, in *Knowledge and Diplomacy,* ed. Jovan Kurbalija and Hannah Slavic (Mediterranean Academy of Diplomatic Studies, Malta, 1998).
3. Bernt von Standen, German Secretary of State and former Ambassador to Washington DC, writing in *The Modern Ambassador: The Challenge and the Search,* edited by Martin Herz (Institute for the Study of Diplomacy, Georgetown University, Washington DC, 1983).
4. Justin Robertson, ed., *Foreign Ministries in Developing Countries and Emerging Market Economies* (Halifax, International Insights: Dalhousie Journal of International Affairs, Volume 14, Summer, 1998).
5. This comment is made independent of my work in Namibia in the Foreign Ministry as a Commonwealth Adviser, but I should add that in fact the receptivity and functional hospitality—and personal kindness—extended to me in Windhoek by Namibian Foreign Ministry professionals and other personalities, has reinforced my conviction that such technical cooperation projects can function well. The Commonwealth Secretariat has taken some initiatives elsewhere too, but I am not aware of the work of other agencies in this sector.
6. Brian Hocking, ed., *Foreign Ministries: Change and Adaptation* (Macmillan, London, 1999). The description of the old and outdated

role of the foreign ministry as a 'gatekeeper' used in the previous paragraph is borrowed from his book; the contemporary role that Prof. Hocking ascribes to the MFA is that of coordinator.

7. Alan K. Henrikson, *Diplomacy and Small States in Today's World*, Twelfth Lecture, The Dr. Eric Williams Memorial Lecture Series, University of Miami, May 22, 1998 (Central bank of Trinidad and Tobago, Port-of-Spain, 1998).

PART I

PURPOSES

1

A Framework for Relations

Practical diplomacy demonstrates that states act in a pragmatic way, pursuing short-term interests as well as long-term objectives in their external relations, interacting with other states. Ethical and normative principles are blended into what is essentially the country's pursuit of self-interest. Scholars studying international relations theory have developed sophisticated, and sometimes complicated, concepts that interpret the behavior of states. A summary of current ideas in international relations theory is given in an extended endnote below.[1]

INTERNATIONAL RELATIONS

A fundamental objective for all countries is to build strong external partnerships around the world, to create a network of friends and allies. In an interdependent world, these ties are essential for the pursuit of one's own interests. These interests cover national security (i.e. safety and survival of the state in all circumstances), as also political, economic, and other benefits, extending to fields such as culture, education, the environment, science & technology, tourism, and the like. States pursue self-interests in an enlightened manner for the most part, seeking to maximize their own gain, but in a way that is also to the advantage of the other partners, since this is the only way to build sustainable relationships. The strengthening of international law in recent years also supports the thesis that norms of international behavior are more widely accepted today, and enforced by the international community, than at any time in the past. We are not in a Hobbesian situation of jungle anarchy, or survival of the fittest. For the most part, diplomacy is not a zero sum gain, in that the advantage of one does not come at the cost of the other, and in most situations, both partners stand to profit. One of Indira Gandhi's favorite expressions was to liken country relationships to the care and nurturing of a plant—that it required the same kind of attention and long-term effort. The analogy is apt.

Over the past four decades or so, there has been an upsurge in multilateral diplomacy. This has been a consequence of the expansion in the community of states and growth in numbers of international organizations, as also the strong emergence of disarmament, economic and social development, international trade, the environment, terrorism and many other issues in the global dialogue. The importance of multilateral diplomacy, and its associated 'summitry', for the settlement of a wide range of issues through global and regional discussions, is an undeniable fact. But to some extent this preoccupation has led to a loss of focus on bilateral relationships, the basic building block in international relations. It is the author's contention that many countries tend to take for granted the work of building country or bilateral relations; all the tools and concepts available for this task have not been given full play. It is possible that in the post-Cold War world, in the absence of a master matrix of competing alliance structures, there will be renewed attention to the bilateral dimension of diplomacy. It is certainly overdue!

A STATE'S DIPLOMATIC PROFILE

The distinction between 'diplomacy' and 'foreign policy' is important. Diplomacy, as the word is used in this book, refers to the way in which a given foreign policy is executed by the foreign ministry (MFA) and implemented on the ground by professional diplomats (who used to be called 'diplomatists', before the term went out of currency, to distinguish them from those who may engage in 'diplomatic' behavior without being professionals in this field). One way of presenting the distinction is to visualize foreign policy as the strategy and diplomacy as the tactics. An experienced British diplomat, Peter Marshall, has written: 'Foreign policy is about what to do and diplomacy is about how to do it.'[2]

How might one view the diplomatic profile of a country? One way is to examine it in terms of its relative **character** and its **focus**. These values can be plotted against a simple graph. There are other criteria that can be used to describe the diplomatic profile. Among the criteria that can be considered are: 'Professionalism' and 'Global Outlook'; or 'Attachment to Rule of Law' and 'Credibility as a Partner'. Such analysis plots the behavior of countries in the international arena, and offers a comparative perspective when we use the same device to visualize the profile of other countries. Of course, such empirical study is based on past action, and can serve only as a rough guide for portraying the character of the state. It does not pretend to offer a reliable indicator of future actions.

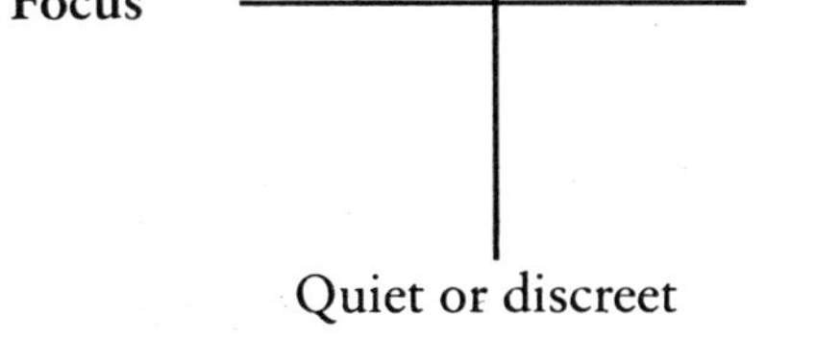

In his book *Diplomacy for the New Century,* Abba Eban[3] has quoted noted Arab historian Ibn Khaldun of Tunisia who observed in the 14th century: 'No social phenomena should be judged by analogy with other phenomena, for if it is similar to them in certain respects, it may yet differ in many others.' In the study of diplomacy, excessive reliance on analogy can lead to serious error. Because a state behaved in a particular way in the past may suggest that in a new situation it may react in a like manner; but the totality of circumstance is never identical. If one relies too much on the past as a guide, and fails to consider the totality of the present situation, one may draw the wrong surmise.

NATURE OF RELATIONSHIPS

From the perspective of one's own state, the potential offered by different foreign states for fruitful partnership, in quality, breadth and depth, and mutual advantage varies from country to country depending on the specifics of each situation. In a very rough way, one may divide countries into three broad clusters—those with whom **special relations** subsist, those with whom **normal ties** are maintained, and those that are of relatively **peripheral interest**.

- ❑ **Special.** The first group usually includes immediate neighbors with whom strong political, security or economic links are customary. For a country like Namibia, such a group may include South Africa, Angola, and the Democratic Republic of Congo, as also Botswana and Zimbabwe, even while the priority attached to each at any time is variable. Singapore regards Indonesia and Malaysia as its most vital partners. Other nations may include in their own special list the US, because of its global reach as the sole superpower. A Francophone country would feature France in its list of special partners, by virtue of typically exceptional links or even an actual situation of dependence. There may be other factors such as religion or ideology that may produce close affinity. In each case, bilateral relationships are handled in ways that are not duplicated elsewhere. One characteristic can be a special mechanism for high-level consultation. The leaders of France and Germany meet at bilateral summits every 6 months. US and Canada have a similar mechanism. Namibia and South Africa have a 'Joint Mechanism' for quarterly meetings of Presidents, accompanied by cabinet ministers, to tackle shared economic projects and other major issues. Relationship building among such countries is highly intensive, using exceptional mechanisms that may involve major agencies of the government and non-state institutions. There is also usually a special method of monitoring such relationships that goes beyond the foreign ministry, involving the cabinet and frequently the heads of state and government as well. The MFA desk officer dealing with such countries has a major task in liaising with different ministries, playing the coordinator role, as feasible. And the mission accredited to such a country is invariably under close scrutiny at home from the highest quarters.

- **Normal.** This covers a broad cluster, with wide variations from top to bottom. A common feature is a sustained use of all the customary diplomatic avenues to develop linkages, mostly without resort to exceptional measures. But innovative methods for advancing interests have good potential here, when used with discretion and balance. Example: joint commissions or an equivalent mechanism for bilateral consultation is often established, but the practical use made of these devices varies. Both the territorial division in the MFA and the mission have ample scope to practice 'integrated' diplomacy, acting as coordinators and as 'value-adders' for the other government agencies involved in the relationship. Often the economic content of such relationships is sizable and acts as a determining element in the relative priority each gives to the other. One pre-requisite for 'normal' relations is that the countries have extended diplomatic recognition to each other, and also recognize each other's governments. They are then said be 'in diplomatic relations', even if resident diplomatic missions are not exchanged. One might add here that even the extreme step of 'breaking diplomatic relations', if and when it happens, does not mean withdrawing recognition from either the state or the government, and usually also keeps intact their 'consular relationships'.

- **Peripheral**. No one of course likes to have his country described by another as belonging to such a list. (One recalls the furor that arose in UK in 1968–69 when a Foreign Office review, the Duncan Report, gave this appellation to countries in Asia and Africa while recommending a complete revision of external goals.) But it is a reality in a global community of 190 states that there are many countries that lie 'beyond the horizon', in terms of partnership utility. It may also be that potential for cooperation, in terms of density of economic and other exchanges, is undeveloped and perhaps awaits exploitation. In such situations, the main relationship building task is 'to keep the pot warm', to carry out friendly exchanges whenever opportunity arises. This can happen when delegations visit the region, or if there is no permanent diplomatic representation, via the intermediary of the permanent missions of the respective countries at the UN, or through encounters at international conferences. Special emissaries may be sent when warranted—such as mobilizing support on an issue of vital importance. Or the country is covered through concurrent accreditation, or a 'non-resident' ambassador. Trade and other exchanges are nevertheless encouraged, and in a dynamic process, one may 'graduate' the relationship to a higher level when circumstances warrant.

An alternative to the above approach is a yardstick suggested by noted US diplomat Joseph S. Nye.[4] This divides countries into those that are a threat to one's survival; those that threaten one's interests but not survival; and finally those that affect one's interests, without threatening them. Such criteria relate to a security perspective, rather than relation building.

The bulk of the methodology sketched in this book relates to the 'normal' bilateral relationship. The clear understanding is that in actual practice the level of cultivation implemented will depend on circumstance. In contrast, when countries handle their 'special' relationships with particular states, virtually all the methods outlined here will usually be involved, besides other intensive techniques as well.

CHANGES IN DIPLOMACY

The 1961 Vienna Convention on Diplomatic Relations, the definitive legal framework for diplomacy that consolidated the accumulated practices of earlier times, states in Article 3:

> 1. The functions of a diplomatic mission consist *inter alia* in:
>   (a) representing the sending State in the receiving State;
>   (b) protecting in the receiving State the interests of the sending State and of its nationals, within the limits permitted by international law;
>   (c) negotiation with the Government of the receiving State;
>   (d) ascertaining by all lawful means conditions and developments in the receiving State, and reporting thereon to the Government of the sending State;
>   (e) promoting friendly relations between the sending State and the receiving State, and developing their economic, cultural, and scientific relations.
> 2. Nothing in the present Convention shall be construed as preventing the performance of consular functions by a diplomatic mission.

The key words are: **representing**, **protecting**, **negotiating**, **ascertaining** and **promoting**. The definition is useful, but evokes a less than proactive image of the tasks involved. It does not capture the full focus and intensity of contemporary diplomatic activities. In her superb analysis of the Vienna Convention, Eileen Denza notes that initially only the four classic functions of 'representation, protection, negotiation and observation' were proposed as the functions of diplomatic missions, and 'promotion' was added at the demand of three member-states (the Philippines, Czechoslovakia and Yugoslavia). Taking into account the evolution in diplomacy in the past 40 years, we need a better definition to portray contemporary work.

During the period that some regard as a classic era of diplomacy, the inter-War years of 1919–39,[5] the prime task of the ambassador and his mission was 'negotiation'. The works of Sir Harold Nicholson, the doyen of diplomatic writing, bear testimony to the way that this concept was implemented at that time. But if we fast-forward to the 21st century, we find that much has changed. Take, for example, the European Union—the most advanced model of political re-engineering that the world has seen, covering the existing 15 members, that is set to grow to over 25 or 27 countries in this decade. Virtually all negotiation responsibility among the members has passed from the bilateral diplomatic missions to the collective entity, the European Commission and the EU Council of Ministers. Negotiations involve not just the foreign ministry but also the line ministries, who have become autonomous in handling their own external affairs.

Yet, if we use the term 'negotiation' in its broadest sense, all dialogue is some kind of negotiation, whether in diplomacy, or in social or personal life! But in looking to diplomacy as practiced today in most countries and regions around the world, negotiation, in the narrow or classic sense remains important, but it is no longer the central task of diplomats. There are several reasons.

A. In most countries, the functional or 'line' ministries tend to handle their own negotiations; even when representatives of foreign ministries and embassies are included in delegations they do not lead. (The Japanese Foreign Ministry recently gave up its unique insistence on leading all delegations.) Partly this is on account of the technical nature of many issues, but it also has much to do with the changed role of the foreign ministry—it is now more the 'coordinator' of external relations, rather than the 'exclusive channel'.

B. The multilateral system has grown extensively, unlike in the past (during the years between the two World Wars, when the League of Nations proved ineffective and bilateral diplomacy became a prominent discipline). The UN Charter provides both a conceptual and operational framework for cooperative relationships among states, as do also the other multilateral institutions that bring countries together, ranging from the Non-Aligned Movement, the OAU, and all the varied regional groupings of states, to WTO and the like. Negotiating peace, or guaranteeing harmonious cooperation is no longer left to each state to work out on its own. Even in exceptional situations of tension and conflict, diplomacy now operates within set and established laws and rules.
C. For many countries, basic agreements covering most typical cooperation sectors already exist, and save in frontier areas (like the environment, or new technology), the challenge lies more in the implementation, than in the drawing up of new agreements and protocols.

There are other priorities that have emerged, replacing the former centrality of negotiation. The diplomat of yesteryear dealt primarily with the foreign ministry of the host country and engaged in confidential dialogue with the authorized representatives of the state. But today the constituencies that he has to cover have expanded beyond recognition. This is directly the consequence of the 'democratization' of foreign affairs, in particular the entry of many actors on the stage, including non-state actors, and the continual erosion of the 'exclusive' position of the foreign ministry. Another major change is 'public diplomacy' which represents a paradigm shift for this profession.

PUBLIC DIPLOMACY

This term carries mixed meaning. In the UK it is often equated with propaganda by the diplomats. One instance is the definition given in *A Dictionary of Diplomacy* by G.R. Berridge and Alan James (Palgrave, London, 2001), which states: 'Not to be confused with open or parliamentary diplomacy, a late-twentieth-century term for propaganda conducted by diplomats.' Many would find this definition inadequate, reflecting old diplomacy attitudes.

Public diplomacy includes a wide range of outreach activities, including advocacy and persuasion, aimed at the various non-official constituencies that influence, or are involved in, foreign affairs. Typically a state carries out public diplomacy both at home, and in foreign countries. Public diplomacy is also a method through which states try and influence domestic and external audiences during a negotiation process, and at the same time convey messages to their direct negotiation partners. We see this, for instance, during EU summit meetings where public diplomacy becomes a facet of negotiation.

It is probably in the US that this sector has received the most attention, and acceptance as mainstream diplomatic activity. It is well organized also in many European states. In India, in contrast, the public outreach work is handled together with external publicity, which is not the same thing. Such organization of work is duplicated in some other countries. (See also Chapter 2.)

NEW TASKS: PROMOTION AND 'OUTREACH'

An alternate short working description of professional diplomacy divides it into five prime tasks that are action oriented:

- ❑ **Promotion**
- ❑ **Outreach**

- **Feedback**
- **Management**
- **Servicing.**

For the purposes of bilateral relationship building the first four are of obvious importance, but in the work of the mission, and at headquarters, the servicing role is no less vital, especially in the contemporary age where good governance issues dominate all discussion of the public services. Therefore, all the five functions are addressed here.

'Representation' continues to describe a core activity of the embassy, but again it appears passive, and is better replaced with words that carry a more dynamic flavor. The place of the old negotiation and representation functions has been taken above by **promotion** and **outreach** as the prime tasks of bilateral diplomatic missions, i.e. the building, consolidation and enrichment of relationships.

- These two tasks encompass a vastly expanded 'advocacy' role, with the difference that the diplomat must try and influence diverse state entities, parliamentarians, business, the media, academia and think tanks, and anyone else who, in the country of assignment, is a decision maker or an influence on foreign affairs.
- Outreach means creating favorable constituencies, and gaining allies, to be used as sources of information, accessing opportunities and networking as needed. One way this is done is by building a 'Top 100' list of friends; whatever the specific method, creating and sustaining connections is a permanent task.
- Outreach also means creating the means and methods of influencing decisions, where this is feasible and permissible in the actual context of the bilateral situation. The keyword is discretion, that old ally of the diplomat, of whom the early French pioneers spoke with such elegance and fervor.
- Promotion relates more specifically to 'selling' the state, using methods that are somewhat similar to those used in the corporate world, except that the scope is wider. In the economic arena it

includes assistance to own exports and mobilization of foreign investment, now regarded as mainstream diplomacy or 'economic diplomacy'. Some countries treat this as a job for specialists from other ministries, while many more integrate it with other diplomatic work. In all instances, economic promotion works best only when the ambassador and his entire team are involved in it, regardless of their work designation.

- For some countries, projection of culture and language are integral to promotion and outreach (e.g. France, Italy and Germany). They believe that these elements define their country's personality.
- There is a public engagement or media role that goes beyond reacting to events and ensuring that one's own side of the story is put across, important as that remains. There are situations where the diplomat has to, on his own initiative, actively create, shape and influence the public perception in the host country. This may involve sailing very close to the activities that are forbidden under the Vienna Convention, i.e. involvement in what some may regard as the internal affairs of the host country. (This is narrated well in former Canadian Ambassador Alan Gotlieb's book *I'll be With You In a Minute, Mr. Ambassador*, covering his experience in the US in 1987–93.)

Some of the methods outlined above, and in the other chapters in this collection, are focused on the work of the foreign service official in a mission, rather than at headquarters. At the latter end the attention is more on 'management' of the missions and on the wider web of bilateral relationships across regions and continents—MFAs now look after not just the political but also the 'integrated' relationship. But the concepts involved are identical, and the differences are more in the primary and secondary responsibilities in particular work sectors. Given the interchangeable roles of the diplomat (between the mission and headquarters), only when specific tasks are excluded at the one or the other place is it necessary to define the location of the work.

FEEDBACK, MANAGEMENT AND SERVICING

Feedback refers to the work of reportage, from missions to headquarters, and at the MFA or headquarters, the writing of analysis, records of discussion and policy recommendations that are the lifeblood of the diplomatic system. **Management** is the task of operating the system, i.e. running the embassies, supervision over them from headquarters, and producing optimal performance from the diplomatic system as a whole. **Servicing** refers to all the routine tasks that are performed, mainly dealing with the members of the public. Examples: provision of consular services and protection to own citizens, responding to queries from businessmen, providing information to own citizens and to foreign nationals, and the like.

It is frequently argued that the joint impact of various forces and developments has made the embassy far less relevant than before, and others players have overtaken the work of ambassadors. The points generally cited in support of this argument include the vast improvement in instant communication and news networks replacing some of the work of embassy reports. Then there are the frequent direct encounters between heads of state and government, at summit meetings and elsewhere, and the way they even sideline their foreign ministries. There are also the burgeoning contacts between line ministries and foreign counterparts; and what has been called 'Concorde diplomacy'—the frequent peregrinations of foreign ministers and other delegations. The facts are incontestable. But one major truth remains: there is no one other than the resident embassy that can continually engage in 'outreach' and 'promotion' as outlined above. And that remains a major responsibility, even among countries that are extremely close or partly 'unified', like the members of the European Union. No one has argued that for the member-states of the EU, which are now even engaged in creating a 'Common Foreign and Security Policy' (CFSP), the bilateral embassy is redundant. In fact their embassies are busier than ever before. The Paschke Report produced in Germany at the end of 2000, examining the role of German embassies in EU capitals, notes that some of the work has changed, but the need for embassies is unchanged.[6]

There is another role that has unexpectedly emerged for the resident embassy, almost unnoticed. This is the task of 'bilateral relationship management'. The sheer multiplicity of contacts has created a new kind of empowerment for embassies, at least for those ambassadors who are in countries other than those of 'peripheral' interest. How does this happen? There are two elements. First, line ministries are engaged in their own external contacts, and they no longer need to pass through the foreign ministry. The MFA cannot keep track of all the details of such activities by the line ministries, even while it coordinates broad policy issues. Second, the external contacts of non-state actors have also multiplied and affect bilateral relationships. The embassy in a foreign country has the nearest approximation to a complete view of these contacts, in practice better than that of any home agency.

The embassy is the only agency of government that follows activities in different sectors and has no responsibility other than monitoring the totality of the bilateral relationship. This enables the embassy to practice 'integrated' diplomacy, advising the foreign ministry and the other agencies at home on possible connections between issues, plus the cross-linkages and leverage available. We will develop this thesis later on.

Consulates and consulates general are subsidiary to embassies and generally work under the latter's supervision. In the past, major powers had a consular service that was separate from the diplomatic service, but the two were merged some decades back, and now the personnel are fully interchangeable in all services. Typically a consulate general does not carry out political or country representation functions[7], and besides consular work (which is its *raison d'être*), it handles all the other economic, cultural, media, education and related activities. A consulate ranks slightly lower, and is headed by a more junior official compared with a consulate general. But nothing prevents these entities from carrying out both political outreach and promotion on behalf of the embassy; they deal with the local province or other sub-state entities and not the MFA of the host country.

OUTER CIRCLE AND PROBLEM COUNTRIES

While many of the tools and methods of relationship building do not obviously apply to that final cluster of foreign countries where one has a rather minimal interest, the desk officer at headquarters dealing with them, or the resident mission that may be located there need not lose heart. In some respects, it is in such bilateral situations of rather minimal mutual interest that there is the greatest scope for individual initiative. Examples abound of heads of mission and officials who through personal dynamism and effort have created a new and higher profile for their countries in particular countries, translating this into economic and other benefit, by way of trade, project contracts and the like.

It is possible to work in such a manner to raise the quality of ties and to 'promote' the relationship to a higher level of mutual advantage. Practical examples are to be found in the way relationships were developed by India with countries in the Gulf region after the first oil crisis of 1973, taking advantage of economic opportunities that arose to win industrial contracts and to secure placement for skilled workers from home.[8] Similar new prospects for gaining access to natural resources, especially oil and natural gas, arose for Turkey and others in Central Asia, after the collapse of the Soviet Union and the emergence of the CIS Republics. Besides these, in every diplomatic service there are instances where a resourceful envoy has been able to transform the existing bilateral relationship.

Much of the above analysis does not seem to apply to situations where there is tension between pairs of countries, and where the *realpolitik* diplomacy is pursued to secure unilateral advantage. One might argue that save in exceptional situations of bilateral antipathy, as sometimes happens between neighbors, consistently hostile international behavior is rare over any period of time. In most cases the methods of diplomacy do not change. But if one state is perceived to be working all the time to secure for itself one-sided benefit, or acting in a manner inconsistent with accepted international behavior, other states put aside notions of mutuality and accommodation in their dealings with it. One could say that in the past, North Korea behaved in this manner but even in Pyongyang, which seemed to revel in its self-imposed isolation in the past, the winds of change have blown and it begins to revert to normal diplomatic interchanges, perhaps in a hesitant manner. There are other states that could match such a description, depending on one's perspective.

Diplomacy as a profession offers no standard template. Some may even question whether knowledge in this field can be transmitted in any way other than practical experience gained through actual work, aided by 'mentoring', as we saw in the Introduction. There are techniques that can be described, and illustrated with practical examples. But there is no substitute for actual work. Very little of this work follows a set pattern, and the action canvas is vast. Self-drive, initiative and even faith in serendipity are vital attributes. So is the ability to 'think outside the box' and use the interconnections that an integrated action field offers. It pays to take advantage of windows of opportunity. Here lie the challenge and the thrill of diplomacy.

QUESTIONS

1. What is the importance of bilateral relationship building in professional diplomacy?
2. Identify 5 or 6 countries that belong to the circle of special partners for your own nation, and describe in a couple of sentences for each the external profile of each of them.
3. What is the prime task of professional diplomacy today? Please give examples.
4. What challenges does diplomacy face today from internal developments within nations?

REFERENCES

1. Denza, Eileen, *Diplomatic Law: A Commentary on the Vienna Convention on Diplomatic Relations,* 2nd Edition (Clarendon Press, Oxford, 1998).
2. Gotlieb, Alan, *I'll be with you in a minute, Mr. Ambassador* (Toronto University Press, Toronto, 1991), Chapter 1, pp. 3–41.
3. Marshall, Peter, *Positive Diplomacy* (Macmillan, London, 1997), Introduction and Chapter 1, pp. 1–20.
4. Rana, Kishan S., *Inside Diplomacy* (Manas, New Delhi, 2000), Chapter 1, pp. 23–32, Chapter 2, pp. 55–59.

NOTES

1. International relations theory can be divided into several clusters. The '**realist**' or *realpolitik* school holds that in the international environment, states act to safeguard their survival and long-term benefits. The safety and independence of the state is its own first responsibility, and moral imperatives are alien to it. This set of theories, in all their variations, is identified with the Greek historian Thucydides, and Machiavelli, the 16th century Italian protagonist of the role of power. In one interesting elaboration, it is argued that while all external actions of the state cannot be directly linked to its survival, the state acts 'as if' this were the case, since survival is a prerequisite to achieving any other goals the state may have. It is easy to conceptualize security as the mainspring, in analyzing the rivalry and tension among European states in various periods of the 18th and 19th century, or Japan's outlook in the entire period of its foreign contact until World War II. Or if we look to West Asia and North Africa (comment: this is a more precise term than the 'Middle East', since the latter begs the question, 'East of what?'), it is evident that concerns over territorial integrity and the survival of nations remain dominant factors for many countries. In contrast, if we look to the Europe of today, a decade after the end of the Cold War and on the edge of expansion into a 'Union' of some 25 plus states, it is hard to postulate security as the basis of inter-state relations.

   In diametrical opposition to the above, there arose the '**liberal**' theory, associated with the names of Immanuel Kant, John Stuart

Mill and other thinkers of the 19th century, that the determinant of state behavior is located within states. State behavior does not respond to the international system, but constitutes it. Moral values orient their actions. It is the social groups, the state institutions and the culture of the country that are the determinants. US President Woodrow Wilson argued that in democracies foreign policy is subject to domestic debate, and others like Cordell Hull went on the ultra-Liberal thesis that war is obsolete. Liberal theory also postulates the benign view that states pursue cooperative partnerships, accepting the principles of mutual benefit, and that they have evolved beyond the threat of mutual destruction.

There are also the '**institutional**' and '**structuralist**' theorists who argue that the action of states is determined by their structures, and that to understand international behavior we must first study the institutions within the countries. Marxist theory is a version of institutional determinism. The believers in 'agency' theory take an opposite view: they hold that the actions of the principal agents have to be understood in terms of their makeup and character, and that individuals play the crucial role.

There are many other variations in theory. In the end, it is clear that no one hypothesis covers all situations. At the best of times national concerns over security do not fade away, but to regard these as an exclusive source of international behavior motivation is a distortion of reality. Contemporary trends within countries, which include increased involvement of non-State actors in external relationships, at home and abroad, plus the blurring of the distinction between foreign and domestic affairs, give credence to many of the liberal postulates. It is useful to keep in view the theory variants, and take an empirical, practical, view of international relations. If we proceed on this premise, *realpolitik* appears submerged but never absent; at the same time, states assiduously pursue cooperative relationships abroad, strongly influenced by domestic concerns, and by domestic actors.

2. Peter Marshall, *Positive Diplomacy* (Macmillan, London, 1997). He also speaks of the substance of international relations and the nature of international society, and the manner in which nations behave with one another; substance and process are 'inextricably linked. Process

affects substance'. Diplomacy deals with process, but this in turn is intertwined with substance. This partly explains the persisting confusion between foreign policy and diplomacy.

3. Abba Eban, *Diplomacy for the New Century* (New Haven, Yale University Press, 1998).
4. Article entitled 'Redefining the National Interest' in *Foreign Affairs,* July–August, 1999.
5. Historians see the 100 years after the Congress of Vienna and until the outbreak of World War I, 1815 to 1914, as the first classic age of diplomacy. At the end of the World War I, when the League of Nations was launched as the first permanent multilateral structure for international peace and cooperation, Woodrow Wilson and Harold Nicholson hailed the advent of 'New Diplomacy', which would be transparent and inclusive. But from another perspective this was also the final phase of colonialism and emergence of independence movements that culminated with the emergence of former colonies as independent states at the end of World War II. With this, diplomacy underwent a paradigm shift, marking the start of post-colonial global diplomacy.
6. At the end of 2001, this report is under examination in Berlin, and under debate in the Bundestag.
7. However, there are exceptions. Before the US opened a 'liason office' in the People's Republic of China in 1972, the US Consulate General in Hong Kong was its *de facto* observation point for China (formal recognition came in 1979).
8. The total number of these workers and professionals that followed them rose rapidly to the current figure of about 2 million in all the countries of the Gulf region taken together, including Saudi Arabia. They account for the bulk of the annual inflow of $12 billion worth of inward remittances sent by Overseas Indians to the home country. A number of other Asian countries derive similar benefit from their workers and professionals in this oil-rich region.

2

Building Political Relations

Under the UN Charter that was framed at San Francisco in 1945 at the end of World War II, the new organization's 50 founder member-states undertook the commitment to safeguard peace and security. As the process of decolonization subsequently unfolded, every state that gained freedom sought UN membership as one of its first acts, in assertion of an independent international personality. This has made the UN a uniquely universal international organization.[1] In accordance with the UN Charter and the basic tenets of international law, the presumption is that friendship and a willingness to cooperate animates foreign relationships between different countries around the world. In addition, factors such as shared interest, subscription to common ideals, and mutual benefit in external cooperation within and across regions and continents, guide countries. All these elements contribute to building strong, mutually advantageous foreign relations. While situations of tension and conflict exist among some countries, the basic presumption is that all states seek good relationships around the world. In practice, how is the task implemented? Is there what may be called a standard methodology for relationship building?

CONCEPTS AND GOALS

It is perhaps only a state charting out its foreign policy course at independence that asks itself such basic questions, but it is pertinent to carry out from time to time a kind of 'zero base' examination of one's own external relationships. One way to do this out is to reassess one's interest in a particular country and examine how this matches actual actions on the ground. Another approach is to examine the concepts that underlie different sets of relationships. The concepts may include:

A. **Security objectives.** National security is the country's first priority shaping its external relations. This will determine the way one deals with neighboring countries, or with potential rivals, or with countries that are antagonistic. Security factors also enter the calculation in dealings with great powers.

B. **Neighborhood.** This is a powerful factor, shaping relations even when security factors do not dominate. Proximity works in a complex manner; handled well, it becomes a platform for cooperation. At other times it leads to rivalry and contestation. The management of relationships with neighboring countries is invariably the first diplomatic challenge.

C. **Shared ideals.** Values or 'ideology' (though this particular term is not much in fashion after the demise of the Soviet Union and the 'socialist bloc') are another factor. Among post-colonial, developing countries, commitment to Non-Alignment and the economic goals of the G-77 group, plus South–South cooperation, can serve as a principle-based connection. After the end of the Cold War, Non-Alignment as a 'Movement' has lost steam, though it continues as a forum for Third World countries sharing some common interests.[2] Religion has been seen as another unifying factor by some states, such as those belonging to the Islamic faith.[3] In practice, such commonalities by themselves are not a powerful basis for mutually beneficial relations, but they serve as a useful starting point.

D. **Mutual antagonism.** Regional rivalry, ethnic factors, history, and antipathy can shape relationships in an adversarial fashion, even among those that are not neighbors. But in today's dynamic post-Cold War world, enemies of the past can become cooperative partners, even while mutual wariness persists.
E. **Matching interests.** Mutuality of interests is usually a strong basis for a lasting relationship; the more so if these shared interests are of a durable character. This may comprise of economic factors such as a good and expanding level of trade, or investments, or the need to work together for exploiting a shared resource.
F. **Legacy.** Whether through past colonial or other contact, or shared culture, religion or language, inherited connections provide a good base for affirmative relationship building. Such elements provide depth and weight at popular levels. The ties between France and its former colonies in Africa are one example.
G. **Momentum.** The development of a relationship becomes a valuable asset, like a 'virtuous circle', in that positive actions create new opportunity for further relationship growth. The reverse is also true and negative developments can create a vicious cycle of downturn, which can be broken only through determined initiative.
H. **Diversity.** A mature relationship is identified by diversified contacts, which permit flexibility and accommodation for differences. The opposite situation is uni-dimensional ties where a single issue can lead to crisis in the entire relationship. India's relationship with the US in the past belonged to the latter category, when divergence over the Non-Proliferation Treaty (NPT) led to a serious downturn in ties. The past decade has seen a maturing of mindsets, where one set of differences are not allowed to hurt progress in other cooperative areas.[4]

In bilateral diplomacy, identification of commonalities lies at the heart of relationship building, the more so in situations where commonalities are not obvious. Countries best respond to one another on the basis of how the other can help fulfill their own objectives, not through abstract principles, nor as a reaction to the logic of an argument presented by the other country. Principles and logic are the idioms in which states speak to one another, but the foundation of relationships is self-interest. In practice, identification of commonality is a dynamic process, depending on elements like the opportune moment, presentation of the arguments, and the persuasion applied, i.e. the full range diplomatic advocacy.

DEVELOPING RELATIONS

Let us assume that diplomatic relations exist and resident missions have been exchanged (or arrangements worked out for concurrent accreditation, or even to have 'non-resident' envoys, who may be stationed in the home country and operate out of there).[5] The standard methods for cultivating relationships at a political level consist of the following:

i. **Initiation of contacts** usually marks the start of new relationships, as for example immediately after independence. The first steps may include a cautious probing of intentions, and contacts to measure the level of interest, and an evaluation of practical prospects for mutually beneficial links. Such informal exchanges that may have taken place prior to formal relations are consolidated and renewed at this stage. Depending on the assessment, this may lead to an exchange of resident envoys, or concurrent accreditation.[6]

ii. **Dialogue and exchanges** of visits at various levels are always useful. These may range from exploratory missions, dialogue at functional or official levels, to visits by ministers, going all the way to visits by heads of state and government. Each move of this kind is preceded by a careful assessment of the benefits that are expected to accrue, and the objectives to be realized. Other factors that enter the calculation include the pattern of past exchanges, reciprocity, and of course the other competing priorities. A landmark summit encounter event is often celebrated with a joint statement or communiqués, but when there are frequent encounters between heads, informal protocol rules are applied, with focus on dialogue and not on ceremony (see Chapter 10).

iii. **Agreements** covering new areas of cooperation are both the end product of expanding relationships and a platform for stronger subsequent actions. Sometimes agreements are concluded in areas of peripheral interest, simply to add to the appearance of closeness, or decorate a visit with an outward image of substance. Usually this is of little value. Experience shows that new agreements or protocols are worthwhile if substantive result is expected, not empty gestures. Accords that are not implemented can become an embarrassment in the future, and also undermine the credibility of interlocutors.

iv. **Consultation mechanisms** are another useful device to signal serious intent to work closely, and produce results. These range from joint commissions meeting annually, often led by ministers on each side, usually covering economic issues. Another method is 'joint consultations' between foreign ministries, at the level of permanent secretaries or even foreign ministers, where bilateral ties are reviewed, new initiatives launched, and the dossiers that may have been blocked, pushed to conclusion. Another method is the creation of special groups of independent 'eminent persons' drawn from different walks of life, to advise both governments on further ways to improve ties (Chapter 9).

v. **Cooperation in functional areas** is yet another means of moving relationships forward. This may cover exchanges in culture, the media, education, science & technology, and 'sister city' or inter-regional relationships. They involve official agencies as also non-state participants, and the latter is of increasing importance in an age when foreign relations are no longer the monopoly of the state. Countries like Germany, France, and Poland have demonstrated the way in which strong people-to-people bonds can be created, overcoming past history

JAPAN'S CULTIVATION OF MYANMAR*

Japan's cultivation of Myanmar in 1998–2000 provides an interesting case study. Having determined that the continuing isolation of that country's military regime was not to the advantage of its Asia policy, Tokyo implemented a series of measures. Initially, careful soundings were made in Washington DC, to put across its objectives to this vital ally, to explain what was virtually the first independent initiative. The US was not convinced, but Japan decided to go ahead anyway. A conference of some 40 scholar–specialists on Myanmar was organized jointly with UK at the foreign policy think tank Wilton Park. Noting that experts regarded the policy of isolating the military junta of Myanmar as locked in an impasse, and no one had an alternative for breaking the deadlock between that regime and the democratic forces represented by Nobel peace laureate Aung San Suu Chi, Japan concluded that Myanmar's entry into ASEAN, and its own Asian interests justified a policy of measured cultivation.

Aid that had been blocked earlier was released, and food aid was imitated. A direct air link between Tokyo and Yangon (formerly called Rangoon) was launched by a Japanese airline. Former premier Hashimoto made a visit as a special envoy in October 1999, and this was followed by a business delegation that was received exceptionally well by the Myanmar authorities. The process also served Japan's larger purpose of articulating an autonomous foreign policy directly serving its interests.

* A visiting Tokyo University professor narrated this account in 1999–2000 at a closed-door seminar in New Delhi.

and ethnic stereotypes. The steps include massive programs of youth exchanges, and links among grass-root organizations in virtually all fields, ranging from administrative entities that lie along the frontiers, to facilities for border populations to attend schools in the neighboring country and to learn one another's language.[7]

vi. **Regional cooperation** has emerged as a strong trend, binding neighboring countries into networks that jointly pursue trade concessions, or establish a free trade area, or cooperation in other areas like economic development, transport, resource exploitation and the like. A good bilateral relationship acts as a building block for mutually beneficial regional activities.

New initiatives are productive when they are well prepared, and take advantage of the right window of opportunity. The reputation that a country creates for its astuteness in the implementation of its foreign policy, i.e. diplomacy, is also a factor that contributes to success.

PRACTICAL METHODS

Political cultivation operates on decision and direction by headquarters and is usually implemented by the diplomatic mission, or by roving envoys, special delegations, or even directly by the foreign ministry, depending on circumstances. In most cases the resident mission is the prime implementing agency, operating under supervision by the headquarters. From the perspective of the embassy, this process is influenced by a number of practical steps that include:

A. An **understanding of the power structure** in the target country, identification of the principal players, and all forms of related 'intelligence', which is no more than close analysis of the ground situation, and determination of the tactical route that is best suited to one's own needs.

B. **Information management** is a key ingredient, related to the above. The Internet and a multiple of openly available databases make information collection very easy, but focus on relevant material and good analysis based on this are harder. Pertinent information along with objective analysis is the basis of sound diplomatic reportage.

C. Creating a **web of contacts**, friends, and allies, and continually building on this, in a proactive manner. The work is incremental, and continuous, but each door opened often leads to another. Networking is a vital instrument of diplomacy. The diplomat engaged in the task has to place in wide context his own role in this process, and avoid personal ego. He or she must pass on contacts to successors, since such work is part of a continuum.

D. In any capital, big or small, embassies are engaged in a real **competition for access**, in which good results may be determined by diverse factors, ranging from social entertainment to personal credibility, ingenuity and chance. Serendipity is always one of the biggest allies of the diplomat. The application of method and purpose to representational entertainment is vital, but so are other elements like social skills and the ability to offer something exceptional, be it cuisine, company or style. The spouse, who used to be overlooked or taken for granted, can be crucial in contact-creation.[8] The diplomatic spouses merit attention from the diplomatic service, and one of the new motivation devices is to pay a special allowance, to encourage the spouse to accompany the diplomat to the foreign assignment.[9]

E. Notions of **status and level** of contacts particularly affect ambassadors, and this applies as well to visiting delegations. Deliberate slights (or protocol mistreatment) have to be considered carefully and dealt with as a form of non-verbal communication by the other partner. But we live in an age when functional factors are more important than outward form, even in this protocol-driven profession. Access and good communication routes should take precedence over status and form.

F. Between headquarters and the mission, and within the mission, political outreach hinges on a **team approach**. Notwithstanding the internal division of work, all members of an embassy form the 'country team', but in the real world conflicts over jurisdiction are common.

G. The **Diplomatic Corps** is virtually an association, even a brotherhood, with its own code of behavior and rites. In the larger capitals, even more vital than the Corps that may include 150 ambassadors or more, are the regional sub-groups. These offer a unique platform for information sharing, analysis, and sometimes even for joint action in the name of a regional entity like SADC or ASEAN, and for promotional outreach. One can join such groups at various levels such as first secretary or counselor, or create one's own group, depending on local circumstance, if there is a vacuum or suitable opportunity.

H. The **old tools of persuasion and negotiation skill** remain the principal weapons in the diplomat's armory. To these professional skills should be added the instruments of integrated diplomacy, the ability to identify trade-offs and cross-linkages, which can help in determining shared interests, and creating 'win–win' situations for both sides. Armed with information, one can search for opportunities to offer to the other side something it seeks, linking this with some action or accommodation that is to one's own advantage. This is the diplomatic doctrine of 'linkage' and 'leverage'.

I. It is invariably better to focus on creating **institutional connections** between counterparts of the two countries, even while the role of individuals is crucial in identifying and forming these links. This permits the relationship to move to a more stable platform, beyond personalities. Institutions outlast individuals.

Former Canadian Ambassador to the US (1987–93), Alan Gotlieb has written about his experience in implementing the theory of 'multiplicity of instruments', i.e. functional contacts between Canadian and US counterparts, which are multiple and self-interested, as the 'backbone of the relationship.'[10] He notes that this went against the notion of centralized control in the Department of External

Relations. 'Management of the relationship became the buzzword.' This sums up the formula for intensive bilateral cultivation.

CULTIVATION TARGETS

Viewed primarily from the perspective of the resident mission, the main targets in the process of building political partners are a bit different today from the past when the focus was primarily on the MFA of the partner country and a narrow circle of authoritative official agencies. The age of public diplomacy has widened the target range.

a) The local MFA remains the first contact point, and the mission needs contacts with it at all working levels. In most capitals the ambassador can meet the foreign minister rather rarely, but good contacts with the permanent head, the permanent secretary or the state secretary, and with the political director, and the territorial division head serve very well. This kind of cultivation depends on subjective factors, personal credibility and professional competence. Even when the MFA is bypassed, as may be appropriate in some circumstance, it is crucial to keep the prime interlocutors there informed—the territorial division, and the functional divisions vital to one's own interests, plus the other key players.
b) The offices of the heads of state and government are the other prime targets. In contemporary practice, the resident envoy finds it difficult to access the heads themselves, save in exceptional circumstance. (Example: Professor Galbraith, as the US Ambassador sent by Kennedy to New Delhi, had written with wit about his direct access to Nehru in the early 1960s, but such exceptional times and personalities are rare.[11] There are many Western capitals where all but the envoys of great powers have much difficulty in meeting even the foreign minister.) But working contacts with the officials in the offices of high dignitaries serves a like purpose. The key is the ability and clout to get one's

viewpoint across whenever needed, sometimes at very short notice, without abusing access.

c) Contacts at the other ministries depend on the density of dialogue and functional need. Broad cultivation of all major agencies of the government is part of basic outreach, but has to be linked to potential for cooperation. This requires involvement of the entire embassy team, with each diplomat covering a cluster of agencies, at appropriate levels.

d) The parliament is a traditional diplomatic partner, and more important now than ever before, not only because various parliamentary committees engage in detailed examination of issues like foreign affairs, trade policy and aid, but also as there is a general trend towards their deeper involvement in foreign affairs. (Like the involvement of non-state actors, this is part of the 'democratization' of foreign affairs that is visible in many countries.) Bi-national parliamentary friendship groups are special entities that play a role through exchanges of visits by parliamentary delegations. In the US and at the Brussels headquarters of the European Commission, plus at the European Parliament at Strasbourg, many countries use lobbyists, as a routine means of influencing regulations and gaining support, much as such activities are 'unconventional' (and not anticipated by the Vienna Convention of 1961). One observer has estimated that in the early 1990s Japan spent a total of $ 250 annually on lobbying, directly in hiring them, plus cultivation through think tanks, institutions and the like.[12]

e) The media, print and electronic, demand in many places local language ability for daily monitoring. Negative publicity is the routine bugbear of the diplomat, but the knee-jerk reaction of countering this with counter-publicity or 'refutation' is seldom productive—though it may be inescapable in certain types of situations. The creation of positive publicity is the more effective route for image building, which is now—or should be—a constant preoccupation of embassies.

f) Business is a prime cultivation target today, directly in terms of reaching out to the major individual enterprises (both those with sizable business interests in the relationship and those that offer future potential), plus the business and industry associations. No less vital are medium and small companies that play a special role in bilateral trade, technology and investments. All embassy officials, regardless of tasks performed, should be seen as contributors to economic diplomacy. For example, the consular official needs to be sensitive to the visa needs of businessmen, meet them personally if opportunity arises and share with the economic sections the data on business visitors, to act as a contributor to economic diplomacy. The same is true of the officials dealing with media or culture sectors.

g) The think tanks, academia, the science & technology community, the social and volunteer organizations and the NGOs, all the elements of civil society that have a special affinity or interest in one's own country are part of the new public outreach. They should be cultivated in sustained fashion by designated officials, with the personal involvement of the ambassador. The utilization of all public speaking opportunities is equally vital, to reach out and build favorable constituencies.

h) Ethnic communities deserve special attention, especially those from one's own country. In plural, open and democratic societies, they may be in a position to directly influence the local political process. (Example: the pervasive Jewish lobby in the US represents Israel's trump card in that country). Even when present in small numbers, ethnic communities are useful sources of information and contact.

MANAGING COMPLEXITY

The issues in diplomatic dialogue are more diverse than ever, and so is the range of players who are engaged in bilateral external relationships—representing different branches of government as also non-state actors. We live in an interdependent world, whose *leitmotif* is globalization, even while many see this as a mixed benefit, one that sharpens the divide between the haves and the have-nots. For foreign ministries and for missions, diplomacy has become a matter of complexity management. Part of that complexity also involves dealing with many kinds of technical experts. The diplomat, whose special knowledge can almost never cover the range of technical issues he encounters, has to grasp the essentials of diverse disciplines, and place these within the integral context of the bilateral relationship with that country. He must also acquire the skill of making inter-connections wherever possible, to find leverage or 'trade-offs'. This is the crux of his professional skill, an ability to interact with experts, understand the essentials of technical issues under dialogue, and relate these to the totality of the relationship.

In bilateral relationships a crisis can emerge through diverse reasons, some of which can be exogenous. No standardized set of responses can be stipulated, but in handling such situations there are elements that can be taken into account, for safeguarding relations and for reducing adverse impact.

a) Diversified relationships show greater resilience than those that are not. In the latter, a single issue can dominate and cause a crisis that embitters the entire relationship. Conversely, one of the challenges of relationship management is to prevent single theme domination in periods of adversity. This can be seen in the experience of many countries. For example, in contrast to the earlier mono-theme India–US relationship narrated above, China and the US, after overcoming decades of mutual hostility, have shown a capacity to compartmentalize differences, and prevent them from poisoning coöperation in other areas.
b) Equally, spreading contacts across different constituencies, political and functional, is a way of minimizing the impact of crisis. This applies in particular to situations of radical change of government. It is a form of political insurance. This is visible

in the relations between countries of West Europe, where sharp divergences in social philosophy and domestic policy do not affect ties between conservative and social democrat governments.

c) Calculations of long-term interest are important when determining responses during a crisis, to avoid foreclosing future options or prolonging damage. This may entail for the foreign ministry the adoption of unpopular standpoints at a time of popular upsurge or hostility towards an external partner. As the saying goes, there are no permanent friends abroad, only permanent interests.

The Vienna Convention remains the framework for diplomatic work, but the content or tasks performed has expanded. An expanded definition of diplomatic tasks—promotion, outreach, feedback, management and servicing—has been suggested in the introduction to this book. On occasion and using discretion, diplomats sometimes transgress into the 'domestic' arena of the host country, in an effort to persuade, to obtain a favorable outcome in legislative or regulatory formulation, or simply to influence an important decision. This is an aspect of sovereignty erosion that is under-studied, but is part of the globalization process in which the sharp distinction between 'domestic' and 'foreign' is often hard to make. States are more directly involved in trying to influence one another than ever before. Further, regional entities like the European Union and ASEAN, carrying out their own policies of integration, also pose special challenges for multilateral and bilateral diplomacy. These are issues on which the response of the diplomatic system is under evolution. The post-War world showed the ways political diplomacy adapted to new situations, like the emergence of former colonies as sovereign states, and the Cold War, in which countries chose between bloc membership and non-alignment. In the same way, the shape of professional diplomacy in the post-Cold War era, which is even now barely a decade old, is yet to emerge fully. We realize for instance that 'public diplomacy' is going to figure even more prominently in the future, and so will the need for the diplomat to deal with a broad range of non-state entities. Even if all the contours of diplomacy of the future are not clear, we can be certain that the process of adaptation to change will continue.

QUESTIONS

1. What are the criteria relevant to the relationship between your country and two of its immediate neighbors?
2. What are the instruments for building relations between states, as one may find from a practical example?
3. As an ambassador, what methods would you deploy in your mission to prepare for an intensive effort to build ties?
4. Who should be the top three cultivation targets for an embassy?

REFERENCES

1. Marshall, Peter, *Positive Diplomacy* (Macmillan, London, 1997).
2. Mellissen, Jan, ed. *Innovation in Diplomatic Practice* (Macmillan, London, 1999).
3. Rana, Kishan S., *Inside Diplomacy* (Manas, New Delhi, 2000), Chapter 3, pp. 61–73, Chapter 12, pp. 313–29.

NOTES

1. The only country of significance that is not a UN member is Switzerland, and Swiss voters have rejected several referenda that have proposed membership. Despite this, the country has been host to the UN's European Office and is a member of several UN agencies, a few of which are also headquartered in that country. In February 2002, Swiss voters accepted UN membership.
2. The Non-Aligned Movement (NAM) now has over 110 members, and remains a caucus of some value at the UN, and holds summit meetings

of member-states every three years (these are also attended by 'observer' countries belonging to alliances). But the focus of NAM is less sharp than before and even participation by member-states has declined in numbers and quality.

3. The 50-odd Islamic states constitute their own organization OIC that works to a political agenda, with the paraphernalia of annual summit meetings and more frequent gatherings of foreign ministers. Despite rhetoric, it exercises limited influence.
4. An example of differences that have been accommodated well is the Comprehensive Test Ban Treaty (CTBT) where the two differed sharply in 1994–96 when the treaty was negotiated, and India abstained. But this, and the nuclear tests India carried out in 1998, has not prevented the growth of a 'strategic partnership' between the two countries.
5. It is customary that diplomatic missions are exchanged on a reciprocal basis, though one country may retain its own embassy in the other state even if the latter does not set up a resident mission, if there are strong factors that are in play. But it is not customary to find in a particular capital say 60 or 70 resident foreign missions, when that country has set up only some 35 missions around the world. One exception to this is Singapore which hosts over 70 resident missions but sends out only some 28 of its own to foreign capitals. This is in part a tribute to the unique location of Singapore as a hub of commerce and transportation, and in part also due to the astute manner in which since the 1970s Singapore has developed the system of 'non-resident ambassadors', who are figures from public life and business, based in Singapore, who travel to the countries of their accreditation a couple of times a year and generally work to promote good ties from a distance. The receiving states have found this to be a useful formula, since it is better than no representation at all.
6. At Independence there is a first wave of embassies that a country sets up and within the next year or two further missions are opened, depending on the funds available and the concrete interests identified—like trade, inward investment, aid and tourism prospects, ethnic factors, and the like.
7. These methods used by West European states after World War II to create a new public support for partnership, overcoming centuries of

distrust and enmity, are a model for other regions. It is interesting that the same techniques are being applied after the end of the Cold War by Germany to create new understanding with border populations in the countries that lie to its east, Poland and the Czech Republic.

8. Alan Gotlieb's book *I'll be with You in a Minute, Mr. Ambassador* gives a persuasive narration of the role of the spouse in building contacts.
9. Spouses are also motivated to accompany diplomats to assignments abroad if they are allowed to work. In the past almost all diplomatic services did not permit this, but the wheel has turned and starting with a restricted list of jobs that the spouse could take up, most services now permit the spouse to work without imposing any conditions, other than the regulations in the receiving state. The latter usually applies the principle of reciprocity in granting work permits to the spouses. A special problem arises for the spouse of the ambassador, but most services now permit them to work as well.
10. Alan Gotlieb, *I'll be with you in a Minute Mr. Ambassador: The Education of a Canadian Diplomat in Washington* (London, Routledge, 1995).
11. The successor to Ambassador Galbraith in Delhi was Ambassador Chester Bowles, on his second assignment to India. He found it hard to sustain the same kind of contacts with Prime Minister Indira Gandhi, as his predecessor had enjoyed with Nehru. The key element was that Indira Gandhi was less accessible than her father had been. As the years went by it became even more difficult for foreign ambassadors to meet her, as I observed in the years 1981–82 when I served on her staff. But even at that time, she was more accessible to foreign envoys than what Indian ambassadors found in many countries, especially in the West.
12. Gotlieb, *I'll be with you in a Minute Mr. Ambassador*, as noted on page 24.
13. A good definition of public diplomacy is needed.

3

Security and Diplomacy

The neo-Realists believe that the mainspring of external relations is the safeguarding of the state's security, and that each country is an autonomous entity that works to this calculation. Since security issues loom large in dealing with adversaries and in situations of conflict, but recede when there is a web of external cooperative partnership, one might say that the diplomat is a neo-Realist in hard times and acts on wider Liberal or quasi-Liberal calculations in good times.

SECURITY CONCERNS

Even the smallest of states zealously safeguard their sovereignty and independence. In fact small states are especially mindful of threats, actual or potential. Take for instance a country such as Singapore, comprising some 3.5 million people living on a small island, hugely dependent on Malaysia even for its supply of drinking water, and hemmed in by the territory of that country and Indonesia. Singapore is today highly prosperous, with a living standard that rivals that of Western nations and an annual per capita GDP of over US$ 25,000, several times higher than of any of its neighbors. But as Michael

Leifer points out in his recent study[1] *Singapore's Foreign Policy*, survival has been its first foreign policy concern and it has practiced in essence the 'diplomacy of vulnerability'.

In the post-Cold War world, the demise of the Soviet Union and its Warsaw Pact group of nations, and the collapse of communism has marked an end to block rivalry. But the US and its NATO allies remain preoccupied with their military alliance, even if the contours of that alliance have changed. Former rivals—the countries of East Europe—are now NATO members, and there is a special dialogue between Russia and NATO. Ethnic strife and tensions in the states of former Yugoslavia have led to direct engagement by NATO, and its operational doctrine has undergone reshaping, extending to an as yet undefined interest in 'out of area' security issues and even wider political objectives. Some may wonder if in the aftermath of the unprecedented terrorist attacks on the US on September 11, NATO will have a global reach. We witness a situation of flux, with an undefined 'New World Order', and a state of transition in international affairs, in terms of relationships between great and lesser powers. The anticipated 'peace dividend' that was to flow from the end of Cold War has not materialized. Instead we see contradictory trends, like a possible reduction in nuclear arms buildup as promised by the Comprehensive Test Ban Treaty (CTBT), on one hand, and on the other, re-emergence of new divergences over new concepts like 'nuclear missile defense' systems, and talk of scrapping old arms reduction treaties. The Bush Administration has also put a question mark over CTBT, to which the previous administration was so committed.

Major powers have security concerns that are qualitatively different from those of smaller states. Theorist Karl W. Deutsche has written: 'The larger and more powerful a nation is, the more its leaders, elites and often its population increase its aspiration in international affairs. The more ... they see themselves as destined to put the affairs of the world in order.'[2]

DEFINITION OF SECURITY

What is national security? One author, Barry Evzan has defined it in terms of 'freedom from military, political, societal, economic and environmental threats'. In reality the definition of security gets broader all the time, as the world shifts to a relative reduction in direct preoccupation with military security to less overt threats that seem a byproduct of enhanced interdependence among nations around the globe, which is summed up in the word 'globalization'.

A small country, say in Africa, does not apprehend a military threat from a major great power located at a distance, be it the US or Russia. But the chances are that it has local security concerns, in the form of perceived threats from strong neighbor countries and from situations of instability or conflict in its region, which may also involve weak neighbors. All too often, boundary issues, and with it ethnic claims of one kind or another are a source of tension and insecurity. In Africa the OAU Charter wisely declares that the frontiers inherited from colonial times are inviolable and are to be accepted as permanent. But this has not prevented the emergence of many situations of conflict over border issues on that continent.

The establishment of good regional cooperation is invariably seen as a safety net that reduces any security threat. This is an underlying, often unstated element in regional cooperation, and a powerful argument in favor of such arrangements that may address issues of trade and economic cooperation. The stronger the web of such regional and cross-regional ties, the stronger is the threshold against regional trans-border disturbance or threat.

During the Cold War era, the notion of 'collective security' gained wide currency, promoted by great powers, to safeguard small countries. Today most observers would agree with Israeli diplomat and writer Abba Eban[3] that it is 'a discredited concept', or at least irrelevant. It is the international system, especially the UN and its Charter, its institutions like the UN Security Council and the General

Assembly, plus the structure of international law, which create an indirect framework of security or at least a set of fallback measures, that a country feels it can utilize if it feels threatened. Regional webs of cooperation and security assurances supplement this, even while these do not generally constitute formal alliances (such as ASEAN).

Wider definitions now speak of 'total security' and 'comprehensive security', which go much beyond military or defense to cover other fields.

- **Economic security** is one of the basic concerns for a majority of countries that feel threatened by globalization, which engenders the feeling that nations are not in complete control of their own economies and are subject to vicissitudes coming from abroad. For instance, most countries have drawn a lesson from the Asian Economic Crisis of 1997–98 that they must have better control over short-term financial flows, and that sound and conservative management of the economy is essential to guard against exchange rate speculation originating from abroad. There is similar concern over the extension of WTO into areas like the environment and labor laws in developing countries, aimed at eroding the competitive advantage of poorer countries without giving them real benefit of market access or investment flows.
- **Energy security** deals with assured sources of energy, especially those covering oil and other hydrocarbon resources, as well as assured supplies of electric power, including hydroelectric power. For instance Japan has a vital interest in assured oil supply, since 99% of total consumption is imported.
- **Food security** refers to assured supply of food. This is an important concept for countries suffering from endemic crop failure that depend on imports. Many countries use this as an argument in favor of high levels of protection for inefficient domestic production of food crops, in defiance of WTO free trade commitments (e.g. the positions taken by the EU and Japan on this issue).

- **Water security** covers assured supplies of water for consumption and river navigation. It is anticipated that the globe would suffer from increasing water scarcity in the coming years. Countries like Bangladesh that lie downstream on major rivers, regard water-sharing as a vital national issue.
- **Ecological security** is a mounting concern; harmful effects of environmental degradation do not stop at the border. For instance, Austria is concerned over unsafe nuclear power plants of Soviet vintage in Slovakia. This is also cited as a factor in favor of positions taken by rich countries over the preservation of equatorial forests in nations like Brazil.
- **Technology security** is a concern for medium-sized and emerging market economies that feel constrained by technology export controls imposed by rich nations, under 'dual-use' restrictions and other similar checks on the flow of technology. Such nations believe that autonomous development of domestic technology, wherever feasible, is a safeguard against an excess of controls from abroad.
- **Communications security** relates to the potential concern of countries with disruptions of the Internet, and the need for autonomous control over communications links. There is also concern over the capacity of major powers to listen in on all communications, through systems like the ECHELON[4] network of the US.
- **Societal security** deals with insidious threats that may be posed by other cultural exemplars, such as Western pop music which may be seen as a threat to traditional values in countries of Asia and Africa, or threats posed in situations of religious sensitivity by foreign missionary groups that carry out proselytizing activities. Another example, the cultural threat perceived by France over the infusion of English words in the French language. Samuel Huntington has theorized on the alleged 'clash of civilizations', what he presents as a growing global menace of religion- and

culture-based conflict. It would take us too far in a digression to examine this complex issue, but there is no doubt that countries that harbor minorities—ethnic, religious or cultural—worry over potential threat to national unity. They view the danger as both internal and external.[5]

- **Demographic security** focuses attention on population issues that have complex impact on nations. Some rich nations, like Germany, Japan and others in Europe face a major middle-term problem of a declining and aging population, and a dependence on imported labor to keep up economic productivity, with the concomitant problems of internal ethnic stress that this engenders. Others like most nations of Africa, Asia and Latin America have expanding populations that place severe stress on resources, and produce movement by economic migrants in search of a better life (e.g. exodus to the West and Australia from the Third World, into India from Bangladesh). Illegal migration is likely to become an acute political issue in many countries.

GLOBAL TERRORISM

The devastating attacks on the World Trade Center in New York and the Pentagon in Washington DC in the United States on September 11, 2001, have pushed to the forefront concerns over **international terrorism.** The modern state is vulnerable to attacks by entities that are not states but groups of extremists, operating from shadowy and fringe territories, hard to pin down, but a very real threat to security. This phenomenon calls for a new conceptual vocabulary. It also calls for a revised methodology of response, of force and diplomacy, to create a virtual global alliance of states and peoples against such actions, and carefully calibrated military responses that address the real culprits. Some lines of response that emerge are:

- All forms of terrorism have to be fought, because terrorist groups are interconnected by motivation, training, and actions undertaken. If one set of terrorists are excused as 'freedom fighters' fighting a cause that is aligned to one's own interests, one quickly finds that down the road the same groups will turn the gun on the former mentors. This has been the concrete experience of the US in Afghanistan (and of India in Sri Lanka).

- Flexible responses, in which technology alone does not provide all the answers, have to be developed. Human intelligence sources are no less vital than communications intelligence. So too are special force teams and a willingness to fight on the ground, since reliance on high technology weaponry is not enough.
- Besides combating terrorism directly, the roots of conflict also have to be addressed. This is the hardest of all, since it suggests that the terrorists are successful in getting their targets to rethink issues. However unpalatable, addressing the source of the problem is unavoidable for a lasting resolution of the terrorist threat. Specifically, the Palestine issue has engendered a sense of desperation and hopelessness that has bred the Islamic fundamentalists. Addressing that issue makes good political sense on a number of counts, especially in that it would 'internalize' some of the anger that is directed today at external targets, including the US.

Past experience indicates that terrorism, drug trafficking and international crime, are partly interconnected. Almost none of the security threats listed above can be resolved simply by diplomacy. The majority of the challenges mandate internal actions within nations. Diplomacy can help to create external conditions that are favorable, and establish dialogue with countries that have congruent interests. Some form of external cooperation is helpful to resolving the different situations. We also realize that none of these issues are amenable to simple defense security-based answers.

One should add that many security issues relate to the structural and systemic problems faced by nations, especially the developing countries. But the wider security problems are not limited to this group of nations. This is one reason that for developing nations, the international relations theory concepts of the Structural or Institutional proponents are more relevant than any of the other competing doctrines. Third World countries also understand that all too often when Western nations refer to the interests of the 'international community' they have in view primarily their own interests, and that there is a limited understanding of Third World perspectives.

SECURITY AND DIPLOMACY

How do these concepts of security relate to the management of bilateral relationships? What are the implications for practical diplomacy? Several lines of possible engagement can be identified, for creating a web of diplomatic structures aimed at security.

a) Safeguarding the **nation's security is the first imperative** of foreign policy and diplomacy that gives concrete expression to that policy. Working diplomats, and statesmen, can ignore this only at great peril. Example: one of the great 'if' of history for India is how the relationship with China might have been shaped if the settlement of the border had been tackled in the early years of Independence in the early 1950s (as a minority in the policy-making group of the time suggested), rather than left aside for later resolution, as Nehru decided. Before jumping to simplistic conclusions based on hindsight, it should also be understood that Nehru, preoccupied with reinforcing the stability of the new nation-state, probably opted for time to strengthen bargaining power, not that he minimized the threat of an unresolved border. But the question remains relevant.[6]
b) The management of **relationships with neighbors**, especially those that are a security threat or concern, becomes the highest diplomacy priority. The very best diplomats should be assigned to these countries, without becoming excessively neighbor-centric. In practice, this does not always happen, and there are instances in different regions of countries diluting attention to their

own areas, in preference of focus on the major Western capitals.

c) Application of pressure and **coercion is a form of diplomacy**, usually practiced by powerful nations against weaker ones. For greater effectiveness, this is often supplemented with incentives and rewards, which is sometimes called a 'policy of engagement'.[7]

d) Creating a sound frame of **regional cooperation** is an adjunct to the above. The finest example of how a set of countries faced with threats of an irredentist and ethnic nature, changed the paradigm, and created an entirely new cooperative partnership is provided by ASEAN. When it was founded in 1967 there were at least four major sets of territorial claims among the original five members, Indonesia, Malaysia, the Philippines, Singapore and Thailand. Today these bilateral disputes are history, resolved through mutual accommodation, and more important, the creation of deep-rooted mutual confidence. ASEAN and China have also managed to evolve a method of putting into cold storage the complex sea boundary issue in the South China Sea that involves several countries of the region. Equally impressive is the establishment of the 'Asian Regional Forum' as an adjunct, which involves all the major powers of Asia and the world in an annual dialogue with ASEAN. In fact ARF is a prototype of a new kind of soft framework for security.

e) Flowing from the above, it is clear that the **settlement of boundary disputes** is a vital step in ensuring long-term security. This is visible in Africa where countries that have resolved old territorial issues, using the OAU Charter as the base for respecting inherited borders, have been able to move on to wider cooperation. In the case of India and China, after the sharp and bloody border war of 1962, the two have managed to work out bilateral arrangements to de-militarize the border region and re-establish broad ranging cooperation. But the absence of a boundary settlement remains a factor of potential instability.

f) No less important is **cross-regional cooperation**, especially linking up sets of neighboring countries that straddle different regions in our conventional definition of regions. This usually hinges on sound bilateral relationships between key countries, since the bilateral relationship is the basic building block of diplomacy. Examples: the concept of 'Mekong-Ganga Cooperation' covering ASEAN countries that lie on the Mekong river and its delta, and India. The initiative in this particular grouping has come from Thailand, which sees itself as a bridge between regions. Another instance is the Indian Ocean Rim Association for Regional Cooperation (IOC-ARC), encompassing countries from South Africa to Australia, including India, Oman and a dozen others. There are similar new putative cooperation networks in Central Asia. The most successful instance of cooperation of this kind is APEC, which brings together the US, China, Japan, all the ASEAN states, as well as Australia and some Latin American countries.[8]

g) Wider concepts of security concerns suggest the need for alert and agile diplomacy that looks to **building issue-specific coalitions** with like-minded nations, putting aside old notions of ideology and division into North–South groupings. It also underscores the value of sound relationships with all the **major power centers** of the globe, even if one does not subscribe to the concepts of multipolarity.

CASE STUDY: AN INDIA–PAKISTAN GAS PIPELINE?

The tense and often problematical relationship between India and Pakistan, now both nuclear powers, is well documented. The two countries have fought three major wars, in 1948, 1965 and 1971, the last of which saw the separation of the unviable entity of East Pakistan and the creation of Bangladesh. The two have also fought minor wars, the latest of which was the clash in Kargil in mid-1999, when Pakistan surreptitiously crossed the 'Line of Control' in Kashmir and was soundly rebuffed after two months of localized fighting. The interplay of security interests in relation to a concrete issue is narrated below.

PREVENTIVE DIPLOMACY

This term refers to heading off conflict before it erupts. In January 1992, in the afterglow of the success of the Gulf War the previous year, the UN Secretary General asserted that the UN could be a more effective instrument 'for peace-making and peacekeeping'. But the mood changed with the re-emergence of differences among Western powers on other world issues. The term preventive diplomacy takes several meanings.

First, a great power approach is to include in it peace-making, the use of incentive, threat and even force to prevent the worsening of a situation or outbreak of hostilities. This demands strong commitment by powers that have a capacity to influence events, to the point of intervention.

Second, it focuses on mediation and/or offers of 'good offices' to resolve problems, by way of diplomatic intervention by single states and by regional groups, and the development of 'confidence building measures', without invoking force. It may involve innovative diplomacy, a proactive application of new methods.

Third, it refers to efforts by non-state activists, NGOs and private voluntary organizations (PVOs), to apply social detection and early intervention, through economic and disaster assistance, as well as other forms of relief. It may be called pre-crisis action to prevent the emergence of a full-blown crisis. This is the theme of an influential book, *Preventive Diplomacy: Stopping Wars Before They Start* edited by Kevin M. Cahill, (Routledge, New York, 2000), revised edition.

In July 2001, the leaders of the two countries held a summit meeting at Agra that proved inconclusive. Prime Minister A.B. Vajpayee has accepted a return invitation from the Pakistan President, though in the aftermath of the September 11 events and the repercussions in Afghanistan, there are new complications.

Discussion on a cooperative project is now on the back burner, but what are the issues?

Pakistan maintains that a settlement of the Kashmir issue is the core of the problem between the two, and without this, no improvement in relations, or even normalization is possible. It seeks to win the valley of Kashmir, even while this is couched in terms of a settlement that safeguards the 'honor of Pakistan' and 'respects the wishes of the people of Kashmir', allegedly the third party in the issue. Once the Kashmir issue is resolved to its satisfaction, all other problems become capable of early settlement, such as normalization of trade (where Pakistan refuses to reciprocate Indian measures, at considerable cost to itself too), movement of divided families, cultural exchanges and the like.

India views Kashmir as the symptom, not the principal problem. In the state of Jammu & Kashmir, which India regards as its integral territory, there are five main components, the Jammu area with a majority Hindu population, the valley of Kashmir with a Muslim majority,[9] and the principally Buddhist Ladakh region; then there are two other parts that are under Pakistan's occupation, Muzaffarnagar and the Northern region (a sizable part of which has been ceded by Pakistan to China). India's goals are to get Pakistan to vacate the large area of 'Pakistan Occupied Kashmir', and to get it to cease its cross-border terrorism. Most countries recognize Pakistan's complicity in aiding terrorism, via training camps, supplies of arms and the induction of foreign mercenaries, including Afghans, in the false name of 'Jihad' or holy war.

India's larger problem is that it regards the domestic challenge of alienation of sections of the Kashmir people as its internal issue, one that needs a political solution, not a redrawing of the boundaries of India and Pakistan in the name of religion. India is a modern secular state, with over 130 million Muslim inhabitants, representing 13% of the people. In contrast Pakistan sees itself as the 'homeland' of Muslims, and is chronically unable to accept secular India, practicing tolerance and equal respect to all religions. That is the crux of the differences, and settlement of large issues depends on Pakistan's acceptance of this reality.

Against this complex background a new issue has emerged some years back, offering both promise and a challenge. Iran, which has vast reserves of natural gas, sees in India a long-term market, and a gas pipeline is the most feasible option to take the gas to the Indian consumers. But an overland pipeline must traverse Pakistan. Alternatives, like a deep-sea pipeline that would avoid Pakistan territory, are both highly expensive and technologically almost impossible, given the deep-sea trenches that must be traversed. Using the gas liquefaction route is monstrously expensive. On the other hand, an overland pipeline would give Pakistan a major permanent source of income. Both Iran and Pakistan are keen that the pipeline be built. India's dilemma is the security of supply, and assurance that gas supply would not be disrupted, the more so as the tribal region to be traversed in Baluchistan, is but under marginal control of Islamabad. How can permanence of supply, on which India would build a superstructure of downstream gas processing, be guaranteed?

The World Bank and major financiers are interested in the project, which is commercially viable. It may also be feasible to work out international and bilateral guarantees between all the parties involved to give assurance of non-disruption of supply. What is the level of credibility or assurance that India can expect, to safeguard its energy and gas supply security? Is it believable against the background of tension and other major problems? Can such a project be executed, and even become a basis for larger mutual confidence and cooperation? One should add another dimension of reality. There is at least one major bilateral India–Pakistan agreement, the Indus Waters Treaty of 1960, that has worked to the satisfaction of both countries, throughout the past four decades of tension and war. So there is limited precedent for sustained cooperation.

The gas pipeline project remains under sporadic dialogue,

principally between India and Iran. There is little chance that it can move forward, until the unsettled international situation, particularly the aftermath in Afghanistan, created in the wake of the September 2001 terrorist acts, eases. The project offers a dynamic case study of the intersection of strong political, security, and economic interests among three countries that remains under evolution, conditioned by the complex bilateral relations among the three. The blend of perceived threat, economic expectation and self-interest protection is worth attention by diplomacy scholars.

QUESTIONS

1. How would you define national security from the perspective of your own country?
2. What are the new ingredients of security, in general, which you feel deserve greater attention?
3. How would you integrate national security issues into diplomacy? Do you feel that the foreign policy of your country pays sufficient attention to security concerns?
4. Please name and explain with reasons a theme that in your opinion constitutes an interesting case study blending security, economic, political and/or other interests?

REFERENCES

1. Cahill, Kevin M., *Preventive Diplomacy: Stopping Wars Before they Start* (Routledge, New York, 2000).
2. Caldwell, Dan, and Mckewon, Timothy J, ed., *Diplomacy, Force and Leadership* (Westview Press, Boulder, 1993).
3. Craig, Gordon A., and George, Alexander L., *Force and Statecraft: Diplomatic Problems of Our Times*, 3rd edition, (Oxford University Press, New York, 1995).
4. Eban, Abba, *Diplomacy for the New Century* (Yale University New Haven, Press, 1998).

5. Haass, Richard, and O'Sullivan, Meghan, *Honey and Vinegar: Incentives, Sanctions and Foreign Policy* (Brookings Institution, Washington DC, 2000).

NOTES

1. Michael Leifer, *Singapore's Foreign Policy: Coping with Vulnerability* (Routledge, London, 2000).
2. Karl W. Deutsch, *An Analysis of International Relations*, 3rd edition, (Prentice Hall India, New Delhi, 1988).
3. Abba Eban, *Diplomacy for the New Century* (New Haven, Yale University Press, 1998).
4. This highly classified network, on which some reports have emerged in recent years, gives the US a capacity also to listen in on all forms of communications around the world, *inter alia* giving it access to commercial and economic information from its close allies as well.
5. After September 11, 2001, it is convenient to view attacks by Islamic extremists on the US as proof of a clash of religion and culture. But that is both over-simplistic and operates like a self-fulfilling prophesy. Virtually every state today harbors multi-ethnicities and people of diverse religions. Almost every large or medium-sized country is a celebration of diversity of different kinds. Countries and peoples do have a capacity to live in harmony with these differences, provided they are not provoked from outside, or within, into developing antagonism and polarization. There is resilience in countries and in the world community to withstand provocation and sustain harmony, but it needs constant cultivation and reinforcement. Despite the civilizing influence of culture, the Hobbesian world of strife and each for oneself is not too far. This situation poses one of the profound challenges of out times.
6. Many commentators have also written about the 'deal' that Premier Zhou Enlai offered to Jawaharlal Nehru on his last visit to Delhi in 1960; Nehru was tempted, but the option was foreclosed by opposition within the Indian Cabinet, as also possibly a premature leak in the press.
7. An exhaustive survey of sanctions and incentives is given in the book

Honey and Vinegar: Incentives, Sanctions and Foreign Policy, by Richard Haass and Meghan O'Sullivan, (Brookings Institution, Washington DC, 2000).

8. The unifying element in APEC is the notion of the 'Pacific rim', a concept that was much in fashion on the US West Coast in the late 1980s during the period I served as Consul General in San Francisco.
9. For hundreds of years there was a minority Hindu population in the Kashmir valley that lived in harmony with Muslims. After the onset of Pakistan-inspired terrorism around 1990, which took advantage of some genuine grievances of the people of the Kashmir valley and political ineptitude by its government, this minority has been driven out of Kashmir through targeted acts of terror. This ethnic cleansing has attracted little notice in the international community.

4

Economics and Diplomacy

Viewed earlier as a peripheral activity best left to commercial secretaries and specialists from other departments, the building of trade and economic relationships has moved to the center of diplomacy. This is an interesting turn of the wheel of history. Even a couple of decades back, commercial diplomacy was seen as a 'black hole' by diplomats pursuing a fast-track career, and paled in comparison with political work. But if we go back to the origins of diplomacy, like the recently transcribed Amarna archive clay tablets of Middle Egypt of the period 1460–1220 BC, and the extensive trade that existed in subsequent centuries among the countries and civilizations of Egypt and West Asia, we see that trade provided the first motivation for inter-state contacts and agreements. Another example is provided in the spread of colonialism in Asia, following Vasco da Gama's journey to India in 1498, and Europe's 'discovery' of the riches of the East Indies. Again the flag followed trade.

CONTEMPORARY IMPORTANCE

Today, diplomatic services place virtually equal emphasis on political and economic work. Rich countries and developing nations alike consider the mobilization of inward foreign investments (FDI) and export promotion as the essence of advancing interests in foreign countries. Over a dozen nations around the world use the Australian and Canadian model of an integrated ministry that handles foreign affairs and external trade;[1] others like UK have achieved similar unity of action with joint new structures that handle trade and investment promotion through the embassy network, under the direct charge of the Foreign Office. Thus economics is a major component of contemporary 'integrated diplomacy'. In a word, economics permeates diplomacy.

In the same way that law was seen as the foundation of diplomatic studies in the past, economics is now the *sine qua non* of contemporary training. (Example: Germany now attracts more economists than law graduates in its diplomatic service.) No diplomat can afford not to master this so-called 'dismal science', both to understand the dynamics of world affairs, and to integrate economics into all his work. At headquarters, politics and economics are intertwined in bilateral and multilateral work. In the embassy, every diplomatic official, regardless of work domain, must weave into his or her job the economic perspective in the same manner that he or she also keeps an eye on the political dimension.[2]

The US–China relationship, in the way it has developed in the past 20 years, is one outstanding example of the way economics becomes a driving force in shaping political relations. Each time the US administration or the Congress has considered human rights issues or the Taiwan issue in a manner that is contrary to the interests of Beijing, US business lobbies that are fixated on that country's immense market potential, become active to 'safeguard' their export interests. This is one way economics becomes a driver of political relationships.

A different example is provided by the way India–US ties have evolved after India's nuclear tests of May 1998. The non-proliferation concerns of the US, some European states, and Japan had led to the imposition of an explicit policy of economic 'sanctions'.

Gradually these sanctions have been modified and lifted, at least in part because of the business attraction offered by this 'Big Emerging Market'.[3] In both cases astute eco-political diplomacy has been marshaled by the country affected, to neutralize adverse political circumstances, using also wide networks of non-state constituencies, especially the corporate communities within the other nation.

Foreign ministries do not generally handle external economic relations (with the exception of Australia, Canada and a score of others that have a combined ministry, as mentioned above). But some monitoring of bilateral economic links is combined with political work in most MFAs, through their territorial divisions. This is in recognition of the fact that economics is a vital and often dominant component of bilateral relations. The other related element is that most diplomatic services combine economic work with other tasks, though there are a number that also have a specialized foreign commercial service (like the US), or handle commercial diplomacy with a combination of specialists deputed to the larger embassies from the trade ministry, and regular foreign service personnel handling this elsewhere.

The four pillars of economic work are:

- ❑ **Trade** promotion, with prime but not exclusive focus on exports.
- ❑ **Investment** promotion, mainly focused on inward investments, but not excluding the home country's outbound investments, where appropriate.
- ❑ Attracting suitable **technologies**, plus technology 'harvesting'.
- ❑ Management of **economic aid**, which is important for most developing countries as 'recipients', and as 'donors' for developed nations.[4]

There is also the larger task of **country promotion**, which supports all of the above, and blends into image building, as well as tourism promotion. Enhancement of the image of the home country is one of the essential tasks of diplomacy that underpins and relates to a wide range of external activities.

A word should be offered on definitions. Contemporary 'economic diplomacy' is broader in scope than the 'commercial' work of the past. As the above list indicates, the tasks go beyond trade, and encompass activities that would not have figured on the work agenda of embassies and foreign ministries even some 25 years back. Three concrete examples are investment mobilization, tourism promotion and management of the country image. Each of these three is relevant to diplomacy, as concrete activity that official representatives today undertake in external relation building. And each of them provides feedback into other elements of the diplomatic process. It is another demonstration of expanded and integrated diplomacy.

ORGANIZATION OF ECONOMIC WORK

There are several different models, if we try and understand how economic work, i.e. trade and investment issues are handled within the MFA. These are:

- **Unified.** There are about 15 countries which now combine foreign affairs and foreign trade (Australia, Canada, Sweden). But in a special twist, under the unified ministry, Australia has a separate commercial export promotion service, distinct from the diplomatic service, though the head of mission plays a unified role in heading both activities.
- **Part unification.** The best instance is UK that has created two special units in the Foreign Office, jointly with the Department of Trade and Industry, to handle trade and investments, manned by a unified diplomatic service.
- **Third agency.** This is the Singapore method, where the MFA largely keeps out of economic work, and the operational tasks are handled by two special entities, the Singapore Trade Board and the Singapore Economic Development Board, under the supervision of the Ministry of Trade and Industry. Each Board posts its own representatives at key locations, placed within the embassy or consulate general. The ambassador and other

diplomats work closely with them in the well-known 'Team Singapore' style. In other instances we see that harmony is harder to establish.

- **Competition.** This is the relatively confused situation in many countries, with the MFA and economic ministries engaged in turf battles over responsibility not only for export promotion and investment mobilization, but also over the handling of WTO affairs, and some other economic groupings. Examples: India, Thailand. One direct consequence is that the diplomatic machine does not make a full contribution to the advancement of economic interests.
- **Renunciation.** The MFA does not play an active role in bilateral economic work, and is glad to hand this over to another ministry. Examples: China, Germany. This does not optimize resources, even if there is little outward evidence of disharmony.

There are also exceptional situations where aid work is concentrated in the MFA, but this happens only with donor countries (examples: Japan, the Netherlands). There are no instances where recipient countries (i.e. developing countries) handle aid work in the MFA. India offers an interesting contrast; it runs a small aid donation program, which is handled entirely from the Ministry of External Affairs. But the inbound aid work is handled exclusively by the Indian Finance Ministry.

METHODOLOGY

Let us assume that the diplomat has a basic understanding of economics, and accepts the logic of complete integration of this activity into his mainstream work. The practical components of economic diplomacy are given below. This list is illustrative, and does not exclude other matching actions.

A. **Analysis.** Understanding the economic dynamics of the target country is an essential prelude. It includes: insight into the principal elements of the local economy; analysis of the export and import basket of the country and its chief regions; the foreign investment profile; technology strengths; and the activities of competitors, actual and potential, gauged against one's own exports and other ongoing economic activities in that country. It is assumed that the diplomat fully understands the economic needs of his or her own country, and that this knowledge is kept updated. (Example: some diplomatic services require diplomats to undertake familiarization tours at home, prior to taking up each foreign assignment.)

B. **Basic guide notes.** Writing a 'commercial note' or briefing guide on the country is useful on several counts. First, it necessitates understanding the basic economic profile of the country, its principal indicators, the organization of the economy, tax, tariff and customs policy, the banking and related structures, system of business dispute settlement, the pattern of the business organizations, the principal import and export players, and the like. Second, such a guide responds to general commercial inquiries from home. The commercial note can be posted on the mission's website on the Internet, and the feedback used to improve the note (it has to be a continual task to updating and improving the material). Third, one's own note can be compared against those prepared by foreign embassies, again for self-improvement. (Example: the US Commerce Department guide notes available on most countries serve as a useful yardstick.) There are other commercial briefing notes to be written, like market reports on individual products, plus analysis covering competitors and their market share, plus the marketing strategies used by them.[5]

C. **Outreach.** This involves the obvious economic partners, like the local enterprises engaged in bilateral trade and investments, or others that have a potential interest. There are also the associations of business, individual enterprises that enjoy clout, and other pressure groups, as well as parliamentarians, academics, the media, specialists in science and technology, plus local constituents like regional and other subsidiary political entities that have a direct stake in stronger economic exchanges.[6] The latter types of local groups are especially important, for reaching out to local businesses, when employment generation and other local economic benefits are involved. A distinction should be made between companies and entrepreneurs who are the prime actors in economic relations, and the commerce chambers and the like who are the intermediaries. Both have their role and value.

D. **Teamwork.** It may go against the grain of internal work allocation, but a 'task force' method is often useful, which involves the entire mission team in handling specified economic tasks (such as export promotion of priority products). Some believe that such wide distribution of tasks treads into the work domain of the commercial or the economic officials, but the advantage is full engagement of the entire team. Outside the mission, advantage can also be taken of own nationals in key positions, like experts on technical cooperation assignments, business representatives stationed in the country, and others, for brainstorming and participation in different kinds of outreach activities. This acknowledges the reality that relationship building is not the exclusive job of the official representatives; others can contribute, if only they are asked! And leadership has to be provided for such teamwork by the head of mission, through personal example.

E. **Delegations.** Dispatch of business mission in both directions is a classic method of promoting trade, investments and all other forms of economic exchanges. Careful preparation is indispensable for good results, consisting of scrupulous program preparation, and pre-arrival match-making, to identify serious interest among businessmen on both sides. This is possible only when comprehensive information is gathered and distributed on specific interests and targets of each participant. No less vital is post-visit follow-up, to gauge results and draw lessons for the future. Thanks to the Internet, it should be possible to try a 'virtual' delegation method, not as a substitute to the real visits, but as a supplement. This is a concept that awaits exploration.

DIPLOMACY AND INNOVATION

Jan Melissen provides an elegant definition of the role of innovation: 'If it is agreed that diplomacy is the management and facilitation of change in international relations by means of adaptation and innovation of the modes of diplomatic practice ... Diplomacy could not be about anything other than innovation.'*

Adaptation to change produces different kinds of innovation. One instance of innovation has been the 'Asia Europe Meetings' (ASEM) launched in 1995 at the initiative of ASEAN, annual summit meetings between itself, other major Asian states and the European Union. ASEM exploits the desire of EU to build strong connection with the economically vibrant Asian region, and envy at having been left out of the other successful new grouping APEC (in which the US is a major participant.) Concentrating primarily at the summit level, without ministerial meetings or any other structural paraphernalia, ASEM focuses quietly on concepts and methods that guide relations among participants. By taking the driving seat, ASEAN also projects itself larger on global stage.

Consider also another completely different level at which a new method was tried out in 1994 and continued since—diplomatic coordination among Indian embassies in major EU capitals. With the support of the Ministry of External Affairs a system of 6-monthly meetings of ambassadors was launched, taking place in the capital that held the rotating EU presidency. Such regular consultation among regional missions was unknown in the Indian system. In December 1994, just a few days before the Köln EU Summit, the German Foreign Office State Secretary who met our group for a briefing and conversation, remarked that we were the first country to have understood the way European unification would require others to begin also to understand and deal with them collectively.

* Jan Melissen, ed., *Innovation in Diplomatic Practice* (Macmillan, London, 1999).

F. **Multilateral Issues.** Basic understanding of the WTO process, and the manner in which it operates in the country of assignment, the following—local attitudes, policy on 'dumping' issues, the dispute settlement mechanism, and positions on different subjects in the multilateral debates—are required information for all diplomats, not just the ones handling economic work. Multilateral diplomacy constantly demands support actions at the bilateral level. The purpose is not just to canvas support from the target country, but also to engage in real two-way dialogue.

G. **Innovation.** Economic work offers scope for innovation and needs a proactive mindset, perhaps more than any other aspect of diplomatic work. Beyond the list of tried and tested methods, involvement of the full mission team has the advantage of producing new approaches and inventiveness. (Example: the use of the Asia-Pacific group of embassies as a regional promotional tool in Germany arose at the initiative of one visionary individual, former Ambassador Tony Siddique of Singapore.) The tools of 'linkage' are also available, making interconnections between what may at first sight appear as unconnected issues, to advance one's national interests.[7]

COUNTRY PROMOTION

All aspects of economic work are subsumed under country promotional activities (trade, investments, and technology). This activity also reaches into other areas, like building positive media and public images, destination promotion for attracting tourists, and for activities that may even include building institutional links in research & development or education cooperation. Example: during the apartheid era South Africa targeted chief executives of major European enterprises with invitations that were ostensibly for tourist visits, on the calculation that such executives would go back with a sharper awareness of business opportunities.[8] Business takes place in all kinds of environments, including situations where countries are hostile, and may not even maintain diplomatic relations, like China and Taiwan in the period right up to the early 1980s when political contact was established between the two rival regimes. But business always goes better when people like one another and find the other country congenial!

In 1991 the International Finance Corporation and the Multilateral Investment Guarantee Association, both based in Washington DC, had published a comparative study on the country promotional methodology of several countries. (This study was revised in 2000.)[9] In the past decade there has been a much greater accumulation of experience, since most countries, regions and even province-level entities in large countries now implement vigorous programs of their own in pursuit of ever-elusive FDI. We all understand that one's own efforts have to be conditioned by awareness of the competitive market for investments.

The hard material for country promotion—the websites, brochures and other distribution material—is produced by the home agencies, and the mission acts as the distributor. But it can also use its ingenuity in adapting such material for local use, selecting the data and positioning for its own website, and using local knowledge for optimal impact. It also often has the prospect for using local opportunities for extensive and intensive contact, without waiting for investment procurement delegations from home

Regions within countries have emerged as entities that engage in their own external relationship building, particularly in the economic sector. For instance, in Germany the state of Saxony regards the neighboring areas of Poland and the Czech Republic as its special partners in creating a high growth 'Euro-region'. The same is true of the state of Baden-Württemberg that also sees itself as a unique locus of entrepreneurship, based on its dynamic medium-sized industry ('Mittelstand') and a concentration of scientific and research institutions, unmatched elsewhere. In France and in Italy too, such high growth regions are seeking a distinct external identity. In the US, many leading states maintain their own networks of representation abroad. For the purpose of 'country' promotion, such regional initiatives aimed at attracting business, inward and outward, are assets that can be used to the advantage of the region and for the country as a whole.

Other methods that are relevant include:

a) An 'image audit' should be regarded as a fundamental prerequisite for establishing a base line and a reference point, for image building and for country promotion, but the device is seldom used in practice. Consequently, an accurate basis for addressing the image issues that are really important at the particular place and time is often missing. This is an expensive exercise that can be undertaken only by headquarters. But for the individual embassy this does not reduce the responsibility for making a good assessment of the local challenges in country promotion.
b) Official representatives are expected to depict a rosy picture of the scene in the home country, but statements by nationals of the target country and third countries often carry greater credibility. This is even truer of case studies. Yet official statements are important, especially when one can demonstrate an ability to 'walk the talk'.
c) All the classic skills of outreach are involved at their peak in country promotion, including social entertainment and a welcoming ambience offered by the mission. There are documented instances

where the efficient delivery of consular services has been a positive factor in image building and country promotion.

d) In one more demonstration of the integral nature of external affairs, tourism promotion is closely allied with country promotion and it is best to use the synergy available by combining or at least coordinating the two activities.

e) One special device in the armory of the mission is the regional approach, locally using a group such as the cluster of SADC ambassadors or the Asia Pacific group of envoys, for joint promotional effort, *vis-à-vis* the local agencies, or regions. It is remarkably productive in gaining access and visibility.

The role of initiative, innovation and inventiveness cannot be minimized. These qualities are fully tested in all branches of economic promotion work.

BALANCED ECONOMIC DIPLOMACY

Can there be too much of economic diplomacy? One commentator has argued that one reason for the inability of the British Embassy in Teheran to foresee the downfall of the Shah in 1979, despite an abundance of warning signals, was that the entire mission team was engaged in pushing British exports, including even the defense attachés. Feedback to headquarters on important political developments is the logical first obligation of any embassy, and preoccupation with other tasks cannot supplant this responsibility. We know from other evidence, including analysis of the role of the CIA and others, that the failure in Iran was in willingness at headquarters to listen to those who offered advice that ran counter to the wisdom accepted in the highest councils.

There are other instances of failure of diplomatic missions to anticipate tectonic shifts within their host countries, which has more to do with mindsets that depend on conventional thinking and 'status quo-ism'. In diplomacy as in other professions, there is a strong case for 'out-of-the-box' thinking and exploring the unthinkable. This is an even greater challenge for the policy planners at headquarters.

QUESTIONS

1. Why has economic diplomacy gained in importance?
2. Give an example of country promotion activities, or provide a model for undertaking this work.
3. What model exists in your country for handling economic work? Which would be the best method in your view, looking to what other countries have done?
4. What work methodology is the most important for economic work in your view?

REFERENCES

1. Rana, Kishan S., *Inside Diplomacy* (Manas, New Delhi, 2000), Chapter 4, pp. 96–127, Chapter 6, pp. 144–48.
2. Berridge, G.R., *Diplomacy: Theory and Practice,* 3rd edition, (Palgrave, London, publication expected in early 2002).

NOTES

1. Two recent studies on MFAs are relevant. These are: Brian Hocking, ed., *Foreign Ministries: Change and Adaptation* (Macmillan, London, 1999); Justin Robertson, ed., *Foreign Ministries in Developing Countries and Emerging Market Economies* (Halifax, International Insights: Dalhousie Journal of International Affairs, Volume 14, Summer, 1998).
2. This is a concept of work allocation that is not universal, but it makes sense, as explained in Chapter 8. Every diplomatic official should keep both the political and economic perspective in view, whether he handles cultural, education, or consular work, or any other task.
3. In the late 1990s the US Commerce Department identified a dozen 'Big Emerging Markets' for special attention in the development of economic ties, also giving political overtones to the exercise.

4. Countries such as China, Egypt and India are both donors and recipients of external economic assistance. Each focuses on providing the kind of aid that is best suited to its strengths, especially technical assistance which leverages domestic availability of high quality trained manpower and the training infrastructure.
5. It is not an easy task for the embassy to prepare commercial market reports of this nature, but the very act of meeting local and one's own businessmen, gathering information, and getting into the study project becomes a learning experience for the commercial officer. He or she finds that there are allies that can be used, like business chambers, trade publications and even companies that possess expert information and may be willing to share some of this on a two-way exchange basis.
6. Serving in Germany in 1992–95, I found it quite feasible to get a regional party body or a newspaper published in a major city, to organize a business promotional event permitting us to reach out to companies in different localities that were attracted by the Indian market but unsure about how to handle problems of distance and lack of familiarity. This is the kind of promotional activity that a resident mission can accomplish using non-obvious local partners.
7. The Diplomatic Corps also offers opportunity for mutual learning, on a basis of confidentiality and credibility; this in turn hinges on making constructive use of opportunity.
8. The cross-over between business and tourism is recognized very well by countries such as Malaysia, Mauritius, Singapore and Thailand, and inadequately by many others in the developing world. Good tourism promotion meshes very well with business promotion.
9. *Marketing a country: promotion as a tool for attracting foreign investment*, revised edition, (World Bank, Washington DC, 2000).

5

Trade, Investments, Aid, and Technology

There is no aspect of external relations, bilateral, regional or global, that is not affected by the 'image' issue. The way one's nation is perceived by others affects state-to-state links in all dimensions, and even more so the relations at the level of people and the non-state institutions. Embassies, foreign ministries and diplomats are considered responsible for the projection of a 'correct' image of their country—even if in reality their capacity to radically or immediately influence their country's image perception abroad may be limited. But proactive diplomacy demands that even in adverse situations, serious and constant attention be paid to the country image. Diplomacy theorist Brian Hocking has written of a survey of 200 US Fortune 500 companies, in which 72% said that national image was significant to external purchase of goods and services, adding that 'company brands interact with national identities in concrete ways'.[1]

TRADE

All countries today pay strong official attention to trade promotion. Many entrust the work to the diplomatic service, while others handle it exclusively through specialist commercial services, 'trade commissioners' and the like.[2] But even these countries that have not seen the virtues of 'integrated diplomacy' (where commercial and economic work is combined with other diplomatic jobs), find it essential to integrate all the work at the apex, in that the HOM is in overall charge. Experience has shown that detachment of commercial work results in inadequate attention to investment mobilization and country promotion, and one misses out on the cross-connections that integrated diplomacy offers.

Many countries have adapted for their own use a fine 'handbook' for commercial officials written by the International Trade Center, Geneva, to prepare their own guidebooks. Such material comprehensively helps commercial officials through the typical work demands of trade promotion, ranging from the preparation of market studies to organizing country participation in trade fairs and specialized exhibitions. Typically, trade development work includes the following:

a) The starting point of export promotion is a careful analysis of one's global exports, comparing these with **existing exports from the home country to the target market**. Any shortfall in the latter shows what needs to be done. For example, if readymade garments comprise 15% of one's total exports, but in the target market one only has a 5% share, it is worth investigating the reasons for this mismatch. These may lie in strong competition from other countries, or some kind of preferences enjoyed by them, or 'non-tariff' barriers that one's own exports face, or simply lack of adequate knowledge of the market by one's own exporters and/or local importers. In such analysis one should, of course, take into account the advice from one's own foreign trade ministry, chambers of commerce and the like. Another approach that is equally interesting is an analysis of the entire import basket of the target country, and the exports to the target market by other countries that one may regard as one's own global competitors. Such a study often provides insights into product groups that may be missing completely from one's own exports to that country, either because trade has not been initiated, or perhaps even because manufacturing capacities have not been created at home. (Example: In the 1990s China's annual exports of soft toys to the EU exceeded $1 billion. India, which could have had a share of the market, had simply not built the manufacturing capacity in this sector, for want of initiative by home entrepreneurs. In part, this was also on account of unfamiliarity with the EU safety regulations; this has changed subsequently, and one reason has also been the development of a domestic Indian market for high quality soft toys).[3]

b) It is customary to focus on one's own exports, but helping local companies to **export to the home country** should not be overlooked, especially when such companies approach the mission for information or assistance. After all, exports and imports are two sides of the same coin, and excessive preoccupation with a single country trade balance is seldom worthwhile, except in unusual circumstances. (Example: Today an embassy can easily guide a local company that seeks information on exporting to the home country towards websites that furnish such information, rather than tell the company to contact its own embassy. Helping local exporters to access the home market is also a way of building connections that become part of the mission's 'outreach').

c) In the 'promotional' phase, especially when dealing with new markets or other opportunities, the mission can play a critical role in supplying domestic export associations and exporters with **market data and insights** gained from broad contact with local importers, visits to trade shows, and dialogue with major players like department store chains and mail-order houses. In dealing with established export products, the mission's focus should be on finding new market avenues. It is possible for the mission to commission local specialists to produce market studies on products of potential export interest, but an alert mission can undertake this work on its own. Even if the resulting study is not of the highest quality, the very act of preparing it sharpens the commercial section's acumen and insights.

d) **New products** should be a special area of focus. Domestic exporters may lack in awareness of products that are not currently in the export basket, and if the mission can work with some of them to gain entry, market forces would take care of subsequent growth. This would happen through the entry of other competitors from the home country and the creation of additional export capacity. This is one area where the mission can make a unique contribution—once exporters from home begin to actually ship out the new product, others will tend to follow them, and thereby create a more-or-less permanent market for the country.

e) **Trade disputes** are a bothersome but important area. The mission can help at the initial or informal phase, in offering 'good offices' and informal mediation, and urging reasonable settlement. It is important to maintain local credibility, while at the same time helping one's own enterprises—and this may involve discretion, using one's own judgment to withdraw from disputes that are best left to formal machinery.

f) Initiation of proposals for **visits by trade delegations** is another worthwhile activity, particularly when local importers have to be convinced of the quality or other attractiveness of one's domestic manufactures, overcoming the kind of 'information gap' that usually exists, particularly for developing countries. Again good judgment is vital, to avoid over-selling business prospects. Strong commitment by the embassy to the trade mission, from program preparation to accompaniment by embassy officials at business sessions at local chambers and to different cities is essential to maximize the impact. The HOM's personal presence, when feasible, is of much value.[4]

g) **'Buyer–Seller Meets'** is another option, varying in scale from a large show that reaches out to a substantial number of local enterprises, to smaller events with just a few participants, which can even be organized on the mission premises. (Example: a small 'business center' located within the embassy can host such small events, where this is appropriate, because of a relative lack of local specialized trade shows.)

h) **Trade fair participation** is the other classic method of servicing existing export markets, gaining market intelligence on new trends, and creating additional opportunities. Even if one does not export to a particular market, visiting trade fairs is worthwhile to make contacts and gain insights. There is an entire tradecraft in organizing fair participation, and it is worthwhile for the commercial representative to understand this, in order to guide home-based exporters.

The Internet offers multiple options for export promotions that are slowly coming into use. One method exploited by business chambers (and private entrepreneurs) is matchmaking among buyers and sellers. This is done via 'portals' that specialize in industry and product segments, and other 'B2B' services. On a not-for-profit basis, chambers of commerce and official agencies engaged in export promotion work have also begun to use these methods. At an even more basic level, small entrepreneurs are now using the Internet for browsing and data mining, to connect directly with consumers and end-users located in distant lands. Two instances: the manual labor-based ship-breaking industry at Gujarat in India and in Bangladesh now uses the Web to locate ships due for breakup and to reach multiple ship-owning clients. Similarly, producers of handicrafts in many regions in the Third World now have begun to break out of the clutches of middlemen by directly establishing connections with importers and retailers abroad, using inexpensive email (e.g. in the remote Kutch region in India that was ravaged by earthquake in early 2001). The bursting of the dot-com bubble in 2000 has not ended the real opportunity that exists for e-commerce, even in remote places around the world.

A method that has not been used extensively so far is to have 'virtual business delegations', encountering foreign counterparts via special portals created by sponsoring business associations and the like. It is a form of B2B contact, but of a promotional nature, based on careful preparation by diplomatic missions, trade offices and sponsoring official agencies that also indirectly affirm the genuineness of the business participants who join in the exercise. This deals with the credibility issue, a major concern in remote contacts.

The mission has the task of aiding and encouraging domestic enterprises to overcome the barriers of unfamiliarity and lack of knowledge of foreign markets, especially via the Internet. The first prerequisite is an attitude of helpfulness, and real commitment to aiding the national export and trade effort. This involves breaking out of bureaucratic mindsets and operating a *de facto* business center within the mission, which can help visiting commercial executives, and provides facilities like phone, fax and Internet connection, if this is necessary in local conditions. In the larger mission such a center is indispensable as a form of marketing assistance.

INVESTMENTS

Increasingly, investment promotion has emerged as the special priority of economic diplomacy. All countries, developing or advanced, are competitors in the race for attracting FDI, since such investments are the best kind of capital inflows, creating jobs at home, and are by their very nature 'tied' to the destination country, unlike 'portfolio' investments in stock exchanges and other fast-moving capital flows that are motivated by short-term gain and are 'volatile' (as shown by the Asian economic crisis in 1998). Many countries use special agencies for attracting investments (like investment centers in many countries, designed to work as a 'one-stop shop', one model of which is Singapore's renowned Economic Development Board). But embassies are prime actors, by virtue of their overseas spread, knowledge of foreign countries, and intimate ground level contacts. Investment promotion work is a classic instance of cooperation requirement between the diplomatic mission and a home agency that is not the MFA—if they pull together, much can be achieved.

a) There are two primary methods that have to be deployed simultaneously—the **extensive and the intensive**. The first involves creating broad 'catchments' of potential investors, through publicity, distribution of promotional material, organizing or participating in investor conferences, business seminars at chambers of commerce and other forms of wide outreach. The second method involves sustained cultivation of target investors, identifying decision makers within the foreign companies being pursued, holding frequent meetings with them, overcoming doubts, providing clarifications and the like. Each has its particularities. The catchment method involves assiduous preparation, but it is mainly the partner organization that attracts the audience. The target method involves homework in identification of potential investors, followed by cultivation. The two methods complement one another.
b) Following from the above, the mission can create a **'Target 10' list.**[5] Considerable preparatory work goes into the identification of the target companies that are to be persuaded to invest. Such work can be initiated from headquarters, or handled by the mission acting on its own, but with the support of the home agencies. But since ground level contact is key, the mission is the indispensable player.
c) Another good method is the **pursuit of major enterprises** in the target country. For instance one can begin with those sectors that are on the home country's investment priority list, making 'cold calls' on leading enterprises in each, to get them to consider investment options. (Example: the embassy can work with a 'Fortune 500' list, to identify likely prospects. Sometimes this works so well that it may take some persuasion to convince the enterprise being visited that the embassy has acted on its own assessment of potential prospects, and not any 'inside'

information!) Approaches of this nature often involve reaching out to CEOs and Management Boards, usually through the HOM who has the rank to gain access. But concerted follow-up involves accessing others in the decision chain in the target company, via the economic counselor and other officials of the mission, which in turn entails teamwork.

d) Supplementing the above is the pursuit of companies that have **existing investments**, to get them to consider other avenues. One method that has worked well is to target companies that had established joint ventures or technology collaborations in the past, and persuade them to consider fresh investments and business partnerships. (Example: India used this method very effectively in Germany in the 1990s). This works well in countries that have a history of past investments.

e) Another sound device is the marketing of **success stories**, especially when recounted by foreign partners, (e.g. the profitable joint ventures, the fruitful technology collaborations). One needs to give them wide exposure, and use them as 'case studies' in promotional and publicity activities. Practical examples drawn from the foreign country are more persuasive than most other forms of promotion. Businessmen are also more likely to listen to other businessmen, than to officials.

f) Use of **all public platforms available** for indirect economic promotion is another tool, by blending in the message into political, cultural and other activities of the mission. This is a facet of integrated diplomacy.

The HOM has access to companies and institutions in the target country, unmatched by others in the mission. But he or she needs preparatory work, staff backup and follow-up, to translate investment potential into actual FDI inflow and joint ventures. With the exception of teamwork examples of 'economic development boards' of some ASEAN states and a few others, we find that there is often a lack of concord between the domestic investment promotional agencies and missions. The major reason for this mismatch in promotional efforts is usually that the missions and the domestic agencies do not sufficiently coordinate their actions. Home agencies focus on narrating their own stories, such as how much things have changed at home in comparison with the past. The foreign investor is much more interested in how the conditions that one country offers are superior to what they get elsewhere. The embassy has a major role in getting home agencies to view FDI promotion from the foreign investor's perspective. The embassy needs to understand the home priorities and take care not to 'over-sell', by making unrealistic promises about conditions at home, or inadvertently misleading the foreign investor in other ways.

A simple method that is now coming into usage is for the home agency to use the diplomatic missions to follow up on investment applicants whose proposals are under examination at home. This can be done by establishing via the embassy a line of communication that supplements other contacts. The embassy proactively reaches out to the investor and offers to help in overcoming bottlenecks or clearance delay. In this manner, an effort can be made to reduce the number of investment projects that disappear between the proposal stage and actual implementation. The importance of focus on this task can be judged from the fact that the percentage of investment proposals that are actually implemented is as low as 30% in some countries.[6] A better 'implementation ratio' is of obvious value.

AID DIPLOMACY

Either the finance ministry or the national planning agency usually handles aid flow management at home, in the aid-receiving country. The MFA is a facilitator, but not a direct player. Since the end-recipients of foreign aid (whether it is bilateral or multilateral) consist of almost all the domestic official agencies, plus non-official users like NGOs and privately run institutions, the work of consolidating their requests, prioritizing them, and handling negotiations with a wide range of donor partners, calls for full-time and specialized effort. The political relationship provides the framework for aid

STATUS OF ECONOMIC DIPLOMACY

Can we declare after this survey of economic methodology that within those countries that practice diplomacy in a thoroughgoing manner, as a skilled profession, diplomacy in this particular field has attained the stature that it merits? The actual situation resembles the proverbial half-full glass. What it has gained in stature in recent years is substantial, but there is yet a long way to go. This assessment is based on my observation, and a viewpoint expressed by one of the most senior diplomats in an Asian country, one who is an acknowledged master of the art.[7] The problems are:

- First, basic grounding in economics of the average diplomat is still very poor. Without understanding the fundamental concepts (such as those relating to macro-economics or international finance), it becomes hard to follow nuances of issues in the multilateral dialogue, or provide informed assistance to home enterprises.
- Second, some prejudice against economic work in favor of political work lingers on. Those that handle political work are still regarded as the elites in the services, and favored for fast-track promotion, or where this system is not practiced, they are favored for the choice assignments.
- Third, too many foreign ministries especially those belonging to developing countries, have an aversion to two-way personnel exchanges at the headquarters, which means that few specialists from economic ministries serve in the MFA.[8] This reduces the prospect of knowledge accumulation via a process of personnel exchange and osmosis between individuals.

The irony is that deficiencies in economic work occur in precisely those states that need to use diplomacy to maximize economic gain, namely a number of developing countries. We see a situation where lip service to the concept of economic diplomacy that is much in fashion, is not matched by real action. One consequence is that it often leaves the diplomatic service isolated from mainstream activities in the country. The other is that the tangible benefit that integrated diplomacy can offer, is simply not utilized. This accentuates the isolation of the diplomatic machinery.

cooperation, and from this policy perspective the MFA should keep an eye on the volume of flows. The MFA should also concern itself with overall conditions that govern aid, at a time when the trend is for a greater degree of imposition of 'conditionalities' (which attach to aid strings that cover utilization, the social and economic conditions of usage, the target domestic recipient groups, and even policy conditions). Thus aid issues become intertwined with broader diplomacy.

Embassies often accommodate specialists from the domestic aid management agency when the country concerned is a major aid provider.[9] But the more usual system is for aid issues to be handled by specialist teams sent from home, for each round of negotiation. The ambassador and his colleagues have an oversight responsibility, to keep good working contacts with the aid administration agency of the donor country, and to advise the specialists on wider political issues, when these come up, especially the application of political conditions. For example, it has been the experience of many developing countries to receive *démarches* from European ministries of economic cooperation and the like on matters relating to human rights, or some other aspect of socio-economic policy in the aid-receiving country (this usually happens because NGOs in the donor country believe that the aid administering agencies can exert strong pressure, or because of the political persuasion of the minister concerned.) In this kind of a situation some years back, India refused to entertain the *démarches* received from the aid agency on political subjects, pointing out that such subjects should be properly addressed through the foreign ministry. Behind such diplomatic dances is the cold reality that aid increasingly becomes a pressure point, in the name of humanitarian and other concerns.

From the perspective of countries that provide aid, there is a trend to merge aid management with diplomacy. For instance, the Netherlands has a unified ministry that handles foreign affairs and economic cooperation, with two separate ministers handling the subjects. Japan has always handled official aid through the Gaimusho, and integrated it into foreign affairs management—to the point where critics of the system decry excessive focus on aid. Japan is also today the world's largest aid donor. In other countries, separate ministries exist but there is close cooperation, to use aid as an instrument for foreign policy objectives. A dwindling volume of 'official development aid' (ODA), from other sources, reinforces the power of this lever.

TECHNOLOGY

Missions may find 'technology harvesting' as the hardest activity to implement, mainly because they are not end-users of technology, nor have specialist knowledge. Naturally it is the home enterprises, public or private, seeking technology inputs that are best placed to engage in this work. But missions can play a facilitator role. It involves:

a) Gaining insight into the technology achievements of the target country, and an understanding of the evolution and needs in the home country is important for the diplomat, even when he or she is not a technical specialist. This activity can provide leads and ideas that can be fed into one's own system, to assist in evaluation of prospects for technology collaboration.
b) Some countries have 'science counselors' within large missions,

to handle the work outlined above and track local developments, to aid institution level S&T cooperation. It is worthwhile to integrate such officials into the investment promotion team.

c) A special effort can be made by the mission to get domestic agencies (like industry associations) to articulate their technology needs and to use the mission as a channel for initial prospection, even while recognizing that for reasons of commercial confidentiality, companies may not be willing to involve the mission beyond a certain point.
d) Using S&T agreements as a vehicle for economic sensitization, and for creating opportunities for investments and trade is another possibility.

TOURISM PROMOTION

This is a specialized area in its own right, but is relevant to economic promotion because there is synergy between attracting tourist visitors and offering the country as a business destination. It is an old adage that business goes easier when one finds the country and its people attractive. The example has been narrated of how during the Apartheid era, South Africa used its magnificent natural attractions to draw in businessmen as tourist visitors to the country. Singapore is another instance of a small state that leverages geographic location, and its reputation as a 'garden city' to attract visitors and to promote itself as a unique business destination; there are many expatriate professionals who live in this place with their families and commute for some days each week to work in neighboring countries. Countries have seen that in the course of efforts to attract FDI it is especially appropriate to blend promotion of tourism and business. It is worthwhile to use the free air passages and local hospitality that are generally offered by national airlines and tourism agencies to journalists, simultaneously aiming at tourism and economic publicity. Good tourism experiences by visitors, and the human contacts established, easily translate into good country images.

WEBSITES

A good quality embassy website that serves the direct goals of economic promotion is indispensable. Those undertaking a greenfield search frequently look at diplomatic mission websites. Providing user-friendly formats, with a wider range of information, hyperlinks to other official and institutional promotional sites, and constant updating are among the elements that have to be addressed. No less important is a 'feedback' function. One also needs to monitor the way the major search engines evaluate one's website, and to engage in dialogue that ensures good attention for the website.

Website security is another preoccupation, since embassy (and other official) sites are targets of choice for hackers and for others intent on political or other forms of protest.

The Internet offers potential for experimentation and innovation *vis-à-vis* economic promotion and since this is uncharted territory one has to accumulate one's own experience for optimal result. Benchmarking and learning via best practices is a good method, looking to home agencies and to international experience as well.

QUESTIONS

1. As a commercial secretary, how would you set about planning an expansion in exports to a hypothetical country of your assignment?
2. Why is investment promotion of importance to all countries today?
3. What would be the elements that you would put on the webpage for your embassy, for the purpose of economic promotion? Give a detailed listing.
4. Please offer an example of your own where tourism promotion has been combined with economic promotion.

REFERENCES

1. Hocking, Brian, *Diplomacy of Image and Memory: Swiss Bankers and Nazi Gold* (Diplomacy Studies Program Discussion Paper No. 64, University of Leicester, April, 2000).
2. Rana, Kishan S., *Inside Diplomacy* (Manas, New Delhi, 2000), Chapter 4, pp. 96–127, Chapter 5, pp. 128–43.

NOTES

1. Brian Hocking, *Diplomacy of Image and Memory: Swiss Bankers and Nazi Gold* (Diplomatic Studies Program Discussion Paper No. 64, University of Leicester, April 2000).
2. Until about 30 years ago a majority of countries had separate commercial services for external economic work, but the trend has been for integration with other diplomatic tasks. A major exception is the US, which has a separate Commercial Service that operates under the US Commerce Department, but at the level of the ambassador the work is fully integrated.
3. The point that emerges from this actual example is that regardless of the assumption of a 'perfect' market by theoretical economists, if competition is free, in the real world even without entry barriers, a simple lack of familiarity acts as a powerful hindrance. In the case of soft toys, we found that a notion that the EU had imposed safety standards for manufacturers to meet (preventing the toy from becoming a hazard for small children) acted as a barrier. Indian manufactures assumed that it would be very difficult to meet these standards. But once they gained the essential knowledge, and felt that they could count on a support source such as the Indo-German Export Project (funded through German technical aid), they gained confidence and were able to enter the export market.
4. At different assignments as an ambassador I found it useful to accompany business delegations. It helped to open doors in some places, and also became a tremendous learning experience on the rapid industrial changes taking place at home.

5. This method is based on personal experience. The number of targets chosen is not important, as long as this is handled as a rolling program, to keep the embassy focused on potential investors who have to be pursued, in a planned manner.
6. This figure is based on India's experience in the post-Liberalization period after 1991. Achieving a higher rate of implementation is crucial in most other countries as well.
7. This comment was made in a confidential interview in April, 2001. The author's observations are based on experience with teaching around a dozen groups of foreign diplomats (each group drawn from over 20 countries from Africa, Asia, East and Central Europe and Latin America) at the Foreign Service Institute, New Delhi.
8. For instance, even today the Indian Ministry of External Affairs refuses to accept anyone from any other ministry or agency for assignment within that Ministry. A small dent has been made in 2001, by accepting two specialists as advisers on defense affairs, but an economist is yet to be appointed, though the idea of having a specialist 'economic adviser' has been afloat for some years. In the reverse direction some foreign service officials do serve in other ministries, including those handling economic affairs, but the numbers are small and too many see this as a kind of exile from the mainstream. There are many other countries where there is a like situation.
9. One new trend visible in Africa is for donor countries to station economic cooperation representatives in one large embassy in a particular region or sub-region, who cover several countries from that base. In practice such an official becomes accountable to several ambassadors, though he spends just a few days each month in a particular foreign country. This adds to the complexity of mission team management, from the perspective of the HOM.

6

Culture, Media, Education, Science & Technology

This catch-all category covers all the segments of relationship building left over when the political and the economic areas are excluded. Each sector—culture, media, education, science & technology (S&T), and even consular work—has its own importance; taken together they can add up to around half of the actual work of the mission. Within an integrated diplomatic service, all officials need exposure to at least some of these work areas at an early stage of their career. With the exception of media and information sectors, the task of monitoring these sectors lies outside the foreign ministry, and is handled by other ministries and departments. (Foreign media issues are customarily assigned to foreign ministries even when there is a separate information ministry.) Some topics are also handled within missions abroad by specialists deputed from other agencies—such as the science or education counselors or advisers in large missions.[1]

CULTURE

Large countries or those with a 'civilizational' self-image usually attach a high value to this sector. A narrow definition of culture covers the performing and the plastic arts, and involves exchanges of delegations of artistes and exhibitions, visits by academics and other specialists, the operation of cultural centers, and cooperation in languages. Other segments like youth and sports exchanges are also usually covered in cultural programs. This is often the working definition in bilateral culture agreements and in protocols or subsidiary agreements that implement cultural exchanges.

A wider definition of culture covers the entire national personality, reflecting its civilization, history and distinctive heritage, plus the genius of its people. It encompasses the value system that the country identifies itself with, as also the language. France is probably the best example of a country that strives to project such an encompassing unique cultural personality. France also expends vast resources in this endeavor. Of course, the external projection of value systems and a distinctive personality is not limited to large nations.[2]

Some countries regard the above goals as too ambitious, involving a greater expenditure of resources than they can afford. But all nations, large and small are preoccupied with the projection of a 'correct' external image, and are highly sensitive to adverse publicity that detracts from their self-perception. In diplomatic work, all the facets of a country's personality—culture, politics, economics, media images, and the like are intertwined, and influence one another. It may be said that the external national image is at the heart of the integrated diplomatic process (see below). Developing countries are especially sensitive to matters of culture and image.

Elements directly relevant to cultural work in bilateral relationship building are:

i. As bilateral relations develop, agreements and protocols covering culture are often among the first to be signed between countries. The implementation of cultural programs is then the mission's prime activity in this sector.
ii. Cultural projection is seldom under the exclusive control of governments, since they are confined to financing and

organizing cultural exchanges under official programs. Hence, for effective projection, it is essential to reach out to autonomous agencies and individuals like artistes, impresarios, and others active in the field, both at home and abroad. In fact cultural work takes on shades of 'public diplomacy'. Missions need to recognize this and use networking methods, to include such non-official partners in their outreach.

iii. Friendship societies, and similar volunteer bilateral groups are vital for local contact. In some countries such groups subsist under direct or indirect official patronage, while in many places they depend completely on private initiative.[3] Discreet support by the mission is customary. Local students who have returned from studies in the mission's country are a useful nucleus around which such friendship groups can be established in different cities, again through discreet initiative by the embassy.

iv. 'Festivals' of culture, stretching over several weeks or months, have become a means of concentrated culture and image projection, with multiple side benefit. The concept was first evolved by India with a year-long festival in UK in 1982–83, with joint official and private support. The event that drew the widest participation was the one that followed in the US, during 1985–86, where official programs were supplemented by thousands of 'associated' events across the country, ranging from performances by local artistes to book exhibitions in local libraries.[4] Other countries have also used festivals for concentrated action.

v. An ideal situation is one where official sponsorship ceases to be the dominant support for cultural exchanges, and where autonomous initiatives by private individuals develop into the main channel. This is the case with exchanges among Western nations. But even then, official guidance remains, focusing also on special initiatives, sometimes in partnership with business and other private sponsors. And missions remain engaged in cultural projection, as always!

vi. An advanced form of cooperation is the 'cultural center', established in the foreign capital, usually functioning under the supervision of the embassy. The optimal management of a cultural center involves clear vision and goals, and adaptation to local circumstance. It also depends on the creation of sound and durable linkages with local partners.
vii. Often popular expressions of culture are overlooked in favor of high culture in official programs. This is true of pop music, and commercial cinema, and such blind spots deserve to be addressed. The cinema and TV exchanges are vital for image projection.
viii. Last but not the least, culture provides valuable connections in other sectors as well. Diplomacy works best through such interconnections.

THE MEDIA

The classic distinction between the print and the electronic media is getting a little blurred through the Internet, since much of 'print' material reaches overseas via the Internet, far quicker than hard copies of journals delivered by mail. But as yet a distinctive set of tactics for handling Internet-based outreach has not evolved.

For headquarters, foreign correspondents, both the resident journalists and those who fly in to cover stories, are a special concern. Usually a dedicated unit in the foreign ministry handles the accreditation and coverage facilities for such correspondents, and monitors the reports filed by them. This requires careful handling, since correspondents are highly sensitive to 'management' by official agencies (or even by their own embassies). Often a kind of 'us' and 'them' mentality develops among the foreign press corps, especially in developing countries. For the receiving country, foreign correspondents play a major role in shaping external perceptions. They offer a channel for projecting new developments and positive images. Negative stories filed by them cause considerable damage.[5]

It is vital for the foreign ministry to constantly monitor the reportage trends and mood among the foreign press corps.

Foreign ministries find it essential to have an 'official spokesman', a senior official with exceptional communication skills, capable of articulating the country's foreign posture, to domestic and external media. This job calls for an ability to think on one's feet, and to keep cool under pressure.[6] Usually this job is separated from media and publicity management, since the spokesman has to master detail, plus closely track international developments and thinking within the government.

Abroad, the mission has the task of regular contact with the editorial offices of at least the major publications, the daily and the business press, as also the influential weekly and other journals, plus the TV networks. This demands the personal involvement of the ambassador, simply because the press or information counselor cannot gain the level of high access that is needed, like meetings with the editorial board. But the information counselor also has his work cut out for him, often needing the support of the entire mission team, particularly when a special effort is needed to get one's own story out, or to implement a campaign. Ideally, all the embassy officials should cultivate contacts with an assigned set of press and TV journalists, on a long-term basis, in a joint activity of the embassy.

Some other practical points:

a) Negative publicity is seldom truly countered with denials or official statements for publication, though gross errors on points of fact, or where reputation is affected, may make such action indispensable. The more effective counter is positive publicity, if possible through the same journal that carried the damaging reports. This is where skills of persuasion and projecting one's own standpoint come into play, as also the relationships built up over a period of time.
b) A publication will seldom agree to bypass or counter the reportage by its own correspondent. One way out is to persuade

the journal to send a special correspondent, or to invite journalists to the home country as part of a regular contact program. Countries in West Europe and North America operate vast programs of 'sponsored' visits, not always with commensurate result, if it is run in a mechanical fashion. Example: major European countries annually invite 30 and more journalists from individual foreign nations; results are often not very evident. In contrast, if the invitation is extended as a special gesture based on a connection that exists already, it may be more productive. Similarly, if the invitation comes from a developing country with limited resources, and is aimed at a journalist with whom the embassy has already established friendship, the results can remarkable. Equally, an invitation to a travel writer produces better publicity than reams of costly tourism promotion ads!

c) The need for prior cultivation particularly applies to TV reportage, where facilitation and an open attitude usually produce good result. Some receiving countries impose rigid conditions on visiting TV teams, including script clearance, supervised recording of material, and can sometimes even demand preview rights. This seldom works in practice, because in most countries material of all kinds can be recorded, using local nationals, or through undeclared foreign journalist visits. It is more productive to cultivate an open atmosphere.

d) A mission can try and encourage programs of sharing news or editorial material between publications of the two countries, though in practice these are not easy to implement, because of their autonomy, different goals and standards of the publications, plus possible problems of language. But cooperation programs between news agencies are often successful.

e) All diplomats need media training, regardless of functions performed. This is because situations may arise, particularly in a mission, where a junior diplomat becomes the spokesman on the spot and cannot duck his or her responsibility of responding to the media spotlight.

SOME EXAMPLES

It is interesting to compare the functional style of the cultural centers of different countries. The French play huge emphasis on language, and have also been innovative in creating entities beyond the traditional Alliançe Francaise, such as the Centre de Sciences Humaines in India. The German overseas offices of their unique political foundations[7] engage in quiet outreach and supplement Goethe Institutes. In the case of the US the external offices of the private foundations are only partly comparable in supplementing the US Information Agency. In contrast, Japan's outreach seems subdued, focusing on niche areas. Chinese and Indian cultural centers too, in different ways, seldom reach the mainstream in foreign countries.

Daimler-Benz (DB) Fellowships, launched some years ago, are an unusual method of creating long-term affinity. From elite universities around the world, a few of the best students in science and engineering are selected and brought to Germany for an annual scientific conference, exposed to company researchers, and given an opportunity to network with their peers, the other 'DB Fellows' (they are now called Daimler Chrysler fellows). The calculation is that they will return home with positive impressions of German technology, and some may end up working for the company as well.

In parallel, the German education system, which has been insular with university degrees that require a minimum of five years of hard study, is both adapting with the introduction of bachelor level degrees, and carrying out sharp marketing to attract foreign students. Attitudes of past complacency that German technology sells itself have been put aside in the face of competitive pressures from other foreign education destination countries.

Past efforts by developing countries to step up media interchanges and establish international new agencies of the South to combat de facto Western monopoly over the news led to nowhere, as did the rhetoric of the 'New Information Order' that was at its height some two decades back. Now the Internet offers low-cost and viable options, but one is yet to see any pan-South initiative.

f) The old adage holds good: the only bad publicity is no publicity. Negative reportage has its virtue and a thick skin is sometimes a diplomatic necessity!

Media work is directly allied with all other promotional activities, and good results produce favorable impact in other sectors as well. This is an aspect of integrated diplomacy.

EDUCATION AND ACADEMIA

Exchanges of students take place mainly at the tertiary education levels, and countries with an extensive academic infrastructure find it worthwhile to give special consideration to receiving foreign students. Besides building people-to-people contacts, exposing students to one's technology, via the hard sciences and the engineering disciplines, is a long-term investment. It creates a base of receptivity in foreign countries, and generally translates into business opportunity. It also wins friends for the future. This calculation lies behind programs of scholarships offered by developed countries as well as by others like China India, Russia and South Africa that have institutions that attract foreign students. Many go for advanced studies on a 'self-financing' basis, and this has become a big business as well, for countries like the US, UK, Canada and Australia.[8]

In the home capital, the ministry of higher education or its equivalent usually handles offers of scholarships. The foreign ministry has a minimal role, besides having officials on selection committees. But for the embassy in the country receiving foreign students they are an important charge. This involves keeping a general eye on their welfare, and acting *in loco parentis* when they are faced with emergencies and personal difficulty. For the mission, sensitivity and a helpful attitude is essential in handling these tasks, the more so because usually home government regulations do not allow for much flexibility or financial discretion for helping students in distress.

Official education cooperation programs generally aim at building institution-to-institution linkages, as this has direct and indirect benefit. This may take the shape of donor–recipient type of activities, or more equal programs of cost-sharing. Those of the latter type are often more successful. In fact, export and import of education technology is a big business that also has far-reaching influence on building country images.

Host country academic scholars specializing in one's own country or region, and other specialists are natural targets for the mission to cultivate, and for the headquarters to consider in their invitations to local personalities for visits. The mission needs to constantly look beyond the obvious to develop wider contacts and relationships in the academic world, including business schools and equivalent institutions. Effective outreach to academic specialists produces results of long-term value in relationships. We witness now an interesting phenomenon. The spread and expansion in influence of TV has had the effect of valorizing academic international affairs specialists in a widening range of developing countries. Talk shows begin to command mass audiences, where such scholars are in demand to explain foreign affairs issues. This represents another aspect of 'democratization' of foreign affairs, and the public involvement of non-official participants.

INTELLECTUAL EXCHANGES

Think tanks and similar specialist institutions are also powerful allies as opinion-molders. In Western countries, and across East Europe, they shape perceptions, and in developing countries too they have an expanding role. For example, an entity like the RAND Corporation or the Heritage Institute cannot be overlooked in the US, either as shapers of public opinion or as influences on the executive and legislative branches. It is also worthwhile for the mission to invest effort into the initiation of regular programs of exchanges between local and home institutions, and ensure that home-based scholars participate regularly in local seminars and conferences organized by reputed institutions.

The creation of special groups for intellectual exchanges on topics like security, disarmament and regional affairs, is one of the options to pursue in creating relationships in the non-state sector. It is worthwhile for developing countries to make more active use of this option, rather than concentrate excessively on 'vertical' connections with countries of the North. As noted elsewhere, ASEAN states have deliberately fostered the development of institutes of strategic and international studies, as a means of expanding interchanges at this important non-official level. In some developing countries, mindsets of reserve by officials and politicians towards one's own academic scholars inhibit such collegial approaches.

SCIENCE & TECHNOLOGY

Bilateral agreements covering cooperation in science and research are another traditional action field for developing bilateral relationships, but the seriousness with which such programs are pursued depends on objective circumstance as well as the initiatives taken from home (e.g. by the ministry handling S&T matters) and by the mission. Since this domain touches on academic research at one end and applications in industry, agriculture and other fields as well, it offers rich prospects for a mutually advantageous result.

While the primary activity is best left to specialists, the embassy can track local developments and facilitate initial contacts, and sensitize local partners on available opportunities in the home country, as also for overcoming bottlenecks. Some large embassies deploy full-time science counselors or attaches, and it is important for the mission to integrate them fully into the team. Linking S&T work with broader economic promotion is of obvious value.

CONSULAR WORK

Often seen as a routine service activity (i.e. the delivery of visas to local nationals visiting the home country for tourism or business or other purposes, and passport issue and related services to one's own nationals), when performed well, consular work becomes a strategic advantage for the mission. For many local nationals it represents the first point of contact with the country; efficient visa services directly aid image projection. For example, offering 'same day' visa delivery can do this, or even better, 'across the counter' visa services—the latter involves only some adaptation in computer applications. The data from visa services can also be put to good use in business and tourism promotion.

The other way consular services link up with broader diplomatic goals is by building positive contacts with one's nationals in the country, invariably sensitive to the quality of consular services. Whether small or large, the expatriate community is a significant resource for the mission, and calls for the personal attention of the HOM. Good and sympathetic consular services become a solid foundation for these contacts. In some countries, especially in North America and in UK, these expatriate communities, even when they have taken up local nationality, are powerful political allies in relationship building.

PUBLIC DIPLOMACY AND CIVIL SOCIETY

Public diplomacy involves the mission in a wider set of relationships with local non-official constituents than ever before. It is part of the changed environment in which diplomacy now functions. At the turn of the last century there was a British Ambassador to the

US who spent 5 years at his post without making a public speech. Today, even 5 days at a major capital without a public speaking function may seem unusual! Depending on local circumstance, public diplomacy may cover some or all of the following:

a) **Public speaking.** Outreach to the shapers of public opinion, and directly to the public via a variety of locally available platforms is part of the diplomatic routine for the embassy. The message may be diffused or of a general nature, or may target specific issues. It is a means of image building.
b) **NGOs.** In developed countries, representatives of Third World countries find it essential to cultivate the Non-Governmental Groups that are engaged in human rights and other social benefit causes, to put across own perspectives, gauge their views and preempt the development of adverse situations. Amnesty, Greenpeace, Transparency International, and War on Hunger are some examples of agencies that shape local public opinion, influence parliamentarians and affect government policy, and for all these reasons they have become the interlocutors of diplomats. (Example: in *Inside Diplomacy* I have narrated the way in which in 1992–93, German policy on World Bank aid for the Narmada Water Project was shaped by the coalition of local, Indian and international NGOs, which left us a bit bewildered, and wiser after the event!) The development of truly 'national' NGOs within developing countries is a delicate challenge, and one that very few countries have been able to tackle, because 'official' sponsorship for agencies of civil society is a contradiction in terms.
c) **Volunteer and professional groups.** These consist of those like the Rotary, the Lions, and many others that play a discreet role of volunteer bodies, which offer a potential for outreach, for country promotion and for building contacts. Their importance varies in different places. Professional groups can also act as partners in outreach and persuasion.

d) **Ethnic segments.** In countries of North America, Europe and Australasia, one's own ethnic populations may exist in significant numbers, with growing political influence. They can be used for the missions for sensitization on issues that are important to the home country, but considerable discretion has to be exercised, to avoid transgression into what can be construed as interference in internal affairs. (Example: the different South Asian communities in several countries, like Canada, UK and US, have grown into a political factor in influencing official policy towards the region.) Even when own ethnic communities are small in number, they can provide valuable advice, insights and local access to the mission.[9]

Culture, media, education and all the other fields offer large potential for relationship building, mobilized through appropriate policy and direction from headquarters, implemented through the missions. It is useful to note that it is only the resident embassy that can optimally perform most of these activities.

QUESTIONS

1. What are the 'narrow' and 'wide' definitions of culture in diplomatic work? What promotional activities fit into the 'broad' definition?
2. Give 3 examples of relation building work in the media sector.
3. What is the importance of the education sector in relations between countries?
4. Why is public diplomacy prominent in contemporary diplomacy?

REFERENCES

1. Rana, Kishan S., *Inside Diplomacy* (New Delhi, Manas Publications, 2000), Chapters 6 and 7, pp. 144–87, Chapter 16, pp. 374–94.

NOTES

1. Within large embassies, it can be that barely 25% of diplomatic level officials belong to the foreign ministry. Some large US embassies have representatives of 30 or more federal departments and agencies. Others may have a smaller range of diversity, but in all such cases the management of the embassy is complicated by the presence of officials who are only nominally under the control of the ambassador.
2. Japan and China fall into a distinct category as countries that have unique and distinctive civilizations, but tend to be 'autonomous', and rather less engaged in external projection of their cultural personalities, compared with some of the European countries. But both do devote sizable resources to cultural work, perhaps Japan more than China. The latter does not engage abroad in the teaching of the Chinese language, unlike others who project their culture abroad.
3. For instance, in UK, US, France and most Western countries (and at many other places too) anyone can set up a friendship association, or a grouping of former students who have studied in a particular country. In Germany, friendship societies come under a special official umbrella, requiring official recognition and receiving in turn a small measure of public funding. In the former socialist countries of East Europe these friendship societies were used as instruments of official policy.
4. The organization of these festivals was one of the most innovative actions in cultural diplomacy undertaken by India. As a discussion at the Brookings Institution at Washington DC disclosed in May 2001, the festival of 1985–86 is recalled even now as the best of a full series of landmark cultural events organized by any country.
5. Journals are duty bound to support their correspondents, but my experience has been that if consistent negative reportage by a correspondent can be documented, the editor will be willing to consider making amends with some other form of positive coverage, and perhaps conveying a suitable message to the concerned correspondent as well. On the other hand, one has to be careful in lodging complaint, since editors are very sensitive to any impression of being pressured.
6. In the case of small diplomatic services there is often no full-time

spokesman, and the civil service head of the ministry takes on this role as needed. This may be practical, but having such a senior official act as the interface for the media means that there is less distance between the policy-maker and the spokesman, which can present problems in some situations. It also removes the element of 'deniability' that may be needed at times.

7. The German political foundations, each representing a major political party, are mainly funded through the federal budget. Besides their responsibility within the country for political education (under a legal mandate), they act abroad as a channel for official aid in the technical cooperation sector. Each of these, such as the Konrad Adenauer Foundation of the CDU party and the Friedrich Ebert Foundation of the SPD party, works in a specified functional area, like entrepreneurship development, labor affairs and the like. These foundations represent a unique method of using the country's political parties in external relation building. They also provide these parties with a window to the world, especially the developing countries, and a source for gathering extensive information and building connections with individuals.
8. Marketing of education technology is big business. In developing countries like India or China, with several tens of thousands going abroad each year for studies at the university level, second and third level universities and institutes from different foreign countries carry out intensive marketing, to attract students. With sizable fee differential for foreign students this is also a very profitable business. In contrast countries of continental Europe do not charge high fees to foreign students (and in fact the level of tuition fees is very nominal). They have lagged behind in active foreign student recruitment programs, but that is changing on account of a need in countries like France and Germany for high-class foreign expertise to meet their own expanding needs.
9. Countries such as India have learnt from Israel the method of mobilizing these instruments as a conscious policy. They now routinely use ethnic allies in the US, UK, and Canada for access to political and business personalities.

PART II

INSTITUTIONS

7

The Ministry of Foreign Affairs

It was the French who first established a permanent office in the administration at Paris in 1626 to oversee the work of their embassies abroad, which became the French Ministry of External Affairs, known by its location as the Quai d'Orsay. Today, every foreign ministry (MFA) is divided into two major components, the territorial divisions (also called bureaus, departments, or directorates) handling bilateral relations with different regions, and the functional divisions that handle specific tasks, like administration, conference affairs or multilateral diplomacy, legal affairs, protocol, and the like. The officials in these sub-units consist of 'desk officers' at the lower rung of the pyramid, to the division or department heads, usually with two layers of supervisors in between.

How do these officials perform the work of building bilateral relation? The subject of the MFA warrants closer study than possible in a single chapter, and our focus here is narrow. One splendid study, cited earlier, is edited by Brian Hocking, *Foreign Ministries: Change and Adaptation*. There are other recent works also covered in the readings at the end of the chapter. But what is yet to evolve is a comparative method, or an identified set of criteria, that can allow us to analyze the performance of foreign ministries. This subject is explored in the penultimate chapter in this book.

DESK OFFICER: MANUAL OF OPERATIONS

A typical foreign ministry 'manual of operations' might assign the following work to territorial desk officers:

- Primary collection, assembling and analysis of data on the subject matters within their competence;
- Preparation of first drafts of minutes, briefs, memoranda, cabinet notes, parliament questions, and speeches on subjects within their competence;
- Drafting of messages to missions;
- Processing of reports from missions;
- Drafting responses to missions' correspondence and requests;
- Any other tasks assigned by superior officials.

Such manuals sometimes provide 'operational hints' or advice. For example, it may be suggested that the desk officers should not wait to be told what to do but should take the initiative; channels of communication should be respected; periodically, or as often as the situation demands, the desk officer should submit briefs on major events. The responsibilities of the desk officer for reports on conferences, the drafting of congratulatory or sympathy messages, speeches and toasts, draft cabinet notes, records of discussion, and parliamentary answers are also elaborated.

ACTUAL ROLE

Within any foreign ministry, the desk officer is the operational base unit of the entire structure. The smooth running of the entire external diplomacy machinery depends on the professional competence of this individual. Hence it is vital for foreign ministries to recognize, and act on this realization, that the good performance of the entire system begins with the desk officer. The training and formation of the desk officer is also imperative because the skills and experience gathered in that job will shape the career of that individual and determine his or her performance in the higher offices that this official will come to hold in later years.

An updated definition should equip the desk officer to handle the following:

a) To become the **unique 'resource person' at headquarters** on the country or cluster of countries handled, (or on the functional areas or organizations that lie within the charge of the desk officer, if the work is performed in a functional division). In an age of 'information overload' fulfillment of this role is judged not so much in terms of the volume of data that one can access, but the relevance of information, plus accuracy and quality of assessment. For instance, the Internet makes it possible to read newspaper articles and editorials published in leading foreign journals on a daily basis. But the material has to be sifted, digested and evaluated. For this purpose the desk officer must use the assessments offered by the embassy in that country, and other sources, including his own judgment. All this is mobilized to become an 'insider' on the country or agency. Equally, the desk officer should be given full opportunity, whenever feasible, to travel to the area under his charge, to sharpen first-hand knowledge, and build contacts. In some systems, junior officials get little opportunity for overseas travel, but even in these situations, professional competence creates its own chances!
b) **Learn to integrate economic analysis with political assessments.** Bilateral relationships today involve almost as much of economics as politics, and the same applies to the international multilateral dialogue. Regardless of whether trade and investment promotion work is handled in another ministry, the desk officer must have intimate knowledge of all the economic issues that are related to his specific cluster of countries, and link these with other subjects in the dialogue, in accordance with the requirements of 'integrated' diplomacy. He must personally master the interconnections.

c) **Master the analysis of reports and special dispatches** received from own missions in the countries or region under charge. This involves integration of data garnered from other sources, as also close understanding of the national policy towards those countries or region. The fact that the desk officer is a member of the team of a particular division and department produces synergy, because he is given the means to relate particular bits of information to the wider picture, and use this in gaining deeper insights. Brainstorming and other meetings at the division and department level are of real value for generating collective effort.
d) Preparation of **records of discussion** is a special responsibility, often involving high-level meetings of importance. MFAs often have guidelines of their own on the writing of such notes, where concentration, accuracy, and brevity are special virtues.[1]
e) Linked with the above two is the preparation of **notes and analysis that guide policy formulation, as well as policy execution.** This includes the work carried out under the guidance of senior officials, plus actions undertaken by the desk officer on own initiative, such as advancing suggestions and producing options, for consideration by senior colleagues.
f) The coordination role of the foreign ministry, within the government, gives the desk officer a special responsibility for **constant liaison with counterparts in other ministries and agencies** that are directly involved in the functional area covered by him. This interface involves discretion and balance, besides regular supervision by senior officials within one's own unit (see below).
g) No less vital is the **responsibility to the public at large**, and to non-state agencies. The actual nature and volume of tasks this entails depends on the country or region covered by the desk officer. For example the official who is in the protocol or administration department may have more frequent dealings with the public than one who is in a unit that handles internal services or a territorial region remote from one's own country. For the

MFA system as a whole, the domestic public dimension is no less than to keep citizens informed of international developments that affect the citizens. This is linked with the process of 'democratization of foreign affairs in the national context. Further, the directives of a 'public service charter'—assuming that one exists—apply equally to all official agencies, even if MFAs often tend to forget this!

h) The **foreign diplomatic missions at headquarters, concerned** with one's charge are another responsibility. Again, an approach based on understanding and helpfulness goes a long way in performing this task well, and in producing contacts and relationships that also help in the optimal performance of the other duties mentioned above. Such contacts should be based on effective projection of the standpoint of one's own country, and building credibility as an '*interlocuteur valable*'.
i) Last but by no means the least are what may be regarded as the normal responsibilities that go with any foreign ministry assignment, the **drafting of letters, messages, speeches, answers to parliament questions, and other notes and documents** that form the staple of the diplomatic profession. A 'non-routine' approach in handling this work, plus mastery over the skills of draftsmanship, is essential.

The above list is not definitive, and there are always other tasks that go with particular desk officer assignments. In all the jobs that the desk officer performs at headquarters, an attitude of performing more than a set 'routine' provides a good mental framework.

SENIOR DIRECTION OF BILATERAL WORK

Much of the above applies, *mutatis mutandis* to the mid-level and senior officials at the MFA who handle bilateral work, typically as deputy directors or directors of territorial divisions (of course, the nomenclature varies). Some MFAs operate with few divisions, entrusting large regional responsibility to each, or clustering sub-units under a bigger entity, like the Africa 'command' within the British Foreign and Commonwealth Office. Others use the formula of multiple small territorial units, like the Indian MEA that has over 15 such divisions, some dealing with just 2 or 3 countries. The Germans have some 40-odd 'Referats' (sections) that are the base units, grouped under two major territorial departments, and several divisions. The US State Department uses the system of 'country directors' to oversee relations with countries of bilateral significance, which suits a large and diversified system. In any format the typical issues, on which the very top MFA leadership determines the outcome, are:

The senior-most civil servant heading the foreign ministry (variously called Permanent Secretary, or State Secretary, or Vice Minister) usually has a collegial group that shares the oversight responsibility. In contemporary practice, like the British Permanent Under Secretary, or the French Secretary General, he functions as the 'Chairman of the Management Board',[2] and is occupied with optimization of the diplomatic apparatus, and relatively disengaged from bilateral or even multilateral diplomacy. The political director general, in typical European terminology, handles much of oversight of bilateral political work. He may even deal directly with the foreign minister on certain issues, always with the knowledge of the top civil servant heading the ministry.

The quality of the MFA structure is another factor of differentiation for many developing countries, which tend to overburden the top official and under-utilize others at the apex. For instance this has been a long-standing difficulty in the Ministry of External Affairs in New Delhi,[3] and analysis of other comparable entities shows a similar situation. Linked with this is a state of flux in the organization structure, with frequent redrawing of responsibility spans and lines of command.

COMPARING FOREIGN MINISTRIES

It might be interesting to have a set of criteria that compare the efficiency of MFAs. The following could be considered as indicators.

- The proportion of personnel at headquarters and in missions. One study (Cascone, *Comparing Diplomatic Services*) notes and compares data among G-8 and EU countries. If we take the headquarters at 1, the numbers in missions are: The Netherlands 0.5; UK 0.7; France 1.5; Japan 1.6; US 1.8; Germany 2.5. The higher number abroad indicates a weaker headquarters for servicing and guiding embassies. The Indian figure of 3.5 shows a particularly difficult situation for its Ministry of External Affairs.
- The number of missions abroad is a guide between comparable nations. The US leads with 160, while France is second with 154. UK has 146, while Japan manages with only 119.
- The size of embassies is another element. It should be no surprise that the US leads with an average number of home-based officials at 58, Germany is second with 35, while UK, and Italy cope with just about 10 each. The proportion between home-based and local staff in embassies is another indicator, revealing local adaptation. Anecdotal evidence speaks of efficient use of people by Cuba, India and Singapore that have low embassy size and reputations for good performance.
- I am not aware of any comparison of budget figures, or even of comparative growth or cutbacks. This offers a useful line of inquiry.

Comparison based on other criteria like quality of reportage and performance in other areas is perhaps near-impossible, except in subjective terms.

PROFESSIONAL SKILLS

There are some skills and personal qualities that equip diplomats to handle well the bilateral diplomatic work that is entrusted to them at headquarters and at missions abroad.

i. Many tasks associated with this profession, at all levels, are 'discretionary', depending on self-motivation. This applies to broad catchment type of information collection and the reading that one undertakes. For instance, the resourceful official can easily track down annual reports of the World Bank and IMF on the target country, or access 'online' the academic journals that carry quality analysis on countries, regions and special subjects. The Internet has vastly expanded the horizon of such discretionary work, and given full play for innovation. But optimal use (for instance to carry out effective 'data mining', or simultaneously consult multiple users on a document using hypertext), demands mastery of this new technique through formal training.[4]
ii. Even for junior officials, there is little in diplomatic work that is of a routine nature. International affairs do not follow set patterns. Except in some particular 'servicing' jobs, like consular affairs, or the administration, repetitive tasks are few. This also applies to a service division like protocol affairs, where one needs mastery of detail and flexibility to deal with the unexpected. Experience shows that a 'can-do' attitude is a common characteristic of diplomats who derive satisfaction from the profession and generally get ahead.
iii. Linked with the above two is the other dominant feature of diplomacy in this age of rapid change—the need for the official to have a broad spectrum of interests. The CEO of one of the world's most successful software enterprises, Infosys Technologies, N.R. Narayan Murthy, calls this a 'broad bandwidth' quality. When applied to diplomacy, this unusual term depicts the need for the diplomat to have a wide range of interests and

capabilities, plus a capacity to absorb new ideas and to be a quick learner. The range of issues that are to be covered in contemporary external relationships is vast. While the diplomat cannot become a master of every subject, he should be able to absorb the central core of the different subjects and to use this knowledge to make 'inter-connections' with other themes and issues. With this goes the human quality of being able to relate to other individuals across cultures. He has to be a 'people's person'. These elements are also features of integrated diplomacy.

iv. It is no longer sufficient for the diplomat to be a generalist, or a 'jack-of-all-trades', to use an old expression. He or she needs a broad range of interests, but these must be grounded in some specialty of his own. Of course there is no one single prescription that applies to all diplomatic services, but one that seems to work for many is to have a blend of one's own specialization plus generalist skills. A young diplomat usually begins with an 'assigned' foreign language that he is required to learn, which translates into expertise in a region or country. As his career advances, the official adds to this other functional skills or special knowledge, e.g. on security and disarmament affairs, or environmental issues in international debate, or on some aspects of legal affairs that are relevant to his own country, or on multilateral economic issues. The range of choice is vast. In this manner, by mid-career three of four special skills would have been absorbed, making him a kind of 'generalist-multi-specialist'. Taken collectively, a range of expertise is thus built up, spread across the entire range of the foreign service hierarchy, not just limited to a few individuals.[5] The MFA's professionalism, and credibility with domestic partners, hinges on the quality of expertise.

v. One discipline that all diplomatists need to master is economics, because it impacts upon much of contemporary relationships among nations. In the past a legal background was regarded as a prerequisite (and there are still European diplomatic services

POLICY PLANNING

In every MFA policy planning is an important activity, whether carried out through a dedicated mechanism or through the 'line' territorial divisions. Henry Kissinger once remarked: 'Policy planning becomes the projection of familiar problems into the future.' That sums up the dilemma of limited ability of planners to think outside the box.

Speaking in Delhi in December 2001, noted strategic thinker and author Richard Haass, now head of the US State Department's Planning Staff, told an invited audience that the steps taken to produce a wide range of thinking include hiring specialists from diverse disciplines, setting up rival teams and 'red teams' that take adversarial positions, plus sensitivity analysis to look at the assumptions and change one or more to see what happens. He added: 'Not all change is linear; we have to prepare for discontinuities.'

We also need to carefully distinguish 'policy planning', from 'problem solving', 'policy implementation' and 'decision making'.

where this position is maintained, but this is changing).[6] Today, an understanding of basic economics, and the interplay between the economic interests of one's own country with the external world, is indispensable for the foreign ministry official, the more so in handling bilateral work. As noted earlier (Chapter 5) this is one deficiency area in many countries.

THE DIPLOMAT'S LONG PERSPECTIVE

The early stage of the career of the diplomat is a time of preparation for larger responsibilities. The years spent at headquarters are a time to gain insights into one's own system, and to use this knowledge to effect when serving abroad in a mission. This helps to overcome a professional hazard—to fall prey to the headquarters–missions or 'us–them' syndrome, failing to consider the perspective of the other. Some other challenges for officials at headquarters are:

a) Opportunities to serve in other ministries and agencies should be seized as a means of widening experience and gaining better understanding of the governmental system, rather than as 'exile' from one's own system and colleagues. Such lateral transfer, for instance to an economic ministry, can become the basis for developing a further functional specialization that adds to one's skill base. It also widens one's contacts.
b) The other option to consider is the sabbatical or opportunity for academic study, raising the level of qualifications through a yearlong course, or attendance at a short-term executive program or the like.
c) In a typical career, choices come up at different stages, for which there can be no standard prescription. It is best for the official to take a long and measured view of career chances. The safe option is not always the best one, as those who have chosen hard or unusual assignments would attest!
d) In most services the fast track to high advancement lies in long service at headquarters. That is where the official gets the chance to serve in the offices of high personalities, and is noticed. The downside is that he or she misses out on assignments abroad.
e) In one of Lawrence Durrell's inimitable novels on life in the diplomatic service,[7] a senior ambassador advises the young Third Secretary to cultivate an idiosyncrasy as one way of gaining visibility and a reputation! While not taking this advice literally, one can still profit through a hobby or special interest that builds on the opportunities provided by the profession.

It is a legitimate aspiration for every young Foreign Service official to 'fly the flag' and serve as his country's plenipotentiary envoy, representing the nation. Mastering work at the MFA, and understanding it as the integral obverse of work in the embassy, is a sure path to higher office—even in diplomatic services that follow the baleful practice of an excess of political appointments to what are highly professional jobs—serving as an ambassador abroad.

THE MFA: NEW RESPONSIBILITIES

Finally, let us look at the evolving responsibilities for the foreign ministry in relation to bilateral work.

First, as Brian Hocking has noted, the MFA is no longer the 'gatekeeper' of external relations, and cannot enforce the demand that all other government agencies use it as the exclusive contact foreign channel;[8] it must play then the role of the coordinator of all external relationships, involved on principal matters, without getting into the detailed management. This role is governed by internal rules of government work allocation. But in practice, another ministry will come to the MFA for advice only if it believes that the MFA adds value to its own activity. For instance, an industry ministry that deals with mobilizing foreign investments from abroad—FDI—will welcome the MFA if it is convinced that the apparatus of missions abroad is of real help in this task, and that this enables it to get out the investment destination message effectively. Or, an environment ministry concerned with global climate issues will accept the counsel of the MFA on the best way to approach a neighboring country for a new bilateral agreement, if it feels that its own concerns will find due place in the range of issues pursued in diplomatic discourse during a major bilateral meeting. This engages the MFA in sensitive internal networking, and gaining acceptance on merit, rather than formal authority. For instance, the British FCO virtually reinvented itself after the Falklands War of 1991, when it was perceived as out of touch with reality. It is one of the best examples of a foreign ministry that has mastered the coordination role.[9]

Second, the MFA should reach out to the organizations of 'civil society' that are engaged in external relationships These are the think tanks and research institutes, academia, the media, associations of business and industry, as well as professional bodies that play a role abroad. This also includes NGOs, and groups that are engaged in 'track two diplomacy' (Chapter 9). Some MFAs have formal mechanisms of contact, where a two-way sharing of information becomes a necessity. A major US advisory panel noted in 1998 that NGOs have used the 'rich connectivity' of the Internet, and some like the reputed World Council of Churches and Catholic Relief Services have played a determining role on the conclusion of an international treaty on land mines; it urged that 'the culture of diplomacy be changed' to include a larger community of international and domestic actors in deliberation and implementation.[10]

Third, Teamwork within the MFA ensures that all officials, top to bottom are *au fait* with policy goals, and apply uniform principles. This demands effective internal communication, both upwards and downwards. For example, volatility of international developments makes it essential that there is a mechanism for rapid daily review among the top management.[11] Yet, there are many MFAs where this is either absent, or handled badly.

Fourth, working partnership with own missions is no less crucial. It is argued in this book that a new empowerment of embassies is taking place now, as 'co-managers of relationships'. It is essential for MFAs to understand this and use the situation profitably. The earlier mission-territorial division formula was that the latter should be the mission's first partner of choice for all contacts at home. The addition is that the embassy too should be brought into the policy process, relying on modern communications, as the single best resource on all issues concerning that country. We move thus from policy advice to participation in policy dynamics.

Fifth, in its human resource (HR) policy, the MFA should use modern techniques of career planning, evaluation of individuals, motivation, and promotion policy, to optimize use of available talent. A special problem in diplomatic services is that unlike in the home civil services, officials are not easily transferable to another career track, and the ones that are passed over for promotion become a drag on the structure as a whole. Some countries have experimented from time to time with the 'golden handshake' and other early voluntary retirement schemes. A few use the formula of placing officials on an enforced leave of sorts, 'awaiting assignment', when there is no job placement possible.[12]

Sixth, MFAs internal management methods need continual updating. This entails corporate techniques where applicable, and monitoring what others do in like situations.

Seventh, the issue of 'good governance' is posed more sharply than before for all the agencies of government, including the MFA. This is at two levels. There is the concept of a citizen's charter that many countries apply to all organs of the government, reflecting the concern that the individual has a right to efficient and rapid service, and that a responsive attitude should be taken by all officials. There is also the wider concept that a good external policy that serves the interests of the citizens of the country is a 'public good' and that this is as important as an efficient water supply system or a good judiciary. This latter concept has not gained wide currency, but a little reflection will show that it is indeed a component of good governance. MFAs have the responsibility of thinking this through and articulating to domestic constituencies the ways in which foreign policy and the diplomatic system serve and advance the national interest.

QUESTIONS

1. How is there often a contrast between the formal and the real duties of the desk officer?
2. What are the personal qualities that a diplomat needs to fit well into his career?
3. What are the priorities for good direction of a bilateral territorial division at the MFA?
4. What is the most important new feature in bilateral work within the foreign ministry?

REFERENCES

1. Hocking, Brian, ed., *Foreign Ministries: Change and Adaptation* (Macmillan, London, 1999).
2. Robertson, Justin, ed., *Foreign Ministries in Developing Countries and*

Emerging Market Economies (International Insights: Dalhousie Journal of International Affairs, Halifax, Volume 14, Summer, 1998).

3. Cascone, Andrea, Italian Ministry of Foreign Affairs, *Comparing Diplomatic Services: Structures, Networks and Resources of the Ministries of Foreign Affairs of EU and G8 Member States* (DiploFoundation, Malta, under publication).
4. Rana, Kishan S., *Inside Diplomacy* (Manas, New Delhi, 2000), Chapter 11, pp. 252–78.

NOTES

1. I have seen a two-page British FCO note setting out guidelines on this point, but have found that most other foreign ministries in fact do not have standard guidelines, or have them tucked away in manuals that are not part of the memory of most working officials.
2. The British FCO deliberately uses corporate terminology. It also borrows from the armed forces the term 'commands' for its principal territorial and functional groupings.
3. These problems are covered in my book *Inside Diplomacy.* The cited studies on MFAs provide extensive information on systemic problems in other countries.
4. The DiploFoundation of the Mediterranean Academy of Diplomatic Studies, Malta, is one of the few specialists in this area, offering a variety of courses that blend Internet technique with traditional learning.
5. Management of all these specialties is the task of career management in the HR division or the personnel administration.
6. For instance, in the German diplomatic service economics has replaced law as the academic specialty of the majority of new entrants.
7. Set in former Yugoslavia in the 1950s, these are among the most amusing accounts of life in an embassy abroad, seen from the perspective of the junior official. Main title: *Esprit de Corps,*
8. This is a paradox because Article 31 of the Vienna Convention on Diplomatic Relations stipulates the MFA as the principal channel for diplomatic communication; in practice however each ministry and department maintains its own network of bilateral ties with foreign partners, and multilateral contacts with international agencies and the like.
9. The Indian Ministry of External Affairs, like many others is often in

turf-battles with other ministries, especially those handling economic work. One particular division head dealing with sensitive relations with neighboring countries, was recently able to establish excellent two-way partnership with the Commerce Ministry and other agencies, by demonstrating to them that the diplomatic apparatus understood their concerns, and working together they could produce a better outcome than through independent action.

10. *Reinventing Diplomacy in the Information Age*, Report of the US Council on Strategic and International Studies Advisory Panel (CSIS, Washington DC, 1998).
11. An excellent book by John Dickie, *Inside the Foreign Office* (Chapman, London, 1992), gives an evocative description of what he calls the 'march of the mandarins', the daily gathering for the 10.30 am meeting chaired by the Permanent Under Secretary.
12. Turkey uses this formula extensively because there are too few jobs at the MFA for very senior officials who return from ambassadorial assignments abroad. One excellent formula is to send them to academic institutions, with the title of 'ambassador-in-residence', as per the practice that the US developed. Customarily the MFA continues to pay the salary for the official, and the costs of maintaining him or her at the academic institution. However, it is vital to avoid an impression that the ones so assigned are MFA 'rejects'!

8

The Embassy and Consulates

In earlier times, some countries maintained two separate diplomatic services, one consisting of those who spent all their time abroad, working in the embassies, and another composed of those whose entire career was at headquarters. The Dutch were the last to operate such a system, up to some 30 years back, but today all foreign services see virtue in a unified system that rotates officials between home and abroad. The bulk of diplomatic missions are of a bilateral character, the exceptions being the missions accredited to multilateral agencies, like the UN Headquarters in New York, or WTO in Geneva, or the Disarmament Commission, or the UN specialized agencies that are located there. The same is true of Vienna, which is the seat of agencies like IAEA, and UNIDO. Then there is Brussels, both the capital of Belgium and the seat of the European Commission and NATO (most non-Western countries have a common mission there that handles all the work under multiple hats, while Western states have separate missions for each). What are the personnel needs in typical bilateral missions, in terms of duties at different levels, and the personal skills this entails?

The bilateral mission is the operational end of the diplomatic apparatus, with no direct policy-making role, but a significant policy advisory responsibility. It is the place where the roles of **Promotion, Outreach, Feedback**, and **Servicing** are played to the full, in relation to the single country of assignment (ignoring the situations where the mission may also handle a concurrent responsibility for representation in another country as well). I have argued elsewhere that because of the work overload at headquarters, and the multiplicity of contacts between nations, official and non-official, the bilateral mission has also gained a new role of '**Management**' of the bilateral relationship. This is simply because there is no other unit of government that has a near-total view of the relationship with a particular country that the mission commands. With this comes a capacity to identify cross-connections between disparate issues, which are available to the alert practitioner for leverage and relationship management.

Some diplomacy theorists have argued that the embassy has become a simple agency implementing the instructions of the foreign ministry, often left out of the information loop by the home authorities. They do not see it as a contributor to policy. True, heads of state carry out direct diplomacy often without even the knowledge of the MFA (Chapter 10). Such exchanges are a fact of life for the entire diplomatic system. But generally the alert mission abroad has local sources to track such direct contacts, such as the offices of the heads of state and government. The MFA and other home agencies can ill-afford to neglect the mission's local contacts and ground knowledge. Further, the same instant communications that place the embassy constantly at the reach of the headquarters in real time, give it the possibility of being consulted at different stages of policy formulation. Intranet-based confidential email exchange systems enable the alert ambassador to keep in close touch with colleagues at the foreign ministry, to intervene judiciously, and in effect 'write his own instructions'.[1]

Thus we see that increasing complexity in international relationships has actually given the bilateral mission an enhanced role and new capabilities. Far from confronting demise, the ambassador and his embassy colleagues emerged as a more active player in bilateral diplomacy. Of course, they are not an independent agents, and the task of relationship management is exercised jointly, and under the supervision, of the embassy's principal partner at home, the territorial division at headquarters.

JUNIOR OFFICERS

Most countries send out new foreign service entrants on their first assignments abroad as third secretaries or attachés, usually 'on probation'.[2] Their confirmation or permanent appointment depends on passing various internal examinations on regulations and financial procedures, as well as usually a 'compulsory' foreign language that is assigned to them. This language becomes the basis of their initial regional specialization. But there are small diplomatic services that do not require foreign languages study as a precondition to confirmation. Generally, the rank of third secretary is a transitory stage for the official under training and promotion as second secretary comes on confirmation in the service. The trainees are placed under the special charge and oversight of the ambassador, and are rotated against different jobs in the mission, so as to broaden their experience.

Like the desk officer at headquarters, the first or second secretary in a mission is the workhorse of the diplomatic system. Promotion to the rank of first secretary may come after around 5 or 7 years of service, and the next step, as counselor comes after about 12 to 14 years of service.[3] Thus the rank of second or first secretary is usually held through more than one overseas appointment, and marks a significant stage in a career.

Reading through the memoirs of diplomats belonging to one's own service as well as others, which cover their early diplomatic career, provides useful information on the service's work parameters, even if the setting of these recollections seems dated to each generation of diplomats and out of touch with one's own contemporary times. All too often, change is more apparent than real, and such books furnish valuable insight.

In a large mission there may be several first and second secretaries, while the small embassy may have only one, who also serves as deputy to the head of mission, become the chargé d'affaires *ad interim* whenever the ambassador is away from the country. Consequently, the duties of the first or second secretary can be clear-cut in a large mission, or within the small mission he or she will become the jack-of-all-trades.

Ideally, every junior official should be given some exposure to economic work and to information duties, regardless of designation, because together with political functions, these three areas lie at the center of diplomacy. Handling some jobs in all the three sectors, even in a supplementary capacity, enriches and rounds out the young official's skill development. It prepares them for senior assignments where each of these skills is viewed in holistic fashion, and woven into the actual task in hand. It also enables the official to understand the interconnections between the core diplomatic tasks. This is the essence of 'integrated' diplomacy.

WORK GUIDELINES

Diplomatic service manuals, when these exist, usually outline the duties of first secretaries in a rather simple fashion. In one such compilation a brief reference to the first secretary simply declares that he should perform the assigned political, commercial, administrative, protocol or information work; supervise the local staff, draft reports, and deliver talks to appropriate audiences. Perhaps one reason for the sparseness of the advice is that the actual work is too varied to be listed. Formal guidelines cannot tell the complete story, but an illustrative, practical listing might cover the following:

a) **Promotion and Outreach**. The principal tasks of the mission, namely reaching out and building productive contacts, also fully engage the first secretary. The actual range of individuals and institutions that he cultivates depend on the work handled, but in diplomacy this is never restricted or confined to an exclusive sector. Whatever the work assignment, the diplomat also pursues targets of opportunity to add to the embassy's wide contact base. The goal is to harness the relations established to gather information, to persuade, and to create new opportunities for advancing interests. One instance of junior diplomats playing a crucial role was during the Cultural Revolution in China in 1966–69, when these language specialists, networking among themselves, became the principal information sources on the hand-written 'wall newspapers' (through which different groups of activists propelled the events of the time). An everyday example is the relaxed, informal relations that these officials are usually able to establish with counterpart officials of the host country, often getting wind of new developments, or details of local thinking, that higher officials are unable to access.

b) **Reportage.** The junior official drafts, and in some cases finalizes on his own responsibility, a sizable portion of the mission's correspondence, periodic reports, and special dispatches. The first secretary is generally not involved in the drafting or writing of the cipher messages, mainly handled by the HOM and the deputy chief of mission, but usually gets to see the outgoing and the incoming messages, and needs to absorb from these some of the skills and techniques that are involved.[4] Indeed, reading through the 'float copies' of dispatches and correspondence is vital learning, and an internal communication method within the embassy, as also within the division or department at headquarters. It is good practice to send out special dispatches written by junior officials over their own signature, with a covering communication from the ambassador or DCM (deputy chief of mission) as suitable. This motivates the official to give his or her best, and deepens personal commitment.

c) **Management.** The job of head of 'chancery' or administration is usually held by one of the first secretaries. In all but the very largest of embassies (where the total number of staff, home-based and local may exceed 50 or more) it is not appropriate to have this handled as a full-time assignment, if only because the embassy then runs the risk of being 'over-administered'.[5] The embassy and the ambassador should keep administrative tasks in perspective. It is important to follow the stipulated regulations, but a mission that is engaged primarily in administration is in effect chasing its own tail. It is far better to have a first secretary handle the chancery job as a sideline. Example: in Germany, our 70-strong embassy had a first secretary (political) who supervised the chancery (and the work of the administration attaché) on a concurrent basis, with no loss of efficiency. But practices vary and in British missions, 'head of chancery' is an honored designation, with some broader internal coordination responsibility as well.

d) **Servicing.** The official handling consular affairs handles this set of tasks, as also by the commercial secretary, both of who interface with 'customers' approaching the embassy for services. The information secretary, involved in wide public contacts, also performs this function. Such tasks place the diplomat in wide public interaction and call for 'people skills', plus sensitivity to human problems. More and more countries use a 'citizen charter' formula to improve service delivery and to overcome mindsets of bureaucracy.

SENIOR OFFICIALS AND DCM

The ranks of counselor and the minister–counselor are customarily regarded as senior, with the latter designated simply as 'minister' in some systems Most countries have also now adopted the US practice of designating, at least in large missions, the embassy's second-ranking official as 'deputy chief of mission' (DCM). Typically these senior officials in the bilateral mission handle tasks that parallel those of the first secretary, but with greater autonomy, often supervising the junior officials as well. As experienced diplomats they function as valuable team members, independently handling projects and special tasks—like media outreach, links with ethnic communities, cultural projection, or economic promotion. In large missions they act as the departmental heads, carrying out independent correspondence, locally and with home agencies, but always under the overall supervision of the ambassador.

The DCM in a large mission handles the day-to-day management, and may also supervise some departments on behalf of the ambassador. In many diplomatic systems he would have served earlier as an ambassador, heading a small mission, and should have demonstrated leadership skills. The DCM's relationship with his own ambassador is of a special character, and demands accommodation and flexibility by both, where autonomy of function for the DCM is traded for basic discipline and loyalty to the ambassador. In practice, this often does not work as well as intended, and situations of friction, even conflict within the mission, are often traceable to problems within this particular equation.[6] In extreme cases, the breakdown in their working relationship may lead to an early transfer for the DCM, but long before this happens, the embassy will have suffered in efficient performance. This is one instance where ease of communication, especially through telephone calls to the foreign ministry colleagues, accentuates such problems of indiscipline.

The larger the mission, the greater the presence of officials from other agencies, ranging from specialists from line ministries that have a sizable stake in the country (covering agriculture, education, immigration, science & technology or the like), to defense attachés and 'undeclared' intelligence officials with 'cover' assignments. Welding them all into a united team is a major responsibility for the ambassador and the DCM. Since the days of President Eisenhower in the 1950s, every US president has made it a practice to address a directive to all official agencies, designating the ambassador as the head of the 'country team' in the foreign state. He has the real power

HR MANAGEMENT

Management of human resources (HR) in the diplomatic service is related to public services in general in the country, even if working conditions are exceptional. Some of the issues that arise are:

- Does every competent member of the service have a fair chance to become an ambassador? This is the case with most well-run services, especially if the definition of the top job is stretched to include also the consuls general. For example this is true of France, Japan and Germany that have large services, but not possible in the US, where the many do not go beyond the position of DCM. Inevitably this poses morale problems.
- Is the system of postings transparent and fair? It is impossible to expect officials to serve with efficiency and enthusiasm in places as different as Madrid and Mogadishu, unless an equitable system of rotation is practiced, responding also to genuine needs of officials and their family commitments. In many systems this is a shortcoming.
- Is grievance redressal effective? The German Foreign Office has an official who receives complaints from personnel at all levels and has high level interface, including access to the minister. Others have their own systems, similar in part. Because of the problems of isolation abroad, it is important to handle this well.
- Does the service practice a rule of the system, or is it a rule of individuals, variable in application? This is one of the problems in many developing countries, also affecting morale and performance.

to send back any official whose presence is judged by the ambassador as inimical to US interests. This contributes to discipline, the lack of which is a perennial problem with internal heterogeneity. But despite these powers, the US blue-ribbon independent task force headed by Frank C. Carlucci (former Defense Secretary and National Security Adviser) reported to the US Secretary of State in January 2001: 'Ambassadors lack authority to coordinate and oversee the resources and personnel deployed to their missions by other agencies and departments.'[7] In other countries where even theoretical power to send back offending team members do not exist, the management problems are more acute.

Sometimes the presence of a significant contingent of non-diplomatic service personnel leads to an 'us-and-them' situation. What works in welding together a team is the quality of leadership provided by the ambassador, not set formulas of formal control. For instance, in the Indian system the best teamwork has been performed where the HOM demonstrates through personal example that each official is valued for the contribution made, regardless of the agency to which the official belongs.

THE AMBASSADOR

More than anyone else, the head of mission (HOM) shapes the embassy through his or her example, work style and personality. Like the captain of a ship, he has overall responsibility as well as latent power, as the personal representative of the head of state, and the leader of the entire 'country team' in the nation of assignment. He is ultimately accountable for the mission's performance, taking the credit as well as the blame for particular events, and in terms of overall performance. And even in an age of instant communication, he faces the challenges of command. These include functional and mental isolation, personal responsibility for the wellbeing of all the home-based personnel in the mission (plus to a lesser extent for the local officials as well), and a frequent need to depend on his own resources.

The skills and experience accumulated over the years reach their fruition at this stage. This is but one of the reasons that career diplomats abhor the notion that those belonging to other walks of life can be parachuted into ambassadorial assignments through acts of political patronage. Such non-career appointments are customary with countries like the US or Latin America or Africa, and almost unknown in classic diplomacy countries like France, Japan, Germany and UK.[8] Objectively speaking, there are very few situations where a non-career ambassador offers something unique for the advancement of national interest that a career official cannot deliver. The exceptions hinge on special circumstances when the political appointee either enjoys special acceptability in the country of assignment, or has personal influence to get things done at home, or both. But the problem with 'political' influence is that it is transitory; changes in government at either end can end it abruptly, at considerable embarrassment to the sending and the receiving state.

The US system of appointment of distinguished figures from public service as envoys dates from the earliest days of its Independence—after all five of the first eight US presidents headed US diplomatic legations abroad before assuming the highest office.[9] But soon thereafter it became part of the spoils system of political appointments, in effect available to anyone, regardless of merit, that had made a sizable financial contribution to the incumbent president. Of the 160-odd US ambassadorial appointments abroad (including permanent missions to multilateral organizations), between 25 to 35% go to people outside the foreign service—especially the high profile ones in major capitals. Some among them are respected figures that have achieved prominence in diverse fields, such as business, academics and public life, unconnected to the president in any way other than affinity in political values. The US is also unique in placing the appointments under the ambit of confirmation by the Senate—no other country has a like procedure. Consequently, reform of the system has often been considered, but there is no consensus on a formula that would eliminate the abuse, and retain the positive aspects of the system, including the right of the president to choose his own team in a constitutional system of delicate power balance.

A corollary to the US system is that all ambassadors offer their resignations when a new president assumes office is re-elected, including the career appointees, who are generally not moved out immediately. Most of the political appointees are replaced as a matter of course, though a few may exceptionally continue in office, at the pleasure of the new president. For the receiving state, one merit of getting a political-appointee US ambassador is that he is likely to have direct access, outside the State Department, to others that exercise a good deal of influence on the unusually collegial policy-making process in that country. If they are lucky, he may even have a pipeline to the White House, or the next best thing, to the National Security Council. Rather few career-appointees can match this.

A final word on the ambassador's bilateral relationship management role that was outlined at the beginning of this chapter. It demands balanced judgment that comes with experience and skill. The envoy learns on the job, starting with a small mission that he may head in a country of relatively low or modest importance as seen from his home capital. There he hones his skills and accumulates knowledge. Major appointments naturally come towards the end of one's career. In the meantime there are also the opportunities to serve in the foreign ministry, at increasingly senior levels, building up an understanding of one's own system of governance, beyond the foreign ministry, that is also connected with a major mandate abroad. The ambassador needs a combination of knowledge and comprehension, innovation and caution, courage and discretion, resourcefulness and the ability to delegate, and above all personal integrity. In a way his entire career has been an apprenticeship for this role.

CONSULATES

Countries with the strongest tradition of emigration have the largest number of consulates abroad (these are Italy, France, Portugal, Greece and Spain). The *raison d'être* of a consulate general or a consulate (the two are identical in function, but the former ranks higher in the diplomatic hierarchy, and is usually headed by a more senior official)[10] is consular work, protection and services for its own nationals living in that territory, and delivery of visas and other related services to foreign nationals. They typically function under the jurisdiction of an embassy, though it is possible to have a consulate even if there is no embassy. This can happen if an existing embassy is closed, for political reasons or on grounds of economy. Even suspension of diplomatic relations does not automatically end consular relations. The Vienna Convention on Consular Relations of 1963 is the international legal framework for these entities, setting out the working conditions, as well as privileges and immunities.[11]

In practice consulates carry out almost the full range of diplomatic work, except that their political interface is with the provincial or regional administration of the receiving country, and they do not directly contact the MFA of the receiving state, or other central or federal government entities. But they carry out the work of promotion, outreach, feedback and servicing in full measure. Their management responsibilities are limited in comparison with embassies.

Non-career appointees, often nationals of the receiving country, head honorary consulates. These appointments require the approval of the receiving country, which may place some conditions on the jurisdiction or even his rank.[12] Some are purely honorific titles, where the appointed individual gives limited local help to the country that appoints him, and 'flies the flag', with no financial reimbursement.[13] In other cases the honorary consul may carry out limited consular work, including issue of visas, for which he may be reimbursed. For the appointing country it is a device to get the help of well-connected individuals, at places where it is not viable to station home-based officials. The crux of the challenge lies in the choice of the appointee, since at many places there are individuals interested only in the social status that goes with it, and have little interest in the work. As often in life, those who actively seek to become honorary consuls are just the kind that should not be appointed, and the ones that would handle the tasks well often have to be persuaded to take it up![14]

PERSONAL CHARACTERISTICS

The quality that mission officials, including the ambassador, need most of all is a capacity for teamwork, because solo brilliance is not nearly as effective as joint effort. The junior official is the foot soldier of the mission, sent off to any assignment that needs to be done, regardless of formal work allocation. At the more senior levels, experience and skills are deployed in sectors where there is need for supervision, as well as autonomous functioning.

How do the qualities needed in a mission differ fundamentally from those needed at headquarters? In a word, the role of promotion or 'outreach' dominates work abroad, far more than at home. Each mission official is in effect a proactive salesman for his country. As for any salesman, this demands intimacy with conditions at home, and zeal to convey this, in realistic and positive terms. He needs:

a) A **winning personality and genuine engagement in personal outreach.** For the junior official, contacts with local officials can often be among the most productive for the mission. At the local foreign office he can treat desk officers as equals, and gather information on attitudes and impending developments through the personal relationships that he establishes. The same applies to any other ministry or agency that belongs to his direct charge. In some respects he has no equal in these contact-building and information-gathering roles, because he is well placed to win confidence and gather material on issues of detail and nuance that more senior colleagues may find hard to access. The effectiveness with which the mission's 'outreach' role is performed at all levels depends on the networking and interpersonal skills of the diplomats. The ambassador is the one whose personal example inspires all the rest, but officials at all ranks have to be encouraged and groomed to become valuable mission resources.

b) The diplomat has a similar **role within the diplomatic corps,** also hinging on personal relationships. In each capital there are usually diverse informal groups of embassy officials, usually 'lunch clubs' where commercial or media specialists and others of like rank meet, exchange information and engage in professional interchanges (this sense of fraternity is particularly solid among the military attachés). Sometimes there is potential for creating a group of like-minded officials of one's own, with the right kinds of contacts. (Example: in the 1960s at Beijing I was involved in the creation of a lunch group composed exclusively of second and third secretaries that my own HOM came to call the 'Tails of Missions' lunch club. Now sub-divided into specialist segments—political, economic, etc.—it survives to the present!)

c) At all levels, when abroad, he has time to **build up specialist knowledge.** The host country is his first target, together with the local language, if this is the local requirement. For the diplomat, language is the tool for access and communication, not the end in itself. Besides the normal knowledge building task of specialization, he also needs an extensive spread of interests because diplomatic work encompasses ever-wider subjects. This is the attitude of constant learning.

d) Building **social and representational skills** is another opportunity. Knowledge of wines and fine foods can help, but this is not the end objective, pleasant as it may be. The professional skill lies more in a winning way with people and an ability to use social contacts in a non-obvious manner, for professional purposes. The junior diplomat is the HOM's special responsibility in the development of these abilities, starting with social confidence building.

e) **Writing ability** is a career-long preoccupation, together with drafting and summarizing skills. These are obvious assets in multilateral diplomacy, where the person that can produce on demand a phrase or other construction of words that bridges divergent ideas is an instant success in drafting groups. The same skill at building compromise and safeguarding one's own interest is no less needed in bilateral work. It is built through observation, and practice.

f) **A special project** becomes a tremendous learning opportunity for the mission team. Examples are a special dispatch of importance, or a local market study on a product exportable from home, or a scheme to streamline consular work, or even a new way to transform the library and periodicals section as a 'resource center'. Any of these provide an opportunity for creative thinking and independent action. The HOM should take care to give credit to his colleagues for the work, and of course guide them as needed.

g) **Technology developments** should be an obvious focus area for the young and the senior official, gaining personal familiarity with the information and communications technology used, or potentially usable, by the embassy. One should seek insights into technology developments in the host country, as a means of remaining well informed on futuristic subjects.

h) The embassy official should **guard his sources**, especially in written reports, if it might conceivably embarrass the source if it is traced back. I learnt the hard way that an urge to establish one's own credibility with details of the source, worked fine until someone at headquarters was indiscreet enough to name the source to his own foreign interlocutor, and the story got back to the original source via his foreign ministry! Practical experience generally shows that besides one's own HOM, one should hold back on sensitive detail.

When a mission official has an opportunity to officiate as the chargé d'affaires, this is an invaluable learning experience, even if the times are tranquil and there are no major developments, bilateral or local. He has the opportunity to mix with other heads of missions, many with vast experience, and even if he is unlikely to be taken too seriously by them, he can learn much simply through observation and a passive listening role in dialogue. He may also gain some insight into the psychological loneliness of the head of mission, who has none to advise on the way he should act, or react, to opportunities and developments as they occur, even in this age of instant communications. He might understand too that the mission is both a branch of the headquarters, and at the same time a distinct unit in a local environment—an environment that is not fully understood from headquarters. These are factors in the complex relationship that he has to sustain with colleagues at home. He then begins to understand the complete responsibility he must bear for his own actions.

QUESTIONS

1. What are the tasks of junior officials in the mission?
2. What are the work areas to which all embassy officials need exposure and why?
3. How do the duties of the DCM differ from those of a counselor heading a department within the mission?
4. List the major responsibilities of the ambassador. Which one is the hardest of his tasks?
5. Which personal qualities are the most important for a diplomat serving in a bilateral mission?

REFERENCES

1. Eban, Abba, *Diplomacy for the Next Century* (New Haven, Yale University Press, 1998).
2. Locke, Mary and Yost, Casimir A. eds, *Who Needs Embassies? How US Missions Abroad Help Shape Our World* (Institute for the Study of Diplomacy, Georgetown University, Washington DC, 1997).

3. Rana, Kishan S., *Inside Diplomacy* (Manas Publications, New Delhi, 2000), Chapter 14, pp. 311–42.
4. Wolfe, Robert, ed., *Diplomatic Missions: The Ambassador in Canadian Foreign Policy* (McGill and Queens University Press, Ottawa, 1998).

NOTES

1. This particular phrase comes from an ambassador interviewed in January 2001, during a survey that I had conducted for a book on the role of the ambassador that is under preparation.
2. Exceptions to this are some small countries in Africa and elsewhere that give diplomatic rank to all home-based officials. Consequently, the ranks of second and third secretary are reserved for support staff and the junior-most diplomatic level official is given the rank of first secretary, even on first appointment.
3. This pattern applies to well-organized services, where human resource management is efficient. There are small services that confront major promotion blockage, which inevitably affects morale.
4. The practice on cipher messages usage varies between countries. Smaller diplomatic services do not use them at all, while in the very largest almost all communication is through this route and all diplomats become adept at usage.
5. My view is based on personal experience and some will surely not agree. European countries other than UK tend to have a full time specialist handling the administration, to whom the internal designation of administration chancellor is applied.
6. During the course of a survey of diplomatic practices, I have not encountered any special training or orientation given in any foreign service on handling the ambassador–DCM equation. Yet there are generic issues, going beyond the particularities of any system that demand serious attention to this problem.
7. *State Department Reforms*, report of the independent task force sponsored by the Council on Foreign Relations and the Center for Strategic and International Studies, Washington DC, 2001.
8. In the majority of Western countries (besides the US) appointments made from outside the service are rare, but they do occur. Typically

at any point in time there might be one or two such persons serving as ambassadors. The Indian system is a kind of compromise, with about 8 to 10 non-career ambassadors in place at any given time, out of a total of about 115.

9. Right until the end of the 19th century, in the first 120 years of Independence the US opened only 'legations' in foreign countries, headed by 'ministers'. One reason was an aversion to royal court protocol of Europe of the time; unlike the ambassador, the lower ranking minister did not form part of the royal court. After the end of World War II, this second echelon of diplomatic entities, the legation, has disappeared from usage.
10. Usually a consulate general has a larger jurisdiction than a consulate. The receiving country, in consultation with the sending country, determines this jurisdiction.
11. Broadly, consular privileges and immunities are narrower than diplomatic privileges and immunities, and are more specifically tied to the actual work performed.
12. Some receiving countries insist that a new appointment should be at the rank of 'honorary consul', which may later be elevated to 'honorary consul general'.
13. Local help may take the shape of looking after visitors from home, organizing programs for delegations, and assisting the ambassador and his officials in contacts with local personalities.
14. In Germany I encountered a situation where a particular set of individuals assiduously pursued the claim of one individual, who somehow felt that he was the best person to represent India in one city. Some years earlier there had been a scandal in another European city over an individual who had been innovatively 'marketing' such appointments to local businessmen who craved the status!

9

Joint Commissions and Other Groups

The institutions of bilateral relations examined in this chapter have one common characteristic. They all involve agencies that lie beyond the foreign ministry in the business of promoting stronger ties with foreign countries. It is not a coincidence that the increasing prevalence of these groups, official and non-official, coincides with the involvement of these actors in external relations in most parts of the world. We also see that one result of these developments is greater dynamism and innovation in the diplomatic process as a whole.

Joint commissions, 'eminent person' groups, and similar bilateral groupings are devices widely used by countries for relationship building. One precondition for their effectiveness is serious intent by both sides to use them for result, and not as prestige symbols—unfortunately the latter is a motivation from time to time! Special non-official groups are also created sometimes within regional groups in unique circumstances. It is interesting to examine the classic models, as also the variations that have developed upon these in recent years.

THE JOINT COMMISSION

This format emerged in the 1950s and was a particular favorite of the erstwhile 'socialist' countries and their partners around the world.[1] A typical joint commission (JC), sometimes also called a 'mixed commission', consists on each side of empowered officials drawn from different ministries, often headed by a minister as co-chairman. The usual JC pattern is to meet at annual intervals, alternating between the two countries, to consider and take joint decisions on a wide range of bilateral issues. The method enables each side to give concentrated attention to priority subjects. The device is useful for taking coordinated internal decisions, both at the preparation and the follow-up phases, especially on complex subjects that might otherwise take considerable time because many different ministries and agencies are involved. It is well suited to state-dominated systems, especially when rigid bureaucracies or poor internal coordination tend to slow down the decision process. As most joint commissions have ministerial status, it also means that high-level governmental clearances can be obtained prior to meetings (usually at the level of the cabinet, the highest executive organ in parliamentary democracies), and that the decisions taken at each session are authoritative. For example, the JC method enabled India and the Soviet Union to develop effective, advanced cooperation models based on the co-production of aircraft and other major items of defense equipment involving a number of agencies on both sides.

Of course the JC system has extended well beyond the socialist nations, and most countries have such institutional arrangements with anything from 20 to 50 or more foreign partners. Foreign ministers head many JCs, but the sheer numbers ensure that various other ministers are also brought in to head many of these. It distributes the burden of servicing the JCs, and one typical pattern is to entrust a particular JC to that ministry that has a major interest in the issues that dominate the bilateral relationship. Thus, the

Minister of Mines might head a JC with a country where many of the dossiers relate to minerals and raw materials. Some JCs operate at much higher levels, when countries invest them with greater tasks. Example: the Gore–Chernomyrdin Commission, created in 1993, was headed by the US Vice-President and the Russian Premier, and worked on eight key bilateral issues.

The functioning and success of JCs depends on several elements:

a) Who is to head the JC? Distributing responsibility among different ministers is effective when there are a number of such commissions, but tension often develops between the foreign ministry and the line ministry that heads the JC, when the latter also has the responsibility for 'servicing' it, i.e. handling the preparation for meetings, the drawing up of a unified stand on complex issues, and generating follow-up. Some foreign ministries create a 'JC Secretariat' that takes care of pre- and post-meeting coordination. That is a good formula, when it works!
b) Is JC membership confined only to representatives of official agencies? In the past the majority were strictly limited to official representatives. But the recent trend has been to open up membership to representatives of chambers of commerce, industry associations, and other economic groups that can make a contribution to the bilateral relationship, or benefit from the dialogue or use the forum for resolving real issues. Countries have found that the JCs that are open to non-state actors work better than those limited to official members.[2]
c) Should the JC have sub-groups? This depends on the breadth of coverage. Where agendas are large, and when a number of stakeholders have to be involved, the actual operational entity may well become the 'joint sub-commission', covering areas like education and culture, or science & technology, as happened with the Indo-US Commission, created in 1982 and wound up in the late 1990s.[3] The US Secretary of State and the Indian External Affairs Minister headed it, and it worked primarily

through four near-autonomous sub-commissions. With a country such as the US, the involvement of representatives of business and the other non-official entities offers the only way to run such groups, because subjects like culture and education are not substantively handled by official agencies. Other models have also shown that the utility of sub-groups covering sectors like the mining industry, or infrastructure development or tourism, hinges on the leadership that one or the other side is able to provide in such detailed dialogue.

d) How often should the JC meet? The general pattern is for annual meetings, but sometimes with particularly active groups, more frequent meetings are useful. As with good architecture, the form should follow the function!

It is the experience of most countries that JCs that are created for symbolic purposes are unable to deliver result. Delayed meetings, or lack of serious content to the dialogue marks them. Sometimes years pass before someone wakes up to ask whether a session should be held. This devalues the mechanism, and the few meetings held become the occasion for officially sponsored jaunts. Eventually such JCs become dormant. Such shortcomings notwithstanding, the JC is an effective instrument in relationship building, provided it is adapted to real needs.

EMINENT PERSON GROUPS

This is both an old and new mechanism. Limited use was made of this mechanism in the post-War era, when special formats like a well known UK–Germany group (the 'Königswinter Group'),[4] and the 'Atlantic Bridge' between the US and Germany, were created. More recently, Germany and India pioneered wider application of the method, among countries that do not have exceptional relationships. The Indian Prime Minister and the German Chancellor decided at their meeting in 1991to create a bilateral 'consultative group', consisting mainly of private individuals, businessmen, bankers, academics, scientists, media leaders, and parliamentarians, empowered with the simple mandate of producing 'practical recommendations on ways to deepen and enrich the relationship'. Both sides saw this as an experiment. Thanks to tight focus on the mandate, the group produced good result from the outset and has since continued with regular annual meetings, each time coming up with some 15 to 20 ideas and leads. Subsequently, Germany and India have gone on to create similar bilateral groups with other partner countries, using varied names like 'forum', 'round table', and the like. The concept has spread. In net outcome, some work better than others. Analysis of the success factors shows that the ingredients for good results are:

a) The non-official participants should autonomously run the eminent person (EP) group, under the designated co-chairman of each side. The MFA representatives provide the financing and participate in an *ex officio* capacity, and should confine themselves to logistics, support and discreet guidance when this is needed. It is also useful to have on the group officials from other key ministries, as long as the total number is small, and they are content to play the role of interested observers.
b) Tight focus on 'actionable' suggestions ensures that the EP group does not become a talk-shop, or a place for repeating the dialogue that takes place in official encounters.[5] In practice, an implementation rate of around 50 to 60% is excellent. This is because inevitably some ideas are either ahead of their time, or are impractical from the perspective of one or both sides. The presence of officials prevents the group from completely 'going off the track'. But safeguarding the EP group's independence is essential.
c) Sometimes the group may create sub-groups, and charge them with the formulation of proposals, or other activities of a conceptual nature. But it would not be typical for the group and the persons serving on it to devote more than a few days in the year to the activities of the group. (Example: the Indo-French

Forum, which became operational in 1997, uses such sub-groups. It also meets, unusually, at 6-month intervals. The Indo-British Round Table also meets twice a year and seems keen to oversee the implementation of proposals, which may become a new activity that gets it involved in fields perhaps lying beyond the capacity of such a group).

d) One factor that works well in genuinely plural societies is that it creates a cluster of influential personalities who develop wide knowledge in the mutual relationship, and come to have a stake in it. This is of inestimable value, since bilateral relationships are truly enriched by such non-official involvement that has a sustained character.

It is possible to have such special groups in different situations. For instance, the APEC forum had at one time created a group of 15 'wise men' charged with charting the future growth of cooperation within this trans-regional group that encompasses countries from the Americas, Asia, and the Pacific. A vital ingredient for success is that the group should be sufficiently empowered, and function in a non-official mindset and style. One indirect value of the EP format is that it recognizes the contribution of 'non-state actors' in external relationships, and in fact acknowledges the plurality of diplomacy actors. This has wider societal value, responding to the democratization urge. The EP group format deserves greater attention in other countries and regions, as a model for creative emulation.

OTHER GROUPS

The US and Canada, two countries as intimately involved with one another as can be imagined for two sovereign and independent entities, did not have any special bilateral consultation mechanism until the early 1970s, when a Commission, headed by the US Secretary of State and the Canadian Minister of External Relations, was created. Since then, of course, the advent of NAFTA (North

American Free Trade Area) and other joint actions covering an array of functional areas, has led to an abundance of bilateral consultation mechanisms. In the case of the US and Germany, at the start of the post-War reconciliation phase, a notional 'Atlantic Bridge' was created, as an umbrella device for a whole series of joint actions, bringing together the leading personalities of the two countries in various fields. This initiative survives till now and has grown into a permanent cooperation mechanism. Other close neighbors have created similar mechanisms for wide consultation, including those in Europe in the early years after 1950.

Among developing countries, such a non-official bilateral mechanism has been relatively slow to grow, perhaps on account of the fact that non-official participation in diplomacy and relationship building has also not been sufficiently nurtured. One exception is the ASEAN group of countries that has deliberately created a series of 'Institutes of Security and International Studies' in each capital, as think tanks that function in an autonomous fashion, and provide intellectual inputs for the benefit of each country and the entire region, and networking with other entities. This is a model that could be well used in other regional entities like SADC and ECOWAS. In South Asia, cooperation among think tanks in individual countries has developed in recent years through non-official initiatives, supported discreetly by the governments and by enlightened external funding agencies and foundations.

TRACK TWO MECHANISMS

In the case of countries that face conflict, or prolonged tension over political, territorial and other issues, a new format that has come into being in the past two or three decades is the 'second track' discussion format. This was well used in the Cold War period by different entities, to deepen understanding and build mutual confidence. Among those who have implemented this from an early time have been religious groups like the 'Society of Friends' (the

NEW APPROACHES

A new mechanism that has become popular is 'strategic consultation'. Invariably it is established between countries that are seeking to make an indirect assertion to the effect that their affinities have increased. In practice it means that officials of the MFA, the defense ministries and other agencies concerned with the political and security environment meet annually (or as mutually determined) for an exchange of views, and a *tour d' horizon*. For instance, in 2000 the first such meeting was held between Indian and Chinese officials, marking a further improvement in bilateral ties.

A different example is provided by an India–EU 'round table for civil society', backed and funded officially, and involving participants drawn from NGOs, development oriented volunteer groups and the like. There are substantive issues of health, education, the environment and other development imperatives where there are sharp divergences, often within the developing countries themselves. For instance, the Indian opponents of big dams are confronted by others Indians, who insist that building such dams is the lesser evil to abandoning development in the name of environment protection. It is not clear if bilateral dialogue, supported by state entities, produces real understanding.

Quakers), think tanks like the Aspen Institute, and special theme groups like the Pugwash Conference that has focused on nuclear disarmament. At a time when relations across the East–West divide were frozen, such private initiatives, almost always with the tacit or explicit support of some of the governments, kept contacts alive and served to transmit ideas and messages. Their contribution to the evolution of events, including the collapse of communism and the end of the Cold War, remains to be fully assessed. In Latin America the role of private groups in the settlement of civil conflicts has also been crucial.

Abba Eban, former Israeli Foreign Minister and master diplomat, has narrated graphically in his book *Diplomacy for the Next Century* how private initiative by a Norwegian social scientist, Teje Larsen, and his contacts with non-official and influential Israeli and Palestinian interlocutors led to what became the Oslo Talks of 1992–93, that led to a substantive peace process, and the joint meeting of Rabin and Arafat with Clinton at the White House on September 13, 1993. This is an instance of a track two process that rapidly graduated to an official dialogue. (We can also see in the current Norwegian involvement in trying to start a dialogue between the Sri Lanka government and the Tamil Tiger militants, the way in which a small country can work for peaceful resolution of complex problems with its own diplomatic initiatives in distant regions.)

Some developing countries, particularly in South Asia, have also used the track two processes. For example, between India and Pakistan there are several such bilateral efforts under way, and the SAARC group of countries in South Asia has other instances of ongoing private dialogue among intellectuals of the countries in the region. Unlike the EP groups, the primary initiative for the track two dialogue comes from individuals active in public affairs, the media or research, though there is often discreet official funding and backing. Funding may also come sometimes from non-official international foundations; usually the amount of money needed is modest. Other features are:

i. By definition, the term track two means that there is no formal official participation, though the individuals who meet, in the South Asian experience, may be retired diplomats or armed forces personnel and others who are unlikely to stray too far from their respective national standpoints. In contrast, at the height of the East–West conflict, officials also took part in such encounters, with the disclaimer that they participated in a 'private' capacity.

ii. Starting from a standpoint of goodwill and commitment to mutual friendship, the dialogue often aims at defining the mutual interests in wider terms than perceived conventionally, as well as feasible means for de-escalating tension.

iii. Invariably the groups report back to the leaders of their countries and to the foreign ministries after each encounter. The countries also find it useful to float trial balloons on new ideas through such groups, which ensures a discreet and 'deniable' mechanism for indirect negotiation, sometimes even taking the shape of 'talks about talks'. When India and Pakistan made an effort to overcome mutual suspicion with Prime Minister A.B. Vajpayee's bus trip to Lahore, across the land frontier in March 1999, track two contacts and discussions among private emissaries had contributed to the summit encounter. In the event, the peace process launched with the Lahore Declaration was sabotaged by Pakistan's large incursion across the Line of Control in Kashmir at Kargil two months later, leading to a sharp and short conflict.

iv. One precondition for the operation of the second track is the existence of some degree of plurality in the countries using the device, or at least a kind of latent plurality, as began to emerge in East Europe much before the end of the Cold War. In contrast, it is not clear, for example, how far the second track would really work with a country such as China, where differentiated positions among independent research institutes, and autonomy of expression is under evolution. Despite such caveats, an interesting track two dialogue was launched in 2001 between intellectuals and academic specialists of China, Russia and India; the first meeting was held in Moscow and another is planned for next year in China.

It is undeniable that the track two provides a means for de-escalation of tension, and for building mutual confidence. In particular it serves to create public opinion in favor of tensions reduction. We sometimes tend to forget that international affairs deal with dynamic situations, and that influencing opinion within the ranks of the 'adversary' is also good diplomacy.

One underlying feature of several of the groups described above is the involvement of non-official agencies and individuals in international affairs. This is an aspect of democratization of external affairs among the domestic constituencies that is occurring in most regions around the world. It forces foreign ministries to practice outreach to these domestic elements, via changed mindsets and some restructuring as well. Such evolution, representing a facet of public diplomacy, shapes the implementation of foreign policy in our age.

QUESTIONS

1. What are the characteristics of a joint commission? How does it function?
2. What are the special features of an eminent persons group? What is a key element for its success? Do you know of any other examples of such groups?
3. What is the rationale of track two diplomacy? Please give your own examples.
4. Why do countries need special consultation or dialogue mechanisms?

REFERENCES

1. Eban, Abba, *Diplomacy for the Next Century* (New Haven, Yale University Press, 1998).
2. Rana, Kishan S., *Inside Diplomacy* (New Delhi, Manas Publications, 2000), Chapter 3, pp. 64–8.

NOTES

1. The prestige factor was important in the way the Soviet Union and East European countries used the JC model, but where the objective circumstances for bilateral benefit existed, it served well to mobilize cooperation opportunities.
2. This was India's experience with the Indo-German Joint Commission

that was established in the late 1970s. The Germans insisted that membership cover the principal business bodies of the two sides, and through them to the individual companies that are active in trade and industrial relations. The result has been a strong degree of realism to the annual meetings, and the development of a problem-solving approach in the government–business dialogue on both sides.

3. The Indo-US Commission was funded by the 'Rupee counterpart funds' that were a residue of US PL 480 food aid during the 1966–68 drought in India. One result of Prime Minister AB Vajpayee's November 2001 visit to the US has been a decision to create a new joint economic group, headed by the Principal Secretary to the Indian PM and the US President's Economic Adviser. This is to have five sub-groups and represents another example of flexible use of the joint group method.
4. Established at the start of the period of German reconstruction after World War II, this was one of the very many institutional arrangements evolved to rebuild durable linkages. There are around 80 participants from each of the two sides, and there are sub-groups where substantive dialogue takes place. Today, with multiple connections among major EU members, the group is less prominent than before.
5. A small but vital decision taken at the first meeting of the Indo-German group became a success factor. The German Co-Chairman of the time, Dr. Ulrich Cartilleri insisted that the final document summarizing the recommendations of the session should not exceed a page-and-half in length; he argued that Chancellor Kohl would not read anything longer than that. The group accepted the advice and at each session one problem has always been to distil the final paper to such length, or in later years, to a maximum of three pages. Such lean final documents are not in the Indian style, but the method concentrates minds wonderfully! And in August 1994, when Chancellor Kohl received the Indian Co-Chairman for a meeting, less than a full day after the end of the session, I saw for myself that the Chancellor had indeed read the recommendations, in the detailed observations he made in support of some of the ideas.

10

Bilateral Summits

Summit meetings between the leaders of countries represent the apex of the bilateral diplomatic process. We use the term to refer to formal or informal encounters between the heads of state and of government; meetings between ministers or even the heads of parliamentary institutions are not included in this category. Foreign travels of vice-presidents are usually not included in this definition.

THE CONTEXT

One feature of our times is that such meetings are more frequent with each passing year. The heads are personally involved in foreign affairs as never before. As late as 1980, a former US Secretary of State recalled the adages of old diplomacy and warned: 'Summit diplomacy is to be approached with the wariness with which a physician prescribes a habit-forming drug.'[1] Abba Eban has written in like fashion more recently in 1998: 'The idea that every difficult condition can be improved by high-level dialogue is one of the more persistent diplomatic delusions ... no situation is so bad that a badly conceived summit cannot make it worse.'[2] Contrast that with the hectic rounds of foreign visits made by British Prime Minister Tony

Blair who in eight weeks after the September 11 terrorist attacks in the US, undertook four separate tours to several states, each time drumming up support for the US-led anti-terrorism coalition.

Another trend is increased informality. Countries like Japan, UK and others in Europe maintain a numerical limit on the number of incoming 'state' visits that are accepted each year from foreign monarchs and presidents, to avoid over-burdening the country's head of state who has to act as host. They have a similar limit for outbound invitations accepted. As noted in Chapter 2, the informal variations on this have grown extensively, and this enables both sides to concentrate on substance, and cut down on the froth of empty protocol or ritual. So while gilded horse-drawn carriages and elaborate state banquets remain on the diplomatic calendar, more and more summits have shifted to business-like formats.[3]

SUMMIT TYPES

Until about 1970, bilateral summits were relatively infrequent. Usually planned with great care, such events fall into distinct categories:

1. **Visits by non-executive heads of state.** These are visits by constitutional monarchs, and by presidents who do not hold executive power. They follow the formal pattern of 'state' visits, or the next lower type in protocol symbolism, the 'official' visit. They aim at goodwill, flying the flag, and underscoring mutual affinity. Constitutional heads do not engage in substantive political discourse, though issues of mutual interest are invariably addressed. By custom, a cabinet minister from home accompanies the constitutional head traveling abroad, since by constitutional form the head acts on advice of his government. (Example: on visits abroad the British monarch invariably has an accompanying cabinet minister; German or Indian presidents do likewise.) In contrast, when an executive president travels to a country that has a constitutional head, the real business of the visit is

conducted not with the nominal host but with that county's foreign prime minister or the chancellor.[4] The reverse situation, a formal visit by a constitutional head to an executive president is increasingly rare as there is no prospect of substantive dialogue. This would apply to a visit by say the Japanese Emperor to the US, important for symbolism, but taking place perhaps once a decade, unlike the annual or even more frequent visits by the Japanese Prime Minister to Washington DC. Most Western countries apply an annual 'quota' for both incoming and outbound full-protocol honor visits by heads of state.

2. **Regular visits by executive presidents and prime ministers.** We speak here of the classic bilateral visit, often planned a year in advance, in response to previous exchanges, aimed at consolidation and augmentation of existing good relations. For example, in the heyday of Non-Alignment, each visit by one of the leaders of this Movement to a counterpart, say the travel of the Egyptian President to India or to Yugoslavia of the Tito era, took place at intervals of a few years, and was planned in meticulous detail. The schedule included events such as an address to the national parliament, a civic reception and the conferment of an honorary degree by a leading academic institution. Some or all of these are now often left out, for reasons of time. The typical bilateral visit format today is a full day devoted to substantive dialogue—between the two heads meeting one-on-one as well as at full delegation level, plus several ministers calling on the visiting dignitary. A meeting with the leader of the opposition is customary. In addition, formal banquets, supplemented by cultural activity are held; visits are made to educational or scientific institutions. A public event is held if the visitor wants to give a major address on a theme of his choice. The guest usually travels outside the capital for a day or more, depending on circumstance. All these variations depend on the guest's convenience and local custom.
3. **State events.** These include the coronation of kings and queens,

some presidential inaugurals (especially in Latin America where it is customary to have foreign dignitaries at these events), and state funerals of high dignitaries. Levels of attendance are carefully noted for bilateral reciprocity when occasion arises. The organization of such events is a demanding task and some chaos is usually accepted in good humor. Protocol arrangements have to be creative to suit circumstance. At Emperor Hirohito's funeral in January 1989, in order to ensure that US President Ronald Reagan would not be placed low on the customary protocol order determined by length of tenure, all foreign high dignitaries were ranked in the order in which the Japanese monarch had made his state visits abroad, of course with the US placed first.

Summits of this nature continue, but with simplified norms and set practices, such as setting limits on the number of the accompanying delegation that the receiving country would treat as state guests. (African and Arab nations tend to offer more elaborate and unstinted hospitality, but even they now exercise economy and apply limits.) The old style summits are now outnumbered by informal visits by heads, dominated by substance and not protocol ritual. The new additions are:

a) **Periodic encounters.** Summits of this type take place between countries which share a great deal in common. Example: the 6-monthly meetings of the French President and the German Chancellor. Depending on the themes, they may be accompanied by other ministers, or exclude all aides, with only an interpreter or note-taker present on each side. Such meetings have taken place in exclusive locations, like gourmet restaurants in the countryside or at famous castles, and are stripped of all ritual. This model of cyclic meetings has not been taken up by developing in different regions. One of the few exceptions is the bi-annual encounter of the Presidents of South Africa and Namibia.
b) **Regional summits.** One positive feature of regional diplomacy is the platform it creates for bilateral encounters of leaders of neighboring states. They take place at regular frequency and

provide a neutral setting for meetings between heads of countries that have strained relations. ASEAN, now encompassing 10 states in South-East Asia offers an outstanding example of such a blend of bilateral and regional diplomacy. In contrast, SAARC in South Asia provides a negative example—the unwillingness of Indian leaders to meet bilaterally their Pakistani counterparts after the military coup in that country in October 1999 has resulted in a long postponement of even the annual summit.[5]

c) **On margins of other events.** The commonest forum for a bilateral encounter is a multilateral meeting, at the UN in New York or elsewhere, usually with elaborate advance planning, and sometimes even in an impromptu manner.[6] Such dialogue keeps contacts alive and permits consultation on issues at the conference that the leaders are both attending. But sometimes the meeting signals a major change.[7] State funerals, as noted above, are also used for such bilateral meetings, though it is rare to have significant business conducted there.[8]

d) **Meetings with a topical agenda.** These kinds of summits take place mainly at short notice, without formal protocol. The visiting dignitary may stop over for just a few hours, concentrating on dialogue with the host interlocutor. Such encounters are increasingly customary. Palestinian leader Yasser Arafat is a seasoned practitioner of such personal diplomacy, traveling incessantly to friendly capitals to marshal political support. With fast breaking developments, as during a crisis, the local embassy in the country being visited is usually 'out of the information loop', not aware of the full contours of the issue. Even in such cases, this embassy can provide information on local thinking and attitudes that the visiting dignitary can ill-afford to neglect.

This listing is not exhaustive and there are other summits that do not follow the pattern, like stopover visits and almost casual drop-ins by leaders. This latter type occurs in Africa and the Arab countries in particular.[9]

SUMMIT VIGNETTES

Bilateral summits can produce high drama, as well as unexpected moments of distraction. An instance of the former is the June–July 1972 India–Pakistan summit held at Shimla between Indira Gandhi and Zulfikar Bhutto, to negotiate the final arrangements after the Bangladesh War of December 1971, including the handing back of some 30,000 sq. km of territory and 93,000 Pakistan army prisoners held by India. He brought with him a large political delegation, including senior ministers, opposition personalities, and his daughter Benazir, then barely out of her teens. (Benazir Bhutto has written that her father warned her to wave to the crowds, but not smile, because of the difficult circumstances of the visit.) The negotiations were difficult and seemed to fail; on the final day a late night meeting of the two leaders, unaccompanied by aides, produced the formula, the Shimla Agreement of July 2, 1972, which commits the two countries to a bilateral process to resolve the Kashmir issue, and converted the 'ceasefire line' in Kashmir to a delineated 'Line of Control'. But that Agreement has not produced durable peace. One issue shrouded in mystery, and an object of bilateral controversy, is whether Bhutto gave some verbal commitments that were later not honored. (See PN Dhar, *Indira Gandhi, the 'Emergency', and Democracy*, Oxford University Press, New Delhi, 2000).

During her November 1981 visit to France Prime Minister Indira Gandhi was to receive a doctorate *honoris causa* at the University of Sorbonne; Indian Ambassador MK Rasgotra insisted that she should deliver her speech in French. She had studied French in Switzerland as a teenager, but had no subsequent contact with the language, and was unwilling to do so. The Ambassador persisted with his advice. Barely six days before arrival in Paris, her Principal Secretary phoned the Ambassador to convey 'firm instructions' that she would speak in English, but the Ambassador stuck to his stand that a speech in English would be badly received. At this point Indira Gandhi, who was present, took the phone and said that this was her own decision; the Ambassador replied that it was his duty to point out that this would cast a shadow on the visit. At this she relented, and with characteristic determination, she then went on to devote three hours each day while in Rome (the preceding destination on her tour) to practicing the delivery of the French text of her speech, with a Professor of French from the University of Rome. The speech, when delivered, was word-perfect and capped an important visit that put the India–France relationship on a higher track. And Rasgotra was appointed Foreign Secretary i.e. the civil service head of the Ministry of External Affairs), shortly thereafter!

The mood at the coronation of Nepal's King Birendra in 1974 was one of amiable chaos, and Philippine presidential spouse Imelda Marcos added to the confusion when she turned up unexpectedly with two plane-loads of friends! Protocol arrangements at the many ceremonial and social events, spread out over three days, were under much stress. At the end of each event, most foreign dignitaries waited 30 to 40 minutes for their cars, escorted by several jeep-loads of armed guards. Everyone took it in good humor.

PRACTICAL VALUE

How real is the utility of bilateral summits visits, and what do they achieve? In an age of public accountability, there are real questions and it is not sufficient to speak in the abstract of the advancement of relations or a deepening of understanding among states. A few responses:

a) A summit may become a landmark event, if it gives a new start or marks a paradigm shift. This was the case with US President Richard Nixon's historic journey to China in 1972, which marked US acceptance of China and led to its entry into the UN, and a shift in the global balance. Such events are rare. Another that was in the making was Russian President Vladimir Putin's November 2001 journey to the US, which did not fully live up to billing as the open launch of the new US–Russia alliance.
b) National leaders get an opportunity to speak directly to counterparts, without intermediaries, to advocate a viewpoint, demand an action (or abstention from an action), or solicit a decision. This is the classic advocacy role of diplomacy. At the minimum this influences countries, offering a perspective that one side may not have fully grasped, not because the facts of the other's standpoint were not known, but because the case is presented in a very personal way, one leader to another. Personal chemistry is always important. Sometimes the dramatic result of actually getting the other country to do what one seeks is possible. For instance, during the first sustained encounter between the British and Indian Prime Ministers in March 1982, Indira Gandhi was able to persuade Margaret Thatcher to agree to contribute to a particular round of replenishment of funds for the 'International Development Association', the soft lending window of the World Bank for the poorest countries, at a level that was beyond the subscription level agreed by the US, and persuade other donors to do likewise. This resulted in getting an additional amount of some $1.5 billion for the benefit of developing states.[10] Contrast this with the virtually unproductive tour that the same Indian Premier made to the US and other Western nations in mid-1971 to mobilize support for a looming crisis, resulting from military repression in what was then East Pakistan and the eventual exodus of 10 million refugees into India. It culminated in the Bangladesh War of December 1971. In particular, President Nixon was unmoved by Indira Gandhi's personal appeal, and Henry Kissinger, present there as National

Security Adviser, has called it the worst bilateral meeting of the Nixon Presidency.

c) Sometimes major declarations or joint statements are issued as bilateral documents that are of world importance, which then become milestones for the concerned countries. One example is the Shanghai Communiqué that emerged from Nixon's 1972 China visit that laid down US acceptance of Beijing's demand that 'there is only one China', foreclosing the notion of Taiwan as a claimant to statehood. One consequence of increased peregrination by leaders is that such joint documents are issued only on special occasions, thus relieving diplomats and their ministers from the task of laborious negotiation of documents that often neither command attention nor hold lasting value.

d) Actions are speeded up because of the bilateral visit; the most common instance is bilateral agreements that may be in the pipeline. There is mutual pressure to sign these during the dignitary's visit, (though by custom, leaders do not personally sign bilateral accords, other than those of exceptional significance). Such agreements are presented as visible symbols of affinity. The same is true of other events or decisions that may be in the pipeline, or photogenic events like the opening of a cultural center or a new chancery building.

e) The visit may produce significant bilateral action. Business links receive a major boost, as seen in visits that mark the signing of major new industrial or construction contracts.[11] It may be that large volumes of aid are announced, as has been the case with visits by Western leaders to Moscow, to prop up the ailing Russian economy. Specific new avenues of cooperation are opened up sometimes, as was the case with the Indian Prime Minister's September 1991 tour to Germany that led to the setting up of the Indo-German Consultative Group (Chapter 9). Indeed, one under-exploited formula is to use the visit as a vehicle for pursuit of concrete issues or 'action points' that are a priority for either side, through a bilateral mechanism that reports back to the leaders after a certain time.[12]

f) A visit facilitates dialogue with a wide spectrum of personalities in the host country, and this may enable the guest leader to assess the second echelon of leadership in that country, and contact leaders of the opposition as well, for instance prior to an election there. This provides continuity of personal contact, vital for stability in relations.
g) The visiting dignitary may be able to make an appeal to public opinion, over the heads of the country leaders, in some situations. This was the case with US presidential visits to Moscow in the Cold War era, when it was often negotiated in advance that at least one of his major speeches would be broadcast live by Soviet TV, on its own networks. The summit encounter may also aim at domestic opinion at home, as was clearly one of President Musharraf's objectives at the India–Pakistan Agra summit of July 2001.[13]

LOGISTICS

For practitioners of diplomacy, visits by leaders demand meticulous preparation, and a total mastery of detail. Protocol work is primarily about management of detail, anticipation of the unexpected and rapid responses to new or unplanned situations. Some of this may resemble petty detail, but this is not a position that diplomats can ever afford to take, because the minor issues can snowball rapidly, and can either make or break a visit.

The world over, the logistical demands made during such visits by national leaders have escalated. Barely 20 years ago, when the Indian Prime Minister traveled abroad, there were no advance visits to oversee planning, nor any movement of officials into the capitals being visited on 'temporary duty', for the actual event.[14] Today, concerns over security and inflation in the size of the accompanying contingent have made one or more advance visits mandatory. Plus, a dozen or more officials are moved into the capital and the other cities in the foreign country being visited to strengthen the mission's capacity to handle the visit. Other countries have seen a similar increase.

Another change is the escalation in the size of the delegations. More and more countries make it a practice to take with the dignitary a collection of parliamentarians and public personalities. Given the stress and time demands of major visits, there are few productive dialogue opportunities for these accompanists, who would surely derive greater value from separate visits spaced out over time. But factors of prestige and a desire to join the bandwagon work against such logic! On the plus side, the visitors are exposed to the country, even if in a hurried and kaleidoscopic manner.

Sizable business delegations have become almost a mandatory accompaniment, and this is a positive development because economics is at the fore of the summit dialogue and we know from experience that the business dimension adds realism. There have been major visits by Canadian Prime Ministers with a 100 or more businessmen in attendance, and Germans Chancellors often travel with 30 to 60. In contrast, Japan maintains the old world formula of not having businessmen accompany visits by leaders, on the premise that this may convey a perception of over-involvement by business in political affairs.[15]

Large media contingents from home are another growing trend, especially the electronic media that are attracted by the visuals of the national leader in a foreign environment. It becomes essential to provide complete media centers for them at hotels and other places visited.

OTHER DIRECT CONTACTS

Presidents and prime ministers engage in direct diplomacy in other ways as well. Some of the ways this happens are detailed below, and these mark an increasing trend of our times.

- Telephone communications between leaders are now frequent. While the major powers have systems of maintaining logs and conversation transcripts, this is not customary in some other countries. It becomes almost impossible for the diplomatic system of such countries to get details of what transpired, even while a general outline is usually available.[16] Personal relations established at bilateral and multilateral summits contribute to the ease with which the telephone medium is utilized, to the point where it has become a major instrument of diplomacy. An often overlooked aspect is that unless both sides use encryption machinery of a robust type, these telephone links are permeable to major intelligence agencies.
- Also more frequent are personal communications between leaders, usually replacing or reinforcing more formal channels. For the country sending the communication there may be an illusion of confidentiality in the exchange, but this may not be the understanding at the other end! In exceptional situations, if there is a special relationship of trust between leaders, such communications can take a personal character and may not be accessible to the foreign ministry—unfortunate both for good diplomacy management and for the historical record.
- In rare situations, leaders may use personal emissaries outside the diplomatic system for communication, and for some negotiation as well. One well documented instance is the secret journey that former Secretary of State Dean Acheson made to Paris during the US-Soviet crisis of 1962, to show proof to President de Gaulle of the existence of Soviet missiles in Cuba, and to seek his support on the ultimatum that President Kennedy was about to give to Moscow. The emissary traveled without the knowledge of the US Ambassador, and went straight from the airport to the Elyseé Palace and back to his special aircraft. Intelligence agencies are often the vehicles of choice by leaders for such 'backchannel' contacts.

ROLE OF MFAS AND THE EMBASSIES

Classical diplomacy scholar Harold Nicholson had warned after the Versailles Conference of 1919 that, 'nothing could be more fatal than the habit of personal contact between the statesmen of the world'.[17] One study of the end of the Cold War examines the Bush–Gorbachev dynamics of the 1989–91 period and quotes former US President Richard Nixon: 'He (President George Bush) believes that if you have a good personal relationship it helps on substance. I believe that unless the leaders' interests are compatible, a personal relationship does not mean anything.'[18] The same study suggests that this personal relationship led to a failure in assessing the competing power centers of the time, and inadequate support to democratization and economic reform.

Of course, not all summits are successful. Some commentators speak of the problem of excess of expectations, or of over-commitment. Whatever the outcome of the summit, it is the permanent mechanism of diplomacy: in particular of the resident ambassador and his embassy that has the task of preparing for the summit, handling the logistics if it takes place in a foreign country, and tackling the follow-up. The embassy handles this in close interchange with the home foreign ministry, and the core functions of both are:

- To prepare thoroughly before the summit. This is not possible if one or both sides distrust the past record between them, or are convinced that personal diplomacy will produce a breakthrough that other contacts failed to produce. The Agra Summit of July 2001 cited earlier, is an instance where the Pakistan President's insistence on bypassing customary preparatory work contributed to failure.[19]
- To anticipate the position the other side is likely to take. At all cost, the home team should not be taken by surprise. Obtaining this information calls for the highest skills, and personal credibility. The Reagan–Gorbachev 'walk in the woods' at the

October 1986 Reykjavik Summit produced high drama when an unexpected Soviet proposal for a complete elimination of offensive strategic arms within a decade took the US President by surprise, and almost led him to agree, to the consternation of his advisers.

- To handle follow-up. Again it is the permanent diplomatic mechanism that has to ensure that this is accomplished with purpose and an orientation for results.
- To smoothen ruffled feathers and restore balance, if things have gone badly. It is the embassy and the MFA that generally have to shoulder the responsibility for failure.

It is a misunderstanding to imagine that summits between heads devalue the diplomatic system or the resident ambassador. Frequent personal contacts between leaders are a positive asset in relationships. Old diplomacy viewed such events with a jaundiced eye because expectations from direct meetings between leaders were higher, and there were spectacular failures from summits. Today's summits do not replace the permanent system of diplomacy, but function as an integral component of the system of international relations. Most of the time, they can provide the diplomatic apparatus with impetus and strong direction. Dean Acheson has written tellingly: 'When a chief or state or head of government makes a fumble, the goal is open behind him.'[20] When results fall short of expectation, it becomes the task of diplomacy to seek new ways of moving forward. Like modern communication, summits are a fact of life, and form one more instrument in a proactive diplomatic system to deploy in integrated diplomacy.

QUESTIONS

1. How does a visit abroad by an executive president differ from that by a non-executive head of state?
2. What are the success factors for a substantive bilateral summit

meeting? How should one work to generate the best possible result?
3. What is the importance of logistical arrangements? Please give some examples from your own experience.
4. How does one's own embassy contribute to a summit meeting of leaders?

REFERENCES

1. Dunn, David H. ed., *Diplomacy at the Highest Level: The Evolution of International Summitry* (Macmillan, London, 1998).
2. Rana, Kishan S., *Inside Diplomacy* (Manas, New Delhi, 2000), Chapter 10, pp. 229–51.

NOTES

1. *American Foreign Policy in the 1980s*, LTV–Washington Seminar document.
2. Abba Eban, *Diplomacy for the New Century* (Yale University Press, New Haven, 1998).
3. Around the world, simplification of protocol is the norm. Gone are the elaborate airport arrival welcome scenes, even in a strong customary protocol capital like Beijing. When there is a state or official visit, the military guard of honor, and the playing of national anthems usually takes place at the presidential palace or similar location in the heart of the city, and even here the ceremony is truncated from the past norms. Also gone are elaborate 'return banquets' by the visiting head of state or government.
4. In practice, this does not present difficulty. It means that while the ceremonial functions have one host, the non-executive head of state, the substantive dialogue is held with the head of government.
5. This is the actual situation in SAARC at the end of 2001, with no meeting of the summit held since 1998, following the military coup that brought General Pervez Musharraf to power in October 1999. India insists on an end to cross-border terrorism support by Pakistan, which the

international community now accepts as a fact, despite Pakistan's denial. In the process, the bilateral dispute blocks regional cooperation.

6. One of the protocol issues that arises is 'who will call on whom?' Some leaders are sensitive on this point, as I witnessed at the Cancun Summit in October 1981, narrated in *Inside Diplomacy.*
7. When Prime Minister Indira Gandhi returned to power in January 1981, after the period of the Emergency (1975–77) and her subsequent ouster in the elections of March 1977, she carried bitter memories of the manner in which she had been criticized in the US. For the next 20 months there was no substantive contact with the new US administration headed by President Ronald Regan. They met for the first time on the margins of the Cancun North–South summit meeting of October 1981, and that brief but decisive encounter set the stage for a full restoration of friendly linkages, including Indira Gandhi's official tour to the US in July 1982.
8. One exception was the funeral of Kenyan President Jomo Kenyatta in 1978, when a chance encounter between the Pakistan President and the Indian Prime Minister in Nairobi led to a new, but eventually abortive effort at normalization of relations. (Source: former Indian High Commissioner A.N.D. Haksar.)
9. There is a story, vouchsafed by a friend, that during a cabinet meeting in the late 1970s Algerian President Houari Boumedienne was handed a note by an aide while he was in the midst of a cabinet meeting. He pulled a face and said: 'We have to now leave for the airport. President Gaddafi has arrived unexpectedly and his aircraft is circling overhead!'
10. This incident is narrated in the dramatic detail of what actually happened in my book *Inside Diplomacy*, pp. 244–6. One remarkable feature was the contrasting style of the two great leaders, the 'take charge' attitude of Margaret Thatcher contrasted with the quiet, unspeaking demeanor of Indira Gandhi who let her principal aides to make the pitch. One net result was the bonding of a remarkable friendship between them.
11. This has particularly been a custom with Western visits to China and some other Asian countries, when the signature of large business contracts is seen as part of the productive gain from the visit.
12. When German Chancellor Kohl visited New Delhi in February 1993, he brought with him a large business delegation. When they were

received by the two leaders, immediately after the one-on-one talks, Kohl told the group that he and the Indian Premier had identified a number of important action areas and that they would meet in Germany a year later to monitor the results on these. The Indian side took advantage of this to prepare as set of specific action points, listing issues that were pending, and this was handed over by Prime Minister Narasimha Rao to Kohl when they met again on the following day. This became a useful device for subsequent follow up. A like method has been used by India on another visit. It has a wider application.

13. The Pakistan President was very successful in using the media, India and international, as an instrument for influencing negotiation, and projecting himself as one who was able to effectively stand up to the demands of international diplomacy.
14. As a mid-level official on the staff of Prime Minister Indira Gandhi (1981–82) I traveled with her on five major tours abroad, to a total of some 20 countries and destinations, including the Commonwealth Summit of September 1981 and the Cancun Summit of October 1981.
15. Information gathered during the author's survey in Japan, April 2001. But in contrast to this formal stance, most observers would agree that Japanese diplomacy is extremely engaged abroad in support of businessmen from the country.
16. During a survey, a foreign ambassador told me of the conversation one of his leaders had held with the Indian Prime Minister. It was from the officials working in the latter's office that he was able to get details that were not available to the foreign ministry at home. There is evidence that even in the US, details of presidential conversations with foreign leader do not often reach the State Department.
17. Cited in John Dickie, *Inside the Foreign Office* (Chapman, London, 1992).
18. Michael R. Beschkoss and Strobe Talbott, *At the Highest Levels* (Little and Brown, New York, 1993).
19. The Cancun North–South Summit of 1981 is an instance of failure of multilateral diplomacy that arose from a decision by the main organizers, Canada and Mexico, to short-circuit the preparatory process.
20. Dean Acheson, *Present at the Creation: My years in the State Department* (W.W. Norton, New York, 1969).

PART III

METHODS

11

Diplomatic Reports

Reports are the lifeblood of the diplomatic process, even in an age when we seem overwhelmed by an 'information overload'. Save in exceptional situations where the mission or the official at headquarters may gain access to valuable information that is not in the public domain, diplomatic reports are no longer the prime source of information for the foreign ministry; information arrives much faster from public sources, like the global TV networks, the print media and the Internet, to give a few examples.[1] But the diplomatic report offers insights that are unique in other ways—the marshalling of information that is of direct relevance to the home government, plus analysis that takes into account the home government's policy concerns, and forecasting needs. Diplomatic reports are also based on the observer's national perspective. In an efficient diplomatic system there is no substitute for reportage focused on the needs of the users, which also includes the other ministries and agencies. This is what I have called the 'feedback' function of the entire diplomatic system, providing perspectives in which information is to be analyzed, and becomes the basis for decision. Reports are the feedstock for policy-making.

BASIC ELEMENTS

Article 3 of the 1961 Vienna Convention on Diplomatic Relations, sets out the functions of diplomatic missions. One of the tasks is:

> (d) ascertaining by all lawful means conditions and developments in the receiving State and reporting thereon to the Government of the sending State.

In choosing the word 'ascertaining', over simply 'observing' or 'reporting', an active or dynamic role has been assigned to the mission in executing this particular function. The premise is that collecting information relating to the receiving state is a core activity of diplomacy.

While feedback is a major preoccupation of missions abroad, the writing of analytical papers and other forms of reportage also occupy officials at headquarters. One example is the perennial job of brief writing, which is almost a constant activity for desk officers and their seniors. (Special kinds of diplomatic documents like the 'action plan', 'management plans' and 'ambassador's instructions' are addressed in Chapter 15, which covers performance.)

Writing diplomatic reports is a craft; some would even call it an art. As with the other skills in this profession, a book or a guide prepared by a foreign ministry may set out advice on good report-writing, but it is through observation and tutelage under an experienced expert that one imbibes real lessons, shaping one's own methods. Some basic elements that can guide the writing of reports are:

- **Balance and objectivity**, looking at all sides of a situation, without bias or selectivity. This also involves impartial assessment of information.
- **Mastery over language**, not for its own sake but to convey ideas in a clear manner, with precision.
- **Completeness**, following the entire chain of events.

- **Accuracy**, checking all the facts, and indicating unverified information in an appropriate way, if this has to be included.
- **Brevity**, accompanied by a logical structure to the report. This includes a narration of the facts, a critical analysis, an appraisal of the current situation, and a reasoned forecast of the way the situation may develop. Where appropriate, policy alternatives need to be set out. Even complex issues can be broken down to essentials.[2] Precise executive summaries have a role.
- **Honesty and integrity**, reporting all that should be conveyed to the government, not selecting the things that it may wish to hear. One must not pander to known views of others, but set out choices and recommendations in a way that facilitates decision.

PERIODIC REPORTS

Each foreign ministry has its own system of periodic reportage by missions, but two frequent staples have been the 'monthly' report and the 'annual' report.

The monthly report is an old institution, dating from before the contemporary communications revolution, when the bulk of diplomatic correspondence was dispatched through the 'diplomatic bag'. The monthly political report covered domestic and external political developments in the target country, providing both factual information and analysis. Such reports were widely circulated, at the MFA and among other agencies interested in international affairs,[3] plus to missions in neighboring countries and in major capitals. This often became a heavy burden to digest, and the monthly report received diminishing attention. Today, in many countries this report has withered away. Where it remains, it is often unread. Few heads of missions use it as a vehicle for conveying meaningful analysis, and a report of this nature compiled by junior officials in the embassy becomes further devalued.[4]

Its counterpart, the monthly commercial and economic report, has a continuing role. It typically summarizes local economic policy and business developments, affecting the home country's export market and trade, plus general information on the local economic scene that is usually not available through other sources. Many countries have the healthy practice of circulating these reports to others outside the government, like chambers of commerce and associations of exporters, since they are real users of the data. It is worthwhile for missions to place such reports on their Internet websites, after deleting anything that can be construed as sensitive information.

The annual report is also an old institution, and remains of value, providing a summary of major developments, political, economic, and in other fields. It can be used by the ambassador as a vehicle for his authoritative evaluation of the year and for forward analysis. Often the annual political report provides inputs for the foreign ministry's own annual report that is customarily submitted to parliament. There is a separate annual report on the mission's housekeeping activities, encapsulating data on finance, administrative issues and logistics, which is important for the headquarters in its oversight over the functioning of the mission.

Some foreign ministries have shifted to weekly 'roundup' reports, covering political and other developments that do not merit a special communication. From the perspective of territorial divisions at headquarters that handles relations with several countries, such reports keep it in touch with developments, and help in preparing summaries for higher management. There are other methods:

- The Germans use an unusual reporting format. Every six months the mission is required to send a comprehensive report on the country, covering political, economic and other developments, as well as summarizing the state of bilateral relations. It is written under the authority of the ambassador, and becomes the basis for a full country review at home. This also has the merit of superior reporting interval, in comparison with the annual report.

- Singapore, with its strong orientation towards performance monitoring uses a monthly 'performance report' in which missions have to respond on three points: the major tasks performed; a list of the reports and dispatches sent by each officer; and details of the new local contacts established. This is a simple, powerful way of performance evaluation.
- In nearly 17 years as a head of mission, I found it useful to prepare a 6-monthly survey of bilateral economic relations. It summarized the status of major projects and issues being pursued, and conveyed an overview of the economic scene, as might be of utility to home agencies, including individual enterprises actively engaged in the target country and national business associations. Leaving out matters of commercial confidentiality, details of new activities were included. It enabled all the players to share information and network among themselves.

SPECIAL DISPATCHES

This is a classic diplomatic reporting format. The distinction between a 'dispatch', and a letter or other form of episodic communication, lies in the depth and intensity of study that precedes the writing, though technically each substantive communication from a mission is a dispatch. One obviously does not include in this category the administrative communications and the financial reports that fill up much of the diplomatic bag in actual practice. One rough way to gauge the work profile of a mission is to compare the proportion of substantive correspondence to administrative communications. This gives a revealing 'teeth to tail' ratio.[5]

Ideally, a dispatch should set out the objective and the issues addressed, go on to cover the facts, then the analysis of this evidence, and finally come to its conclusion or prognosis of the way events are likely to shape up. Some boldness in prediction, or expression of opinion, is far superior to a dispatch that concludes the narration

COMPARING DIPLOMATIC REPORTS

Diplomatic reports see the light of public scrutiny many years after the event, when documents are released under the laws or rules in various countries. This makes it hard to compare the reports written by different diplomatic services. One exception is the EU which has a system of joint reports prepared by two or more embassies in foreign capitals since 1994, some of which are accessible to all members.

I recall as a desk officer in 1965–67, we used to receive at the Ministry of External Affairs at New Delhi British Foreign Office 'reprints' of selected dispatches by British Embassies, bearing the security classification of 'Confidential' or the even lower 'Restricted'. This was a form of Commonwealth information sharing that withered away around the early 1970s. Printed on light blue paper, usually running to four pages, these dispatches provided us with a barometer to judge our own dispatches from the particularly active missions like the embassies in Beijing and Moscow. We noted that the British dispatch scored in elegance and terseness of expression, but our own special dispatches were of like quality and prescience, and sometimes better.

It would be interesting to be able to compare, with living contemporary examples, the ways in which different services write their reports.

with ambivalence or prevarication. It is the business of diplomats to render honest, intelligent advice. And being too timorous or unwilling to express an opinion cannot fulfill that role. Courage to go against the perceived wisdom at the headquarters, or the preference of someone in power is no less vital. Thus the dispatch is a reflection of personal integrity.

The circulation of dispatches written in missions, among other missions, is of utility, because it keeps missions informed of the perspective from different participants in the dialogue, and leads to cross-fertilization of ideas, besides obvious information sharing. With MFAs increasingly using their own 'intranets' for communication, it is all too easy to mark messages to a number of sister missions. On the other hand, there is a real danger of information overload. But it is generally better to run this risk, than leaving it to headquarters to copy dispatches to other missions.

For the HOM at the termination of his mission, a 'farewell dispatch' is the vehicle to summarize his experience in a particular assignment, and convey his overview of the country, as also a prognosis of the bilateral relationship. Such dispatches merit wide distribution. As institutional records, they convey a special flavor of the place and the time. This tradition is not universal, but deserves to be emulated; it should not be left to the option of the individual HOM.[6]

Another end of assignment document that is mandatory in most diplomatic systems is the 'handing over note' which the HOM addresses to his successor, usually following a prescribed format (though there are many foreign services which do not use a standard format, and suffer in consequence). Given the fact that unlike other professions, diplomacy does not permit a physical handover from one ambassador to another, much less a period of 'understudy' or overlap, this is the principal means for institutional memory transmission to the new envoy. In fact, comprehensive handing over notes should be obligatory for diplomats at other levels, (and for MFA officials as well.) An ideal note should convey information on local institutions, personalities and processes, plus all the special features of the assignment and country. It should also give confidential assessments of local interlocutors of importance, plus of fellow envoys from other countries, within one's own regional group and the diplomatic corps, as also pen sketches of the officials in the mission, home-based and local staff. An ideal note would be consulted by the successor for the first several months of his assignment, to refresh memory and to compare his own first experiences with the advice of the predecessor.

CIPHER MESSAGES

In the age of the Internet, and the intranets that are increasingly used by diplomatic services for rapid and 'firewall'-protected secure communication, the old name 'telegram' lingers on in some foreign ministries as a reminder of days long past. The cipher telegram or 'cable'—in the days before the telex machine, when it really was a telegram or cable—was sent through commercial channels, or via a point-to-point radio link. Such coded messages exchanged between headquarters and missions are basically in the nature of instructions and dispatches based on these by way of response. Or they may report on local developments of importance and on dialogue with officials of the receiving country. Brevity and urgency are two essential ingredients. The distinctive feature of such messages is that they are transmitted by the most rapid means available, and on receipt at headquarters, these are widely distributed, usually in a predetermined pattern that applies to such cipher messages. This latter is the USP—the wide information sharing, making such messages a powerful tool for getting one's ideas and analysis read by virtually all the decision makers in one's own hierarchy. They usually carry a security classification, and the rule of thumb is that the higher the classification, the greater the attention the message receives. The sender can usually select the recipients to whom the message should go, and this also enhances its effectiveness.[7] Some countries use the encrypted fax as a means of transmitting confidential messages.[8]

Both outbound and inbound coded messages are distributed widely, to 20 or even 40 recipients. Copies customarily go to the offices of the head of state and the head of government, the foreign minister, the permanent secretary and all senior officials of the foreign ministry, as well as agencies like the external intelligence organization, and where appropriate, other ministries. Often colored paper is used to draw attention to such communications, for purposes of secure handling and to convey priority.

When sent from headquarters, the coded message typically conveys instructions, or a briefing on a development that needs to be shared with missions, by way of background information, or material to be conveyed to the other government.

When sent from the mission, it communicates developments and analysis that calls for a decision, or becomes an input into the decision process. Such messages often convey the contents of discussions that may be a response to a démarche, or a position statement on an issue vital to either or both sides. For the head of mission, who is almost always the originator of the message or at least the clearing authority—since this task is seldom delegated to others, save in the very largest missions—it is a mechanism for conveying his personal assessment and views. The HOM soon learns that these messages can be used as an instrument for gaining visibility and building a reputation, but overused or mishandled, the same instrument can also destroy credibility. Overuse is a frequent professional hazard for the HOM. 'Cipher message diplomacy' is a subtle art.

BRIEFS AND WEBSITES

The mission needs a standard collection of briefing material, for privileged visitors and for the general public, as per the norms set in different systems. The usual material includes:

- An unclassified 'country brief', setting out the basic features of the host country, its systems, and a general description of the bilateral relationship.
- A similar briefing note mainly focused on the bilateral relationship, bearing low classification, to be used for briefing official visitors from home.
- A 'fact sheet' or similar short 1-page document that gives the country data in simple and digestible form, particularly useful in countries where such information is hard to come by.
- A standard 'commercial guide' for businessmen seeking initial

information on the country, updated annually or more frequently. This is ideal for potential exporters from home looking for new markets.

- Health and safety advice for tourists, where this is appropriate.
- Guidance material covering consular issues, like advice on registration at the embassy for own nationals, or guidance on passport renewal. Similar notes are also useful for local citizens on visa procedures.

Much of this material can today be posted on the mission's website, for easy access by all. This also carries the responsibility for updating the material on a regular basis. Visa application forms should be provided on the embassy website, for easy download by applicants, both as a service to users and to save needless correspondence.

REPORTS AND ANALYSIS AT HEADQUARTERS

At headquarters, there is need for reportage on foreign countries that partly matches the material prepared by missions. Diplomatic reports at the MFA include the following:

a) **Analytical briefs:** Territorial divisions usually prepare these on the basis of reports sent by the missions, with the difference that they offer the wider perspective that a foreign ministry is expected to furnish. These become the basis for decisions on policy or on tactics of foreign affairs.
b) **Policy papers:** These differ from the above in explicit design, because they examine policy issues, and are prepared after considerable internal groundwork, plus dialogue with many officials and even other agencies (including the embassies concerned). They set out several options.
c) **Briefing papers:** A major requirement is for internal 'briefing notes', often furnished at short notice to senior officials, to other

ministries and to the offices of the president or prime minister. Word processors allow speed and flexibility in the production of such briefs, but a frequent complaint in many capitals, from the perspective of the end-user located outside the foreign ministry, is that the quality of the material in terms of content and relevance is inadequate. The reputation of the foreign ministry depends on the quality provided, because the briefs are read directly by principals, who invariably have high expectations, and their own sources of information as well. The professionalism of the foreign service is tested in this way.

d) **Talking points:** A special kind of brief consists of 'talking points', prepared often as an attachment to the brief, setting out the points that the high dignitary is advised to make in his dialogue with the other side. It is essential to furnish not so much the basics (which would be known to the principals), but the details and specific points of the arguments. One must anticipate in the talking points the issues that the other side may raise, and provide appropriate responses.
e) **Records of discussion:** These notes summarize discussions held by own senior officials or ministers with foreign interlocutors, and are usually prepared by the junior official at the meeting. Most MFAs have internal guidelines on the writing of such records; invariably it is important to be accurate, to summarize essential points, and to produce the draft rapidly, for approval by the concerned senior official. When the records cover important internal meetings, the need is usually for a careful record of the decisions taken. But there are occasions when complete summaries of discussions of internal meetings are needed (for example, for inter-ministerial meetings.)

The internal notes and policy papers, as the principal written documents at headquarters, call for the highest expression of skill and acumen. The qualities needed for good performance are the same as narrated above.

DOCUMENT DRAFTING SKILLS

The drafting of documents requires a specific kind of skill that is distinct from the general demands of diplomatic reportage. The young diplomat finds himself engaged in drafting reports and special dispatches of different kinds, and preparing records of discussion and the like, again in draft form for others in the hierarchy to finalize or approve. Others in the chain prepare drafts for even higher authorities to finalize, such as drafts of speeches delivered by ministers and by heads of state or government. Thus regardless of level or experience, the working diplomat is constantly engaged in producing drafts, or revising drafts prepared by others, for final approval at much higher levels.

Diplomatic documents are in a special category, in that these involve either another government to which the document is eventually sent, or the document becomes part of public record, or a formal agreement. Typical documents of this kind are:

- A formal diplomatic note, sent to one or more governments, customarily written in the third person, with formal salutations at the beginning and end.
- An *aide mémoire* handed over to one or more governments, ranking lower in hierarchy than the formal note.
- A *bout du papier*, or non-paper, lacking in formal status but nevertheless handed over to another government.
- The text of an agreement, protocol, or an 'exchange of letters' that may be annexed to either of these.
- A joint communiqué or declaration between governments, usually issued at the end of a formal high-level visit.
- A press communiqué, issued either by the government on its own, or jointly with one or more countries.
- A resolution containing the decision by a conference, cast in a customary format, with a preambular section followed by an operational section.

Drafting such documents calls for a special skill that is not easy to define. Besides precision, a command over language and skills noted earlier, it entails the following:

a) The capacity to articulate issues with clarity (as often the case with a press communiqué), combining this with an ability to use words without giving anything away, as may be the need at other times.[9]
b) A felicity with code words and diplomatic shorthand that safeguards one's own position, and persuades the other side to compromise on one's own favor, as much as possible. This is particularly a skill needed in negotiating joint documents like communiqués and declarations.[10]
c) An ability to find words that offer a tactical compromise between contesting standpoints, without deviating from the essence of one's own position. Of course, the other side will have its experts trying to do exactly the same; to prevail one should be able to offer something that appears better, and more palatable to the other side.
d) An easy interpersonal style can be leveraged into automatic membership of drafting groups where the final conferences documents are hammered out, and a position of quiet authority in such key groups.

PROBLEMS OF REPORTAGE

What are the pitfalls of diplomatic reportage? Is there a downside?

- 'Over-reportage' is a professional hazard. It is easy to wax eloquent on the internal political developments, or on nuances of economic policy of a distant nation, perhaps overlooking the real interest that this may evoke at home. A realistic yardstick of likely value at home should be applied.
- 'Under-reportage' is a more serious deficit, and is potentially dangerous. It is safer to report a bit in excess, and live down the occasional comment on this, rather than fail to report a poten-

tially major development, simply as one did not want to bother headquarters with an excess of detail.

- There are lazy diplomats and missions that get through reportage responsibility superficially, sending material culled from the press, or even the texts of speeches by local high personalities, supplemented with some quick comments. The Internet offers vast opportunity to plagiarize in such manner. This is plainly unprofessional.

The record of diplomatic systems in predicting the unexpected is uneven at best. At the time of the fall of the Shah of Iran in 1979, there were many diplomatic observers that anticipated that the regime was on its last legs, and in most cases the warnings were ignored in major capitals. There were academic scholars too who had advanced like predictions.[11] Other major events were not anticipated at all, either by diplomats, or scholars or the media. One instance is the Soviet invasion of Afghanistan in December 1979, whose reverberations still continue to roil world events. Another more glaring event that no one forecast in any kind of reasoned analysis was the collapse of the Soviet Union in 1989, the tectonic political shift in East Europe, and the end of the Cold War. Foreign ministries and intelligence agencies share equally in such failures.[12]

A weakness may be that diplomatic systems are slow in challenging conventional thinking, or in questioning basic assumptions. Some foreign ministries have set up policy planning units and think tanks that are charged with thinking 'outside the envelope' and examining the unthinkable.[13] More than embassies, policy units in foreign ministries should be tasked with such responsibility, to question assumptions and to engage in alternate scenario development.

BUILDING INSTITUTIONAL MEMORY

Foreign ministries are repositories of institutional memory, and usually contain special units like a 'historical' or 'documentation and treaties' division to handle this task. They act as the repository for formal treaties and agreements (which multiply with great rapidity and call for special procedures to collect these from all the functional or line ministries, for centralized safekeeping and access). Their parallel task is less obvious, but equally vital, the building of the institutional memory of events and making this accessible for the future. This is done in different ways.

a) One way of handling important historical documents is to reprint these after editing, making available source material for internal use, or eventually for scholars, after the customary time limit for such documents. Some countries apply a 30-year rule, while others wait for 50 years before even limited release of classified documents.
b) A variation on the above is to scrutinize several dossiers that may belong to different units within the foreign ministry, and even the missions concerned, after a significant event, to produce a selection of material that narrates the main story. This internal exercise becomes the basis for an effort to draw lessons from the event, or guidelines for the future, after discounting for the unique character of each incident.
c) Information technology permits endless possibilities for cross-indexing and cross-referencing of documents via 'hyperlinks' and the like, in a manner impossible with physical documents. With the use of appropriate software, this enables new approaches in building institutional memory, at headquarters and within missions.

In a real life incident, a chief of protocol confronted with carrying out the complex arrangements for a state funeral had his team search urgently for the papers relating to the pervious occasion when such an event had been handled. He was mortified to find that the file, when located, contained but a single piece of paper—clearly the main papers were stored away elsewhere. He abandoned the search, and went on to handle his task unguided by past experience. But when the job was done, he narrated all his experiences in a long note that might serve as a reference point for the future. But unless that note is stored, or at least indexed using IT technology, there is no certitude that his successor in the future, making his own feverish search for past precedents, would manage to lay hands on that document! These are the hazards of building memories.

We tend to assume that in the major diplomatic establishments institutional memories are strong. In large systems the mass of documents to be handled creates its own problems. For instance, in a new study Stephen Cohen has contrasted the strong background documentation that Indians managed to produce at bilateral negotiations with the US, with the State Department's own patchy memory.[14] Another study points to the limitations of the UK's Foreign Office with knowledge management.[15]

IMPACT OF THE INTERNET

With many foreign ministries shifting to dedicated 'intranets' as a global communication mechanism, for dispersed offices at headquarters and for dialogue with missions, some common trends are visible.

a) Communication is 'flatter' than before, with reduced concern for hierarchies. For example, a draft can simultaneously be sent upwards along the chain, to all, including to the principal who has to take a final decision on it (or accept it as a draft of a speech). The amendments suggested by different officials can be indicated, for example as hypertext annotations.
b) Sending copies to two addressees is as easy as sending to twenty. This leads to overload of reading material, but this is not in itself a disadvantage. One needs sharper skills of focus and discrimination.

c) Indecisiveness is penalized. Once a person hits the 'send' button, the message is in the system, and cannot be called back for further editing or change.

For efficient use of the Internet, missions need their own websites, as part of public diplomacy, setting out country viewpoints to reach target audiences, for local contact building, and to respond to those seeking information. Most consular information, visa application forms and the like can be shifted to the website. (It should even be possible to issues visas on the Internet, with due security and safety, and this will affect the size of missions, since such 'back-office' work can be handled from headquarters.) Ideally websites should be part of a pattern established by the MFA, but allow also local flexibility for the mission. Imaginative use of websites is vital.

Not all the consequences of the Internet age are fully apparent as yet. And we are yet to see how contemporary information and communications technology will shape the reportage function of diplomacy. Responding with flexibility and imagination to these ongoing changes is part of the current challenge.

QUESTIONS

1. Why are reports sent by embassies to the MFA important even in an age when information comes rapidly from multiple sources?
2. What in your view is the most important periodic report?
3. How does the special dispatch differ from a periodic report? What should be its main attributes?
4. What qualities are important in notes and analysis prepared at headquarters?

REFERENCES

1. Marshall, Peter, *Positive Diplomacy* (Macmillan, London, 1997), Chapter 9, pp. 154–64.

2. Rana, Kishan S., *Inside Diplomacy* (New Delhi, Manas Publications, 2000), Chapter 3, pp. 73–9.
3. Berridge, G.R., *Diplomacy: Theory and Practice,* 2nd edition, (Palgrave, London, 2002).

NOTES

1. Even the most extensive of the intelligence agencies like the CIA cannot beat global 24-hour TV networks in rapid coverage of breaking news, and in providing 'real time' coverage of major events as they occur. But saturation coverage that they provide is offset by the weakness that it is highly selective, and with a short attention span. Much that happens around the world, especially 'soft' news, is outside their reach, and this is partly true also of much of the print media. But there are serious journals like *The Economist* and *Le Monde* that can compete with the best of diplomatic reportage.
2. During the one year I spent working in the Prime Minister's Office in New Delhi in 1981–82, the standard rule for any paper going to Indira Gandhi was that it should not exceed a page and a half in length, in double space. This was a splendid method for concentrating on the essential, and cutting out verbiage.
3. Thus typically the monthly reports would go to other ministries interested in foreign affairs like the defense ministry and the intelligence agencies.
4. There are excellent compilations of events that are produced commercially, like Keesing's Record, Africa Diary, and Asian Recorder. These serve as valuable reference material, on events and dates. The Internet offers many other reference options.
5. One reason for an excess of administrative correspondence is excessively tight management control from headquarters, and very limited delegation of administrative and financial powers to missions. The modern way is to delegate wide powers to missions and hold them accountable for delivering on performance (see Chapter 14).
6. In the Indian system such end-of-assignment dispatches are not mandatory, though the 'handing over note' is a requirement.
7. For example in the US system, a message carrying an appellation that

only a limited distribution is to be given (NODIS) usually commands the highest attention and actually reaches out to the most influential decision makers. Herz, Martin F., ed., *The Modern Ambassador: The Challenge and the Search* (Institute for the Study of Diplomacy, Georgetown University, Washington DC, 1983).

8. Cipher message systems depend on the science of cryptography, a fascinating but arcane discipline. The code-makers (who originate and provide the operational material for the systems) and the code-breakers (intelligence agencies like the National Security Agency of the US that is reputed to have a budget larger than that of the CIA, and the equivalents in other countries), play a cat-and-mouse game. In reality, a good portion of diplomatic cipher messages are readable by the great powers, sometimes after a bit of time on the code-breaking effort. The only truly 'unbreakable' cipher is the 'one time system', which is completely random and uses no algorithm or formula. But it is cumbersome to use.
9. The late Indian Foreign Secretary T.N. Kaul was a master of the quick repartee that gave away nothing. He once briefed the press at the end of a bilateral meeting by saying that it had been 'friendly, forthcoming and fruitful.' When reporters protested that this was a cliché that said nothing, he said: 'Fine. Let us call the discussions cordial, constructive and cooperative!'
10. Happily for practicing diplomats, this hardy staple of state and official visits, the joint statement of communiqué, has gone out of fashion with expansion in summit encounters. Such documents are now issued only on special occasions. But expansion in regional and other conferences has lead to an even greater surge of conference declarations, resolutions and the like.
11. With remarkable prescience, Prime Minister Indira Gandhi had spoken in 1976–77 of the dangers of over-supply of sophisticated arms to Iran by the West, and the dangers that this might pose for that country itself.
12. The study by Michael R. Beschkoss and Strobe Talbott, *At the Highest Levels* (Little and Brown, New York, 1993) notes that until as late as September 1989, US Ambassador Walters predicted that German unity would come 'in five years time'.

13. This is one of the responsibilities assigned to the policy planning unit in the British Foreign and Commonwealth Office in London. It is not clear how far this has been successful.
14. Cohen, Stephen, *India: Emerging Power* (Brookings Institution, Washington DC, 2001). The special Indian system for handling documents bearing the highest classification is particularly outstanding.
15. Kurbalija, Jovan, *Knowledge and Diplomacy* (Mediterranean Academy of Diplomatic Studies, Malta, 1999).

12

Cross-Cultural Sensitivity

Practical diplomacy involves dealing with countries that present varied cultures. Multiplication of constituencies in the foreign partner state adds to the diversity.

WHY CROSS-CULTURAL SKILLS?

The cultural diversity issue is posed for the diplomat more sharply than before on account of some new elements. First, the breadth of diversities is far greater than what confronted the earlier generations of professionals, in a global community of some 189 UN member-states. Second, we live in an age when diversity is celebrated, and burnished with pride more than ever earlier. Third, within countries, there are sub-state diversities that have gained new impetus around the world, and this adds to the cultural management challenge. We see this in differences, between regions, communities and religious and ethnic groups. For instance, the same Europe that is witness to the world's most intensive political unification process via the EU, now enjoys greater diversity at subsidiary levels. Fourth, the professional diplomat is less homogenous in background and training, and his/her values are no longer cast in the same template as could be assumed even a few decades in the past. Further, this diplomat has dealings with a far wider range of government officials and those outside the government, especially the civil society representatives, academia, and other constituencies, at home and aboard. Taken together, all these elements constitute a strong cross-culture management challenge.

The prerequisite to cultivating cross-cultural skills is to develop an understanding of the other culture, through a study of its history, its value system, and all the other specific factors that identify and differentiate it. Regardless of pride in one's own heritage, notions of superiority and rejection of the other have to be put aside. This is much harder to actually practice, than to accept it intellectually. Genuine curiosity and a desire to learn is a good guide to moving to the higher plane of cross-cultural understanding. The principle to absorb should be that different societies and peoples have evolved their own distinct qualities that are neither superior nor inferior to other ones. Diversity is what human society as a whole celebrates, and the factors of commonality are more profound than surface differences.[1]

Opinion is divided on whether it is worthwhile to categorize different cultures, in order to train diplomats. This has the danger of creating and reinforcing concepts of 'stereotypes', and a false impression that another culture is identifiable by rigidly categorized behavior or value systems that are common to all. In reality, there are a huge number of variations and many individuals and groups that differ radically from notional stereotypes. Indeed, one of the tasks of diplomacy is to convince others to view one's own nation beyond simple stereotypes. Therefore entrenching new standardized, rigid images is counterproductive.

Another perspective can be taken. As long as caution is exercised, cultural categorization is a useful tool for analysis, and is not intended for classification into absolute categories. It offers a first basis for approach, one that is replaced with the experience one accumulates over time, which enables one to move beyond the stereotypes. This analytical method is a tool for learning, which gives an insight into the kinds of differences that are encountered, and the adjustments one has to make to deal with cross-cultural situations.

LEWIS CLASSIFICATION

In his book *When Cultures Collide: Managing Successfully Across Cultures*, Richard D. Lewis has divided cultural characteristics in three broad types, to argue that different nations and their peoples exhibit these traits in varying degrees. The categories are titled 'linear-active', 'multi-active' and 'reactive'. I personally find the last term reflecting a bit of inadvertent cultural bias, and prefer instead the word 'autonomous'. Some countries are identified as the exemplars that exhibit the most extreme symptoms of the three cultural types. If we adhere to the Lewis classification, some of the typical traits in each group are:

LINEAR ACTIVE	MULTI-ACTIVE	REACTIVE (OR 'AUTONOMOUS')
introvert	extrovert	introvert
patient	impatient	patient
quiet, speaks to the point	talkative	silent, good listener
likes privacy	gregarious	says little
plans ahead methodically	plans grand design, impatient with detail	looks at general principle, masters detail
does one thing at a time	several things at once	reacts
works fixed hours, appointments need notice	works any hours, will receive at short notice	flexible, much prefers systematic method
dominated by timetable and schedules	timetable unpredictable	reacts to partner's timetable
compartmentalizes projects	lets one project influence another	sees whole picture

(cont'd...)

LINEAR ACTIVE	MULTI-ACTIVE	REACTIVE (OR 'AUTONOMOUS')
sticks to facts	juggles facts	statements are promises
job-oriented	people-oriented	people-oriented
accepts favors reluctantly	seeks favors	protects face of other
follows procedures	pulls strings	inscrutable, calm
completes action chain	completes human transaction	reacts to partner
uses memoranda	rarely writes memos	plans slowly
dislikes losing face	makes excuses	must not lose face
rarely interrupts	interrupts frequently	does not interrupt
separates personal and professional	interweaves personal and professional	connects social and professional
limited body language	unrestricted body language	subtle body language
mastery over procedures, 'devil is in the detail' mindset	excellent at human relations, cross-cultural skills	keen understanding of systems, looks to the grand scene
easily upset over the unexpected	handles 'chaos' well	accommodates the unexpected
principle more important than context	will bend principle to context	seeks to harmonize principle to context

Abridged and modified from *When Cultures Collide*, p. 41, fig. 7.

Lewis asserts that different countries exhibit these three kinds of characteristics in varying degrees. The ones who reflect the Linear Active traits in the most acute form are the Germans, the Austrians and the Swiss, while arch-examples of the Multi-Active type are Italians, Latin Americans, Arabs, Africans, Indians and Pakistanis. This latter group is too wide a cluster, and much clearer differentiation is required. Research into unraveling the distinctions that actually exist among Africans, Arabs, and Latin Americans is obviously insufficient. The Japanese, and to a lesser degree the Chinese, are held to be typical of the Reactive kind.[2]

Some would find the Lewis method to be too broad in its categorization, and over-simplified. Other disadvantages:

- Surely not everyone that belongs to a particular culture exhibits the attributed traits.
- It can lead one to make erroneous assumptions, if it is used as a rigid guide.
- Identification of 'country' stereotypes ignores the national sub-groups within a state, as also difference along other ethnic, religious or linguistic sub-categories.

But if used with caution, such classification also offers advantages. These are:

a) We can use it as an initial device for identification of the traits that are likely to emerge in cross-cultural encounters, as flags or warning signs to look out for, without relying on it either excessively, or exclusively.
b) One can plot along a scale or graph the typical blend of characteristics encountered at each cross-cultural encounter, as a kind of personal or practical guide.
c) As one builds up one's own knowledge based on experience, it becomes easier to identify those interlocutors that fit into the stereotype and those who do not. This enriches one's insight and perception.

At seminars with business representatives I have used the Lewis classification on several occasions, on the premise that Germans tend to exhibit many of the listed characteristics of the Linear Actives and that Indians show most of the traits listed against the Multi-Actives.[3] This approach has met with general agreement, though some observers have found it to convey implied criticism, and a bit disturbing in its directness. The method is useful in cross-culture training for businessmen, helping them with initial orientation, and sensitizing them to become observant.

EXAMPLES

The complexity of cultural attributes can be illustrated with some examples. When I reached Algeria in 1975, I was told that the cultural style of the officials of that country was one of dourness, rigidity and relative insularity—all traceable to the terrible war of liberation that the country had waged against French colonialism from 1954 to 1962, with an estimated half to one million of the ten million population of the time killed, and another three million displaced as internal refugees. This made Algerian officials and others secretive and uncommunicative—a complete contrast to the gregarious Egyptians and other Arab national types. The Director of the Asia Division in the Foreign Ministry (who later became a good friend) advised that I should understand this and adjust my expectations accordingly. A wise British Ambassador conveyed further insight (during one of the many customary courtesy calls I paid on various diplomatic colleagues), that the Algerians would typically observe a foreign envoy for a couple of years before they made up their mind if he or she could be trusted. If they decided favorably, all kinds of doors would then open up, and the same officials who had been inscrutable or difficult earlier would become communicative. This was precisely what happened, and the relationships eventually established with Algerians became highly productive, as well as personally rewarding.[4] The point this illustrated was not that the general perception regarding Algerian stereotypes was wrong, but that it dealt with surface characteristics, and overlooked the deeper attributes.[5]

The lesson offered is that there are different layers of cultural behavior that have to be discerned. We all deal with the surface, but the diplomat is concerned even more with the underlying elements. He needs to peel back the layers, in the task of building sustained contacts across cultures.

Even an outwardly homogenous society, dominated by one single ethnic and linguistic heritage, like Germany, presents different cultural sub-categories, each with subtle differences in behavior. The Bavarian of the South is quite different from the Ost Fresian of the North, and both differ again from the Prussian type that may be found in the Berlin region. Naturally, individuals will differ in terms of their own distinctive behavior, but the regional types offer some clues on 'typical' mindsets.

Take a country like India with an extreme, layered and pluriform of diversity.[6] If a foreign businessman comes and seeks to understand the kind of behavior and value systems he will encounter in the country, the first question confronting him is the region where his potential partners are located and the 'community' to which they belong. (There is no easy definition of the word community as it is used here; it relates to the distinctive caste sub-grouping, of which there are many hundreds in the country.) A score or more of them are very prominent in business, like the 'Marwaris' of Rajasthan, originally traders who moved throughout the country some centuries back leaving their famine-ravaged land, and set up trading and later manufacturing business. They account for some 30% of total business in the country. Another community prominent in business is the Chettiyars of south India. While some of the value systems of the two are similar, in other ways they are as different as chalk and cheese. But despite these differences we can speak of some more-or-less-common Indian business characteristics.

It is through examples that cross-cultural behavior is perceived and understanding inculcated. It is useful to make a record of one's own cross-cultural observations.

PRACTICAL APPLICATION

We use a category-based analysis (like the Lewis method) in order to sharpen skills of observation and technique of handling cross-cultural interactions. The following elements are important in practical application of the theoretical concepts.

a) One should first develop an objective understanding of one's own culture, looking to history and the source of different traits, plus comparative strengths and weaknesses. This will build a foundation for cross-cultural understanding.
b) To be adept at cultural understanding does not mean that one should adopt the cultural style of others, or abandon one's own cultural characteristics. The aim is to reduce the distance from the 'other', and to gain insight, (using the term in the sociological sense of a cultural entity that is used deliberately or unconsciously as a contrast to one's own.)
c) No one can be a master of all knowledge or a practitioner of cultural styles of even of the countries in a particular region. Looking at the problem in terms of detailed knowledge, in any case, is the wrong method. The better method lies in the attitude of mind with which we approach diversity; an objective analysis of foreign traits helps to accept differences, and develop understanding.
d) One professional hazard for those who live implanted in foreign lands (diplomats, businessmen or others), is the lapse into an 'us' and 'them' mindset, which becomes especially acute in situations of adverse bilateral relationships, or at locations where negative factors are predominant. This also happens when closed societies are encountered (like in the communist countries before the end of the Cold War), where local contacts are severely restricted. Diplomats—and foreign journalists and businessmen—stationed there fall back on intensive interchanges among themselves. For example, this happened to diplomats posted in China before the gradual opening up there after 1979; in the earlier time contacts with locals were non-existent, and the foreign community in Beijing functioned like a closed enclave.[7] The same can happen at other locations where physical hardship or insecurity is acute.
e) There is a reverse risk, of 'localitis' or an excessive solicitude for

the foreign country and culture, among diplomats who have been at a post for too long a time.[8] It is essential to have empathy for the host country; indeed a basic diplomatic duty is to dispassionately represent the viewpoint of the host country to the home government. But carrying it to excess is a danger. Cross-cultural understanding should not degenerate into aping the foreigner.[9]

f) Language is closely connected with culture. Learning a foreign language involves imbibing much of the culture, in a natural fashion. This is one more reason for diplomats to develop language skills. No individual can master the language at each country of assignment, but the diplomatic service as a whole should be able to offer language competence, at various levels of seniority, covering all the countries and regions that are of importance in external relations.

g) At negotiations, having officials who speak the language of the partner is of enormous value. But even when one has mastered the foreign language exceptionally well, it is wise to negotiate in one's own primary language, not only for reasons of convenience to the entire home delegation. There is usually a subtle change in one's personality that is projected via a foreign language, and it is better to be true to oneself in one's own language. This danger is especially acute with 'hard' languages like Arabic, Chinese or Japanese.

Cultural understanding is linked with other professional abilities, including receptivity to non-verbal signals, many of which are culture specific. The development of one skill reinforces the other abilities (see the following chapter).

Traditional diplomacy presupposed communication ability as a fundamental skill that was honed through practice. Today, the addition of many layers of diversity in international contacts demands explicit training in this area. But as always, the practitioner must integrate theory with actual practice, and continually adapt his learning on the basis of experience.

QUESTIONS

1. Do you think that cross-cultural studies are useful in diplomacy? Please offer some examples of your own if possible.
2. Where would you place your own country on the Lewis classification? And how would you place France and Russia in terms of the characteristics?
3. Please give three examples of your own that show different cultural traits in a single country.
4. Please give an example of non-verbal signals that can be received better through good cross-cultural abilities.

REFERENCES

1. Lewis, Richard D., *When Cultures Collide: Managing Successfully Across Cultures* (Nicholas Brealey, London, 1993).
2. Ulrich, Karl, Chaudhry, R.S., and Rana, Kishan S., *Managing Corporate Culture* (Macmillan, New Delhi, 2000).

NOTES

1. In the 1950s a unique photo exhibit was put together by the US Information Service, called 'The Family of Man', a collection of some 500 black-and-white photographs by the world's greatest photographers, including Ansel Adams, Henri Cartier-Bresson, David Douglas Duncan, and many others. It showed graphically the human unity that underlies all cultural, ethnic and other differences.
2. Again, this is an inadequate distinction, because the cultural mindsets encountered in Japan are much more akin to an island nation that had only the remotest historical contact with the outside world, until the 17th century. China is different, even while it exhibits its 'Middle Kingdom' complex of a relatively autonomous culture that traditionally absorbed the foreign invaders and made them Chinese. Korea, sandwiched between China and Japan has its own specificities that a student of East Asia has to master.

3. Indians deal with diversity as a fact of life from childhood, because there are few countries in the world that encompass a bigger variety of differences; ethnic, religious, cultural, linguistic, regional, and in almost all aspects of society. Within each sub-region and religious or linguistic group there are communities or sub-castes that follow different practices in food habits, ritual, and social custom. This equips Indians to handle diversity with ease, even while few of them receive formal cross-cultural training. This and the related human management skills are perhaps a factor in the relative success of Indian corporate managers—there are currently some 20+ CEOs of Indian origin among the Fortune 500 companies in the US.
4. In business circles there was an identical impression of Algerians, then dominated by massive state enterprises. For example the hydrocarbon monopoly company SONATRACH was reputed to be tough and ruthless in its dealings with foreign enterprises. Yet a wide range of Indian business representatives, from Indian public enterprises and private companies, found that once initial unfamiliarity had been overcome, human contact with local counterparts was invariable excellent, and they were fair and scrupulous in business dealings. The key was to win their trust—which was hard for many Westerners, because of the baggage of historical memory and ideological fixation of many Algerians.
5. These and other cross-cultural experiences are narrated in my book *Inside Diplomacy.*
6. Within a single state India perhaps offers greater diversity than any other. Virtually every religion of the world is found here (with Christianity and Judaism having come to South India before Christ); it has some religions that are not to be found anywhere else, like Jainism and Sikhism. Besides the 14 official languages, each with its script and literary tradition, there are around 500 dialects. It is divided into 28 states and numerous sub-regions. The diversities of ethnicity, climate, fauna and flora, and of social customs, cuisine and attire are no less.
7. Stationed in Beijing in the 1960s and again in the 1970s, I recall that those of us who were Chinese-language speakers overcame this with contacts built up assiduously with a handful of Chinese who were then permitted to engage in such contacts (like interpreters working

in embassies, language teachers and the like). Such informal contact groups became a way to break out of isolation and to deepen understanding, in the midst of difficult circumstances.

8. This is one good reason for limiting the duration of diplomatic assignments abroad to three or four years.
9. On November 21, 2001 Indian newspapers carried a report about a Western ambassador observing the Ramadan fast during the Muslim holy month, as a gesture of empathy. One gains little understanding or friendship through such public gestures, which may be interpreted in a foreign country as a crude attempt to play to the gallery.

13

Diplomatic Signalling

Signals are a means for conveying messages.

WHAT ARE SIGNALS?

In diplomacy, signals serve as a substitute for language, which is the direct method of communication. The signal must have:

- an originator,
- a method or channel of communication,
- a recipient,
- a means for both the sender and the recipient to verify, if possible, the authenticity of the message and its receipt on arrival.
- a sender and a receiver with a common protocol or system, without which the communication might be misdirected or not understood on receipt.

Raymond Cohen, author of several works that have focused on non-verbal signals, has written: 'States have become adept at extra-linguistic forms of communication ... (these) do not replace language, rather they complement, illuminate and supplement it.' As far as diplomacy or dialogue between nations is concerned, non-verbal communication that Cohen identifies has three main characteristics.

- It must be *deliberate*. The receiver of the signal or observer has to make an *assumption of intentionality*. But diplomacy involves communication across cultures, and it is not always easy to be certain that a diplomatic signal has the same meaning in different countries. This makes it essential that effective signals are not culture-specific, or hard to discern in other cultures. Example: The wearing of a particular attire at an event of significance, when images are captured and broadcast around the world, may signify a hidden intent, for positive projection or for negative reasons. When national leaders visit their troops in the field, like President George W. Bush in Kosovo in July 2001, they don ordinary combat outerwear, to underscore identification with the ordinary soldier. At one negotiation session with Israel, late Egyptian President Anwar Sadat was photographed wearing a tie that bore a design that some commentators identified as a 'swastika' motif. This was firmly denied by Egyptian spokesmen.[1] Was it is subtle gesture of provocation? We do not know.
- Sometimes ambiguity of intent is also part of the signal, to convey some degree of doubt, or to leave room for denying the signal at some point in the future. If the gesture is explicitly acknowledged as a signal, it may lose its effectiveness; hence it is often *ambiguous* and *disclaimable*. (Example: The 'diplomatic cold' or illness of convenience permits one side to offer an excuse that is probably just an excuse; but the other one cannot be absolutely certain.) And the side making the signal is able to insist on the genuineness of the indisposition with a straight face. Many years ago there was an Asian envoy in Beijing who suffered from a weak bladder and needed to use the rest room in the middle of an event like an official diplomatic banquet. He was invariably at pains to explain to those seated at his table that he was leaving momentarily and would be back. He was mortified that someone might imagine that he was staging a walkout—which was fairly customary at the time in the context of sharp ideological differences!
- The observer has to draw an inference regarding a signal, from

the *timing*, *context* and *convention*. This is where the rules of protocol, the customary convention of diplomatic discourse, and of course the time and manner in which the signal is delivered have to be taken into careful account. Diplomacy offers rich potential for creativity in signals. For example, a deviation from protocol becomes a way of sending a positive or a negative signal. This may take the form of the hierarchy level at which a foreign dignitary is met at the airport, or who receives the foreign visitor for a meeting. Similarly, a social gesture honoring the visitor, like a lunch, or some other function, is also a signal, especially when it is not mandatory under local custom. (Prime Minister Indira Gandhi was a consummate master of the symbolic gesture; there was a clear but subtle distinction between the foreign visitors she received at the office table and those who were offered the sofa seat!) The repertoire for such gestures—and signals—has become wider in recent years with the easing of protocol and introduction of flexibility in diplomatic usage. Thus, against the classic classification of visits by heads of state and government into 'state', 'official' and 'working', there are many variations in the latter category, and new sub-types like 'stopover' visits, 'official working'[2] visits, and even informal summits involving more than one foreign dignitary (as noted in Chapter 10).

The signal arsenal includes verbal communication, where the context may give the words a supplementary or nuanced meaning. For instance, a suggestion made in a social setting, outside of a negotiation process, may indicate a trial balloon, or a probe to gauge the intention of the other side, while retaining the option of 'deniability'. It would usually not be possible to refer to it in the formal talks, and the response would have to be equally indirect.[3] Then there are those signals, which are conveyed via the media, or intermediaries. With the profusion of cable TV, 24-hour news channels and the 'electronic global village', the use of the media as a vehicle of signals is more common than ever before, and numerous instances can be found of diplomatic signaling through this medium. For instance, a day after the inconclusive India–Pakistan Summit at Agra in July 2001, there were public statements from the foreign ministers of the two states that conveyed differing perceptions of the use of the media in diplomacy. India's Jaswant Singh declared at Agra on the morning of July 17, 2001: 'When it comes to bilateral or international issues, we do not and cannot negotiate through the media.' Pakistan's Abdul Sattar asserted a differing perspective at a press conference held some hours later in Islamabad: 'In contemporary diplomacy it is impossible to separate official talks from interviews with the media.' The problem arose because the two sides had not established ground rules in advance on media briefings—i.e. the summit preparation had been inadequate.

Another category of signals are words or written statements that are not accompanied by action, or by action that is at variance from what the words had indicated. This may apply to situations of threat, or some form of tension in relations between states. Such signals are relatively easy to read and confirm the adage that what counts more than words is action. At the time of the India–Pakistan conflict of 1965, as a means of exerting pressure on New Delhi, without engaging in overt action, the Chinese Foreign Ministry took the very unusual step of issuing an 'ultimatum' through a diplomatic note, over an alleged loss of some dozen yaks and some 40 odd sheep, across the India–China border in the Tibet region. A time period of 72 hours was specified for making good the loss. At the precisely indicated time, the Indian Ministry of External Affairs sent a reply to the effect that there had been no abduction of sheep and yaks and the so-called ultimatum was rejected. But the point was well understood that China had made a low-key gesture of support for Pakistan.

One should note that unlike language which is an explicit form of communication, signaling usually involves subtlety, and depends on receptivity by the signal-receiver or observer. Diplomacy today operates in a vastly more diverse setting than, say 50 or even 30 years ago, and professionals conform less and less to a single template. Consequently, the cultural context is of obvious significance. For example, a physical embrace between political leaders in conflict has greater significance than the ritual 'abrazzo' between two Latin American personalities. One example is the powerful signal of reconciliation sent by President de Gaulle and German Chancellor Adenauer in the 1950s when they held hands as they stood at the Verdun battlefield cemetery.

The media is an important channel for signals. But in an interconnected world where 24-hour news channels carry 'real time' images of major developments, signals via this route are powerful, but hard to control. For one thing, they reach out to all, and audience targeting is difficult. This has to be kept in mind while using the medium. This is particularly true of messages meant for the domestic constituency reaching out to external audiences. One example of astute use of the media emerged during the Gulf War in 1991 when the Iraqis permitted CNN to remain in Baghdad during the hostilities, to transmit images and to convey their own diplomatic messages to the world, more powerfully than they could have done in any other way.

BODY LANGUAGE

As in all kinds of human interaction, body language supplements other forms of communication.

- There is the form of greeting and the options it offers for signals, like the warmth of a handshake, which specialists call 'access ritual'. Premier Zhou Enlai was noted for his habit of looking directly into the eyes of each person with whom he shook hands, even at a diplomatic lineup that might stretch around three sides of a reception hall. The Beijing diplomatic corps of those days used to say that a foreign envoy could measure the day's state of relations in the warmth conveyed!

- Facial expression is the simplest form of body language, and most directly readable—an expression of smile, frown, seriousness, or that of a visage at ease. Equally, the true exponents of communication are those who master emotion and use facial expression as a controlled tool.
- Yet other signals are conveyed in loudness or quietness, punctuality or its absence, and even the use of 'personal space'. Some years back, during a state visit to Morocco, the late King Hassan kept Queen Elizabeth waiting for some ten minutes, surely not by accident, but to assert a notion of 'royal prerogative' of his ancient monarchy, and indirectly assert equality with a major power.
- One form of signal that is instantly effective relates to 'inconvenience display', when a host goes out of his way to do something for the guest at the cost of personal inconvenience, like coming to the front entrance steps to receive him, or coming to the airport when protocol does not mandate this. Of course, such a gesture in reverse powerfully conveys a snub.

THE VALUE OF SIGNALS

Cohen points out that one way of looking at diplomatic signals is to analyze their significance.

a) The signal may reinforce speech through action.
b) It may give a clue as to the weight of the verbal (or written) message.
c) It can be used as a discreet indicator as to the current stage of the relationship.

One simple example is the manner in which an envoy is received at the foreign ministry when he is summoned to receive a message. The interlocutor's tone of delivery can lend weight to the formal communication. So can politeness, certain rituals such as reception and sendoff, and even the 'tea or coffee' ritual, by their presence, absence and manner of execution. In a Western capital, an ambassador may find it hard to call on the foreign minister in the normal course; but if this dignitary delivers a protest personally, it lends weight to the seriousness of the issue.

Signals are part of a dynamic process which evolves in value, depending on time and the circumstance. For instance, one of the classic signals of diplomacy, the 'withdrawal of an ambassador for consultations', used to convey a measured degree of displeasure; it continues to be used, but mainly between countries that are practitioners of 'old' diplomacy. In many post-colonial states it would not be understood, and this may be one reason why, for example, Africans seldom use this gesture with another African state, save at the stage of a real breakdown in relations. It may also be that the world over, the ambassador is no longer the unique vehicle of contact, and his presence or absence is less remarkable than before. Some observers have noted that no country, which has withdrawn an ambassador for a period of time in a gesture of political disapproval, has derived benefit from the move. It has often had the reverse effect of not having a senior envoy at post when he is needed the most, a situation of difficult relations.[4]

One point that often receives less attention than it deserves is 'receptivity' to signals. Just as the 'sender' needs to be sure that the message is understood as intended (assuming that he has not deliberately chosen to be ambiguous), the 'recipient' needs to be sure that what he has understood is indeed a real message! Failing this, situations of confusion arise. Individuals tend to display oversensitivity to what are seen as personal slights; this is a function of one's ego. It can lead to situations where an unintended meaning is read into an innocent gesture, or even a mistake. (Example: In *Inside Diplomacy* I have narrated the personal hostility that we faced from an important German minister in 1991–92. The situation was serious enough for the Indian Finance Minister to instruct me when I took up appointment to that embassy in May 1992, to do everything possible to assuage and win him over. His hostility owed in part to a protocol snafu a year earlier when he accompanied the German President to Delhi, and had been left behind at the Indian Presidential Palace when the car convoy departed with customary flurry and speed, for one of the day's engagements. He perceived in this error a deliberate slight; there was another innocent error of judgment on that same visit which also aroused his ire. It took a year to win back grace, and happily, establish even better mutual understanding!) The moral is to make sure that a perceived signal is indeed a signal. The difficulty in discerning signals is complicated by the complex cross-cultural environment in which we now function.

Countries can miss out on major signals of the most obvious kind, and later wonder in hindsight how this happened. One glaring instance is the appearance of Edgar Snow on the Tienanmen rostrum on October 1, 1970, at the Chinese National Day parade review. He was a long-standing personal friend of Mao Zedong, the author who brought the Chinese Revolution to notice in the West with his classic *Red Star Over China* published in 1937. But the importance of exposing him to the Chinese public at the symbolic core of the nation on the most hallowed day in the calendar, went much beyond this—except that the gesture was unread in Washington DC for a while![5] Developing these skills of discernment, involves an ability to filter out conventional thinking, which may become a kind of baggage or background noise preventing absorption of the intended signal. Equally, one must avoid the sin of over-analysis. Balance between these is not easy to achieve. 'Lateral thinking', the innovative thinking tool advanced by Edward de Bono helps one to look beyond the obvious.

Signals also get distorted during transmission. Again, it was at the May Day parade of 1970 that Mao conveyed a major message to India, shaking the hand of the Indian chargé d' affaires and telling him that the two countries could not go on quarreling as they had since the Border War of 1962. While the gesture was under evaluation in Delhi, the news was leaked to the media, and trivialized under Indian newspaper headlines as 'the Mao smile'. The value of the

SYMBOLS AND SIGNALS

Symbols can become powerful transmitters of signals. Mahatma Gandhi, the father of India's Independence understood this exceptionally well. On his return to India from UK and South Africa, this Lincoln's Inn lawyer, habitually attired in Western suits, adopted the simplest of Indian attire, the *dhoti* in its short version, usually with a bare upper body. Churchill called him a half-naked fakir, but by that simple statement Gandhi identified himself with the poorest Indian, the overwhelming majority of the population. This simplicity was extended to other areas, like travel by the lowest class on the railway, and a diet restricted to the common man's food (and goat's milk). Once when he was holding forth on his simplicity, Rajkumari Amrit Kaur, the princess who had given up her inheritance to join his movement, retorted that only his supporters knew how much it cost to keep him in simplicity. Gandhi laughed uproariously!

In 1929 when the colonial administration unwisely imposed a tax on salt, the ordinary man's staple, Gandhi seized on this opportunity with the famous Dandi March, launching a civil resistance movement to symbolically produce salt by evaporation, refusing to pay an unjust tax. The signal caught the imagination of the masses and galvanized the nation, giving new impetus for Independence.

On her October 1997 state visit to India, Queen Elizabeth decided on a symbolic gesture that had not been made even 50 years after Independence, to visit a site connected with the brutality of colonial rule. The natural choice was Jallianwala Bagh in Amritsar, where in 1919 the worst single atrocity had taken place. Some thousands of men, women and children who had gathered in an enclosed garden were machine-gunned by one General Dyer in what accounts of the time called 'a display of power, not control of disorder'. Several hundreds were killed and over a thousand were injured. Unfortunately, the Queen's 'brave gesture' (as *The Times* of London called it) spun out of control even before she reached India—the mood of the post-Independence generation had been miscalculated. When journalists asked at a pre-visit press conference by the High Commissioner if the Queen would convey an apology, he replied that this was 'out of question.' Visiting the memorial the Queen signed the visitor's book, but conveyed no comment or impression despite local requests. Prince Phillip, not renowned for tact, compounded matters by declaring to his Indian protocol liaison official that official accounts of the numbers killed were 'vastly exaggerated', quoting members of Dyer's family! The media seized on this remark with glee. (Strangely, that visit staggered from one disaster to another! In Chennai (Madras) there was a fracas over a 'second banquet speech' by the Queen that was apparently demanded by the visitors, and then not delivered. To cap it, accompanying Foreign Secretary Robin Cook's remarks on Kashmir provoked a media storm and official Indian displeasure. It is said that when planning President Clinton's 1999 India tour, this case was studied as a model of how not to organize a state journey.)

signal was eroded, and it took some more years of quiet effort to begin the process of normalization, which took visible shape in 1976 via the return of ambassadors to the two capitals.

CURRENT CONTEXT

Cross-cultural studies are an essential part of the diplomacy curriculum of today, precisely because the world is more complex, response times are shorter, and diversity exists at so many levels.

This begs the question: can the diplomat master all the needed cultural knowledge?

This query parallels the search a decade back for 'Euro-managers', to handle increased integration in Europe, cross-border business, and personnel movements across countries, within transnational enterprises. It was soon realized that no one could, or even needed to master the cultural traits and customs of each European country. The diversity was vast, and each particularity impossible to imprint in one's memory. In order to function effectively, the manager needed instead a quick learning ability, an open mind, and an acceptance of diversity. This particularly involved a non-judgmental attitude towards other cultures and peoples.

It has always been part of the traditional set of diplomatic qualities that the practitioner must adapt to different situations, and this includes culture. We may add to this, adaptation to diplomatic signals that are culture-specific, in terms of receptivity.

In doing so, there is one concept that can be borrowed from Japan, the distinction between 'surface communication' (called *tatame*), and the inner meaning or true intent of the interlocutor (called *honne*). Both have to be observed, but the latter is the more important indicator of the real meaning of the dialogue or communication. This encompasses the signals received and sent, including those that are non-verbal.

To sum up,

a) The sender has a wide choice of signals that enable him to reinforce, minimize, change direction of, or even replace the formal communication.
b) Ambiguity is also an available option, if it is chosen with deliberate intent.
c) The existence of a common cultural context, or understanding, helps in validating the signal, for both the sender and the receiver. Diplomatic convention used to furnish this in the past, but today

not all countries rely on the same conventions or 'style'. This makes signals a matter of cross-cultural understanding also.

d) The diplomat, in his role as potential recipient, needs to develop sensitivity to reception, filtering out any unintended gestures from the real signals.

e) It probably helps a foreign ministry to develop in its own institutional memory, a collection of signals sent and received, in order to train and sensitize officials in the actual working environment of the country and region.

QUESTIONS

1. What are the main attributes of non-verbal signals? Please offer your own examples.
2. Give some instances of body language that has accompanied diplomatic gestures.
3. Why are signals invaluable for diplomacy?
4. Please explain the link between cross-cultural issues and diplomatic signals.

REFERENCES

1. Cohen, Raymond, *Theatre of Power: The Art of Signaling* (Longmans, London, 1987).

NOTES

1. In India, the Swastika is a venerated Hindu symbol that is thousands of years old, and there is almost no ritual where it is not used. Indians resent that the Nazis usurped this symbol for their evil purposes. Many of the older Indian films begin with a prayer where this symbol is clearly displayed; during film festivals held in East Europe in the period of communist rule there, these scenes had to be cut out!
2. This particular version is a Washington DC innovation. It falls between

'official' and 'working' visits, with some ceremonial trappings that are absent from purely working visits.

3. I had an experience of this in Germany in 1994. In the course of an informal Sunday afternoon social function, the Foreign Office State Secretary advanced a suggestion to resolve a particular issue that was so unusual that it left me without words for a moment. I gave a completely non-committal response, not even mentioning that the idea would be communicated to my government, because I was certain that the suggestion would be unacceptable. The next day I decided that since I could not officially refer to the trial balloon that the State Secretary had floated, I would simply send a letter to the Foreign Office Director dealing with the subject, essentially reiterating our standpoint, and seeking early action, without mentioning the trial balloon in any way. Some weeks later I learnt that the Foreign Office too had doubts about the idea that had been floated to me, but they were under pressure from elsewhere to make a sounding, and hence the signal—made in a way that did not put the suggestion on the bilateral record!
4. This was precisely India's experience when it withdrew its Ambassador to China in 1961 (and China immediately reciprocated), on the eve of the crisis that led to the border war the following year. Both had to manage their embassies for some 15 years with fairly senior officials, actually of the rank of relatively mid-level ambassador-rank officials who only carried formal designation of chargé d' affaires, *ad interim*.
5. During that same final visit that Edgar Snow made to China, he also made an indirect gesture towards India that reflected the gradually improving India–China climate. I had met him a couple of years earlier in Geneva at the home of a Swiss academic friend, and sent a note to Mr. Snow, to the effect that I would like to call on him briefly. He phoned me after some days, recalled our earlier meeting and said that he would come to the Indian Embassy (where I was serving as a First Secretary), to meet me. He overrode my protestation and came to the Embassy in his Chinese limousine, for a friendly conversation that gave nothing away by way of hard information, despite my discreet effort! But the fact that as Chairman Mao's guest he saw nothing wrong in visiting us, in a capital laden with symbolic meaning and subtlety, indicated that the thaw in our relationship was real.

14

Bilateral Negotiation

In the era of classic diplomacy, negotiation was regarded as the central function of diplomacy. Indeed, the doyen of diplomatic writing of that age, Harold Nicholson, defined diplomacy as 'the art of negotiating agreements', agreements that could be ratified. Today we would define the core tasks of diplomacy in wider terms, principally covering promotion, outreach, feedback, management and servicing (a working definition that is more proactive than that set out in Article 3 of the 1961 Vienna Convention on Diplomatic Relations, as noted in Chapter 1).

Negotiation of bilateral and multilateral agreements remains one of the important external relation tasks of governments, but the MFA is not always the lead agency in representing the country in bilateral negotiations. This is because the range of subjects covered in negotiation is infinitely wider than in the past. For instance, in working out a protocol on cultural exchanges, representatives of the MFA and/or the embassy may have a role, as advisers or as observers, but on an agreement covering double taxation avoidance, or on a trans-border electric power supply arrangement, they would probably leave it to specialists to negotiate the accords, stepping in only in situations of impasse. Individual diplomats may find that in an entire career they have hardly played any role in bilateral negotiations, either because the main framework of bilateral cooperation has already been set, or because the kinds of accords under dialogue have primarily involved the functional ministries and their specialists. This does not minimize the importance of study of the principles that govern bilateral negotiations, but places the subject in a realistic context.[1]

Multilateral negotiation is one of the core tasks of multilateral diplomacy, and this remains unchanged, whether at the UN at New York on political and other issues, or at what may be regarded as permanent negotiation conclaves like the WTO for trade, and the Disarmament Commission at Geneva. We leave this out of the present survey, but many of the principles of bilateral negotiation apply there too, with appropriate change.

OBJECTIVES

In a classic definition, Fred C. Ilke has pointed out that negotiation presupposes common interests and issues of conflict. The object of bilateral negotiation is to resolve an issue that cannot be solved unilaterally, through one's own actions. Engagement in negotiation almost implies a willingness to achieve a compromise;[2] somewhere between one's own maximum goal and the absolute minimum that one is willing to accept. There are instances of countries engaging in negotiation to get full vindication of their claim, i.e. acceptance of the maximum position. One side, or both, may assert this as a bargaining stance. But unless one side is in a position to coerce the other to accept this (in which case it is not a negotiation between autonomous entities that exercise independent judgment), getting all of one's claims accepted by the other usually involves giving in on something else—i.e. there has been a process of 'give and take' or a tradeoff.

In more typical situations, the object is to get the other side to accept an arrangement that suits one's own side to the maximum extent that is attainable, while giving up the least of what one is willing to concede. To put it plainly, each one tries to get the most and concede the least. The basics involved in negotiations between nations are not different from those in commercial negotiation, even if the grammar and the syntax are different. In both, a balance has also to be found between short-term or one-shot gain, and building up credibility and a long-term reputation, so as to facilitate future business. Ego, prestige and 'face' are also involved in both, though it may be argued that it is in exchanges between nations, especially in situations of conflict and disagreement the subjective factors are at their most acute. There is an abundance of examples of countries that have been unable to reach an agreement even when issues can be resolved, on account of false notions of prestige. There are countries which consciously subscribe to the concept that a 'win–win' result is superior to unilaterally winning the negotiation.

Bilateral negotiation involving sensitive political issues has one sharp difference from all other forms of negotiation—the process is complicated by the invisible presence of other stakeholders at the table, particularly the domestic opinion of the two countries. This may take the form of a passive presence, or become an active element in the negotiation via the mobilization of these forces by either of both sides through the media and publicity. This is an instance where the line between 'external' and 'domestic' issues becomes blurred, and the negotiators have to simultaneously handle the dialogue at two levels, directly with the foreign partner and indirectly with domestic constituencies in both countries. (See Robert Putnam's 'Two Level Game' theory.)[3]

NEGOTIATION STAGES

We may broadly distinguish between four stages of the process: preparation, pre-negotiation, negotiation, and finally, follow-up.

a) **Preparation.** This is a crucial stage, often underrated. The establishment of an internal consensus is the key to smooth implementation. Example: the traditional Japanese 'ringi' system of internal consensus building is slow and involves officials at various levels, representing diverse agencies, and participating in what appears as a rigid process. But one major merit is that once an agreement is reached it can be implemented instantly, as all parties are already on board. In a top-down process, or in one where the decision has not been fully consensus-based, an agreement or decision can be blocked or undermined from within the system. Other elements:

- An analysis of one's own strength, direct and indirect.
- What are the aims and limits of the other side? What are its likely style, tactics and arguments? Is there a hidden agenda? The collection of all external information relevant to the negotiation, including other exemplars, information on the individuals involved and anything else relevant from the perspective of giving information on the other side.
- Analyze how the other side perceives one's own style, and the cross-cultural factors involved.
- Mobilization of all internal information relevant to the task, alternatives, options, and fallback positions.
- Internal consultations with the stakeholders, generation of a consensus and setting out of a shared goal. Identification of 'BATNA'—the 'best alternative to a negotiated solution'. This would provide the irreducible minimum threshold that would not be crossed, since in that case the negotiated solution would be worse than the one that could be applied without negotiations.
- Equally important is the identification of the BATNA of the other side, which may also be called the 'resistance point', or the irreducible goal of the other side. It is only if there is a settlement range between the resistance points of the two sides that there is a realistic possibility of a solution satisfactory to both.
- If one side appears more eager for the agreement, it may

lead the other to extract some form of payment for entering into negotiation.

- Formation of the negotiation team, identification of the leader, internal dialogue within the delegation, and political clearance for all major issues.

b) **Pre-negotiation.** This is also called the stage of 'negotiation about negotiations'. At the Vietnam peace talks held in Warsaw in the 1970s at the initial stage much time was spent on the shape of the negotiation table. Behind the semantics of table geometry were the real issues of the status of the different partners, and the settlement of this after a long-drawn process facilitated the actual dialogue. There were similar long-drawn preliminary skirmishes at the Korea Armistice talks in 1951. To minimize the value of this stage is to risk the process itself. Sometimes the principals may try to leap over this phase (as in the India–Pakistan talks at Agra in July 2001), in the expectation that personal chemistry, and momentum of the direct dialogue may break a logjam. But the danger is that it may lead to a misunderstanding of the ground rules, and at least in the short-term, to a breakdown in talks. This was precisely what happened at the Agra summit.[4] Other factors:

- Exploratory dialogue to clarify the conflicting interests, and a determination as to whether there is a realistic prospect for a solution satisfactory to both.
- Establishment of the agenda, usually an essential pre-condition, worked out through diplomatic channels. There are instances where this is handled at the negotiation itself—but the result is often delay and blockage.
- Other preliminaries, including the identification of the venue, frequency of meetings, and other logistics.
- Issues of confidentiality and disclosure to the media—particularly important for political discussions. In the absence

of agreement one should be prepared to use the media, and through that, public opinion as indirect participants in the process, used to exercise influence on the negotiations.

c) **Negotiation.** This can be a straightforward process, or may be drawn out over many sessions and even years. It includes the formal sessions of bilateral negotiation and the informal exchanges that may supplement it. All too often, breakthrough comes in the latter, via social functions and one-on-one meetings. The former provide opportunity for informal sounding of ideas and floating of trial balloons, in a manner that does not commit anyone and has 'deniability'. (Example: after the Geneva talks of the 1950s Chinese Premier Zhou Enlai said that the most constructive breakthroughs of the discussions occurred during the social functions.) The ideal format is one that is flexible and practical, taking into account the convenience of each side, including the needs for internal consultations and approval from principals. Where issues are complex, or even with technical issues, it is useful to have a system of agreed minutes, or some form of an interim document, even of a non-binding character, to serve as a dialogue benchmark, to avoid repetitive discussions when there are several sessions spread over time. The main stages are:

- The 'initial' stage when the opening statements are made, calling for perceptive listening to hear the hidden message as well. The dialogue at this point may appear ritualistic, but it sets the process in operation.
- The 'exploration' stage when tentative sounding is carried out, often in varied settings. Hidden signals and non-verbal communication is important.
- The 'formula' stage where the broad approaches or themes are covered. It is essential to secure agreement on these before moving on to the next stage.

- The 'details' stage where the fine print is elaborated and agreed. Sometimes this becomes the battleground for the major decisions. Or there may be no clear distinction between the two stages.
- The 'packaging' stage where the fine print and all the details are tied together. The closer the agreement appears, the greater the sensitivity and the need for caution. Where feasible, the implementation process should be built into the agreement.

d) **Follow-up.** In the euphoria of a successful negotiation this can be overlooked or minimized in value. Many agreements are self-enforcing, and some need an enforcement mechanism. Generally, an agreement which is asymmetrical—for instance, giving a larger advantage to one side—may present problems of enforcement, if the other side finds it expedient to resile from it.

- A full assessment of the implications of the agreement, and its consequence on other relationships and issues. Careful identification of the necessary follow-up, immediate and over time.
- Communication of the results to the stakeholders and to the public at large, to create the optimal conditions for implementation.
- Actual implementation, keeping in view all the parameters of the accord.
- Elaboration of the lessons and insights learnt from the negotiation experience and incorporation of this into the institutional memory. All too often this debriefing is ignored.

Not all problems are amenable to negotiation. The timing of the commencement of the process depends on objective conditions and it becomes the task of diplomacy to create the external conditions that would be conducive to the launch of the process, including outreach to public opinion in the foreign country. Often, the challenge is to influence public opinion at home in favor of negotiation and an eventual compromise solution. This is largely a domestic political issue, but given the intermingling of domestic–external affairs, the diplomatic apparatus can also get involved indirectly in helping in the molding of home public opinion.

THE HARVARD METHOD: 'PRINCIPLED NEGOTIATION'

After an extended study, Fisher and Ury have identified a novel approach to bilateral negotiation as it applies to commercial enterprises and countries, which they have defined as 'principled negotiation' (PN). This is offered in contrast to what they have called 'positional bargaining' (PB) that frequently leads to blockage and impasse, because countries proceed from set positions and the negotiation becomes a battle of wills. Examples: In the early stages of the Kennedy–Khrushchev discussions on nuclear arms control, each side took adamant positions on numbers and scope of inspections, without looking for ways in which the concern of each could be addressed by looking at the inspection method and the real needs of verification. In the India–China border talks of 1960, each offered its own set position, making virtually no effort to identify commonalities or go beyond the formal stance.

Offered as a superior alternative, PN operates through 4 major elements.

A. **People.** 'Separate the people from the problem.' This means:

- ❑ Perceptions: put oneself in the shoes of the other side; discuss perceptions; act in a manner that challenges the perceptions of the other side; make proposals that are consistent with the values of the other side but not their perceptions.
- ❑ Emotions: recognize emotions and treat them as legitimate; don't react to emotional outbursts; use symbolic gestures.
- ❑ Conversation: listen attentively and ask questions; speak to

be understood; speak about own self and not the behavior of the other side.

B. **Interests.** 'Behind adversarial positions there lie interests that may be common. To satisfy interests usually several options are available.' Example: at the 1978 Egypt–Israel Camp David talks, Egypt sought sovereignty over Sinai, Israel wanted security; the reconciliation came in de-militarizing much of Sinai.

- ❑ Identify interests: what are the basic concerns of the other side? What are the consequences, for the other side, of not doing what you seek? Realize that each has multiple interests.
- ❑ Talk about interests: the other may not know what you want; make own interests come alive; put the problem before the answer.

C. **Options.** 'In trying to share the pie, one is operating only in a single dimension.' There should be a creative search for options.

- ❑ Obstacles: premature judgment hinders imagination; assuming a fixed pie means looking for a single answer; solving the other side's problem is part of one's own problem; brainstorming can be used (this is very similar to the well-known de Bono thinking methods).
- ❑ Shared interests: they often lie latent; taking care of the interests of the other side makes it easier for them to do what one wants; opportunities have to be developed.

D. **Criteria.** 'Looking to criteria may offer solutions.'

- ❑ Prepare in advance: standards that are fair and legitimate; also fair procedures.
- ❑ Method: frame each issue as a joint search for criteria; reason and be open to reason; yield to principle, not pressure.

PN is clearly superior to PB. The challenge is to creatively apply these methods in real life situations and to develop procedures, approaches and styles that are based on one's needs.

AGREEMENT TYPES

Agreements can be divided into four broad types:[5]

- **Extension agreement**, which continues an earlier arrangement, with such change that either side requires. This may typically cover trade, tariff rates, or transit arrangements, or indeed any agreement established earlier.
- **Normalization agreement**, which ends a stage of tension or abnormality. It may, for example, establish diplomatic relations.
- **Redistribution agreement**, which leads to sharing of some benefits, on a 'zero-sum game', where advantage to one comes at the cost of the other. This may be a border agreement on territorial claims, or river water sharing agreement, or a maritime agreement.
- **Innovation agreement**, covering some new activity, which is not a 'zero-sum' arrangement, and both benefit. This could cover a new trade arrangement, or a hydro project or transport corridor construction.

The nature of the negotiation process is influenced by the kind of agreement. In practice a redistribution agreement is the hardest to negotiate, while an innovation agreement needs especially careful preparatory work to win acceptance for the gain that it offers to both sides. Such agreements also have to be cast in a manner that is not asymmetrical. An extension agreement in contrast should generally be the easiest to negotiate, unless there are special circumstances.

THE MEDIA AND CONFIDENTIALITY

The element of confidentiality in negotiations is vital where major issues are involved. It is a democratic right of the people to be consulted on foreign policy issues, and one characteristic of our times is strong public interest in major foreign issues. Any sensitive issue is inevitably as much domestic as external, as we can see from the experience of any country. But when negotiations take place in the full glare of publicity, it is impossible to develop new approaches, or make a creative search for commonalities of interest, if each stage of the discussion is reported to the media and to public opinion. The result is likely to be PB, and not a new search for solutions under the approaches of PN.

Sometimes basic approaches may be identified in a confidential discussion at the pre-negotiation stage. But in the majority of successful discussions covering hard issues that have separated the participants over time, some segment of the discussion has taken place behind firmly closed doors. Example: the secret Israel–Palestine talks at Oslo in 1991 sponsored by Norway. In many respects this is one of the hardest issues to tackle in contemporary negotiation processes.

NATIONAL STYLES

Understanding national stereotypes can help in understanding the other side, and in preparing for the negotiation. But one must treat such theoretical concepts like 'country styles of negotiation' with caution, offering indicative data that needs to be tested in the field, but not as immutable rules that provide all answers. With these caveats, it is useful to try and identify and familiarize oneself with the conventional wisdom regarding the negotiating style of the foreign partner. There are excellent studies, based on practical examples, many taking into account the cultural ethos of the country and its historical heritage. This is particularly true of countries that possess distinctive cultural styles, rather dissimilar from one's own. This takes us into the area of cross-cultural studies, as also the art of signaling, both of which contribute to negotiation technique. The craft of diplomacy borrows from, and depends on, a wide array of human behavioral sciences.

QUESTIONS

1. What are the objectives of negotiation? Illustrate with your own example please.
2. Which stage of negotiation would you regard as crucial? Please offer an example of agreements that were not implemented.
3. What is Positional Bargaining? Can you offer an instance other than what is cited in the text above?
4. In the Harvard Method, what is the striking element that you find different from conventional approaches to negotiations?

REFERENCES

1. Fisher, Roger and Ury, William, *Getting to Yes: Negotiating Agreements Without Giving In* (Hutchinson, London, 1981).
2. Fisher, Roger, *Beyond Machiavelli: Tools For Coping With Conflict* (Penguin, London, 1996).
3. Evans, Peter B., Jacobson, Harold K., and Putnam, Robert D., *Double Edged Diplomacy* (University of California Press, Berkeley, 1993).
4. Zartman, I. William and Berman, Maureen, *The Practical Negotiator* (Yale University Press, Yale, 1982).

NOTES

1. In a 35-year career, I recall having been involved in the bilateral negotiation of agreements, protocols and the like, on barely five occasions. This excludes the negotiation of joint communiqués or similar texts, or normal diplomatic démarches, which can also be defined as falling within the ambit of negotiation in a broad sense.
2. There are exceptions to the general notion that negotiation implies willingness to achieve compromise. A country may engage in negotiation as a device to temporize, or as a tactical device to distract attention from other intentions it may harbor, for example, to undertake unilateral action.
3. Initially presented as an article in an academic journal, it is also narrated in Peter B. Evans, Harold L. Jacobson, and Robert Putnam, eds, *Double-Edged Diplomacy* (University of California Press, Berkeley, 1993).

4. This particular summit meeting will provide substantive material for the diplomacy analyst, especially as major elements of the process were played out in public view, when Pakistan used the sizable presence of 24-hour Indian and foreign news channels to play out the Two Level Game, and the Indian side found itself unprepared for this (see Chapter 13). The full inside story of what transpired was not disclosed and the two sides decided to resume the dialogue later but until November 2001 there has been no indication of resumption, and the aftermath of the terrorist acts in the US in September 2001 has complicated the situation. It has not been contested that it was at Pakistan's insistence that India reluctantly agreed to drop insistence on establishing prior understanding on the agenda and meeting parameters. The two countries are unlikely to use the device of non-preparation in the future.
5. This classification is provided by Gordon A. Craig, and Alexander L. George, *Force and Statecraft: Diplomatic Problems of Our Times*, 3rd edition, (Oxford University Press, New York, 1995).

15

Performance Enhancement

The introduction of management techniques into diplomacy is a new trend. It is evident from empirical experience that objective criteria and the monitoring of performance is possible in this profession, which earlier seemed immune from such innovation. This evolution is linked with concern in different countries over improved governance in all public services.

We now know that a performance audit contributes to efficiency and this is best done through institutionalized methods in the diplomatic service or elsewhere, in preference to reliance on individual brilliance. High and clearly articulated performance standards are also a collective motivation device. Traditionalists may argue that such ideas sit ill with the 'plenipotentiary' powers of envoys and their status as personal representatives of heads of state, to say nothing of the style of classic diplomacy. But in practice, running a mission is conceptually little different from running a national subsidiary of a large multinational company, even if the product on offer is different. The UK Foreign Office underscores this parallel with the world of business, by calling its top decision-making body the 'Board of Management', headed by the Permanent Under Secretary. There are other MFAs that use borrowed terminology, like 'corporate services' for what used to be called the establishment and services divisions. 'Corporatization' is also visible in other diplomatic services, through application of costing yardsticks for services (as in Germany) and wide business approaches in all public services (as in New Zealand).

We need to look to the empirical data, at the methods and the actual experience of different diplomatic services, to identify the different ways in which performance is monitored. Of course, there is no single standard or 'optimum' method. The situation in individual countries depends on historical evolution and the perceived needs of these countries. At the same time, there is little evidence of deliberate emulation among MFAs, or even close analysis of the experience of others—except in the case of the European Union. (The EU dialogue mechanism among government agencies includes a monthly forum for exchanges among the administration heads of foreign ministries. Borrowing ideas on MFA management methods is particularly strong among the major states. Regular exchanges of personnel, to work within the MFA and embassies, also helps.) Consequently, in most countries we encounter parallel development of methods that are undergoing experimentation. We also find that there are a number of countries, especially in the developing countries of the South, where performance appraisal has not yet developed beyond rudimentary methods. It underscores the point that foreign services are all too often slow to adapt, without some external stimulus. It also reflects an inadequacy of training—and awareness—at senior levels. There is no reason that a lean and efficient diplomatic service should be the monopoly of rich countries!

FOREIGN SERVICE INSPECTIONS

One old—and traditional—method of performance appraisal has been the Foreign Service Inspectorate system, a standard feature in all the large diplomatic services, usually implemented by a small group of senior officials who travel around the world, inspecting missions in a regular cycle. Typically they look at staffing levels, work performance, as well as a myriad administrative issues ranging from morale to levels of allowances, maintenance of properties, local staff optimization, and the like. Each mission is inspected at intervals that may range from 5, 7, or even 10 years. Even with rapid communications and frequent travel abroad by home-based officials, most diplomatic services regard the inspection system as an essential method of ensuring standardization and monitoring efficiency, and the system continues as a permanent feature.

A typical example of what is the German system; the 'Inspector General' is an official of the rank of a ministerial director, the second echelon in the Foreign Office, just below the permanent heads, the two state secretaries. Two more officials at the next lower rank assist him, and between them they circumnavigate the world, inspecting each mission at an average of every 5 years. A great deal of preparatory work is carried out before the actual visit. The team leader holds a dialogue with all the officials in the Foreign Office and the other ministries that are the main interlocutors of that particular mission. He also sees a copy of every outward communication sent by the mission under inspection in the six months preceding the inspection. A confidential questionnaire running to several pages reaches each home-based official in advance of the arrival of the inspector; it is to be filled out and handed over when he reaches the mission, and forms the basis for a lengthy personal interview with each. As a confidentiality safeguard, the inspector destroys this document before he leaves the country..

The German inspector looks at logistics and a whole range of administrative issues, but his main focus is on substantive matters, like the level of staff; either cuts, or infrequently some additions, follow the visit. He also assesses the performance of the mission and its head. A copy of his report is shown to the HOM who has the right to offer comments that are considered along with the inspector's recommendations.

The system seems to work well, and is mirrored in the ways the other major countries carry out their own inspections. The US has a well staffed 'Inspectorate' and all embassies are visited once in two years. The UK, France, Russia and China have similar systems. Regardless of other methods of performance monitoring, such physical inspection is an essential tool to ensure that the country's diplomatic outposts located in far-flung regions operate on a uniform set of methods, and enforce standard regulations, in personnel and other matters. It should be added that inspections are different from financial audit, which is a special task handled in most systems by professional audit specialists drawn from outside the MFA (though it is sometimes combined with inspections).

AMBASSADOR'S INSTRUCTIONS

It is not surprising that the French, inheritors to the logic of Descartes, operate an elegant system of formal instructions for their ambassadors. On appointment to a new assignment, the envoy-designate carries out a customary round of meetings with foreign ministry officials and with the senior representative of the other official agencies that would be his dialogue partners. This is a standard practice in all countries (with some adding a set of visits to other cities and regions that have a major stake in that particular bilateral relationship). The outbound French envoy thereafter encounters most of them again at a plenary meeting with the Secretary General.[1] There he receives his 'instructions', a written directive prepared expressly for the time and the country of assignment, on the manner in which he is to discharge his mission, the objectives and the priorities. Six months later he comes back to the Secretary General with his 'plan of action' for fulfilling his instructions, plus a demand for additional resources, if this can be justified.

It is interesting that most other countries have not found it necessary to have such a formal system of issuing 'directives' to new envoys. For example, the Germans have not used this system. But two years back, they began a system for the new ambassador to attend a final pre-departure session chaired by the state secretary. Senior representatives from all the Foreign Office departments concerned with that country attend, and based on the dialogue, a briefing paper is prepared for the ambassador. He comes back in 6 months with his action plan. In contrast, UK leaves it to the envoy to set his personal goals, though this is naturally done in consultation with headquarters. There are other major powers that employ an annual system of forward planning. But one may argue that the annual plan is not the same as explicit 'instructions', and there is clear merit in the French system. (Example: At two of my missions, Mauritius and Germany, in complete ignorance of other systems, I attempted to write out my own instructions. It evoked mild interest from the Ministry of External Affairs in New Delhi, but was personally useful in setting out action priorities and points of reference during each assignment.)

ANNUAL PLANS

The US experimented with an annual planning cycle for missions since the 1970s and now has a system of 'Mission Program Plans' that are worked out jointly by the concerned bureau in the State Department and the mission. Resources are tied into the plan. UK also has a system of annual plans prepared by the ambassador, which have to integrate with the 'milestones' that are determined for each geographic region by the Foreign Office. New Zealand requires missions to plan two years ahead, in detail for the next one and in indicative terms for the subsequent year, and later carry out a self-assessment of targets accomplished. Singapore has a very similar system, but goes one better in delegating to missions a vast amount of flexibility in the use of its budget. While the mission obviously cannot change salaries and allowances, purchase of cars, furnishings, rent ceilings and local travel are all left to the mission's discretion, as long as it delivers on performance and meets the set targets.[2]

Of course, the audit system to monitor the way funds were actually utilized also remains, and this audit is part of an inescapable financial monitoring common to all countries. UK too gives to its missions wide discretion on the use of the allotted budget. (How much mission–headquarters correspondence would be avoided if such discretionary authority were more widespread, provided a parallel and strong system for preventing abuse also could be established?)

In many countries, ideas and practical experience in operating such annual plans have evolved in the past two decades. Whatever the format, the crux lies in articulating the 'targets'. Some performance goals are easy to set, like visits of delegations, exchanges of cultural activities, and even numbers of reports to be written and cities and constituencies to be covered. In service segments like consular work, and in dealing with business queries, again targets can be set in terms of response time, reduction in complaint levels and the like. In segments such as culture and education, visits by groups of artistes, or the number of inbound or outbound students, and the utilization of scholarships are the kind of goals that can be provided. Then there are areas where only an indicator can be used, because the outcome does not depend solely, or even principally, on the actions of the mission; trade growth, or investment inflow are good examples. But even for indicative purposes, these sectors can be included in the mission's objectives, since this provides a goal to work towards. Of course, in assessing performance at the end of the year, due allowance has to be made for the efforts it has deployed, and the factors beyond its control that have affected actual performance. Used well, it becomes a splendid guide and reminder for activities to be undertaken, and in addition serves as a self-monitoring tool. When targets are shared among missions within a region, the system also becomes a promoter of new ideas and an emulation device. On the other hand, if the annual planning system is applied without setting targets, one is left with an incomplete device that does not fully use its potential, nor deliver intended results.

PERFORMANCE METHODS

British experience with the use of corporate techniques is related with the efforts launched by former Prime Minister Margaret Thatcher to strengthen public accountability in public services. The result is that UK is ahead of most countries in disclosing the functioning of public services, goal setting for ministries, and the setting of performance milestones. EU countries are emulating the British experience. But as an article in *The Economist* indicated in May 2001, the pendulum is now swinging the other way; there is doubt over the method as it concentrates the work of government departments in areas where output is measurable, at the cost of other activities of long-term benefit that are hard to quantify. Such tension between different objectives and methods is perhaps inevitable as the way ideas move forward.

I used the annual target method at five assignments as head of mission (and had the satisfaction in 1980 of having these plans officially adopted as a standard device for the Indian system.) In the Indian system, the preparation of annual plans received serious attention for a while during the tenure of Prime Minister Rajiv Gandhi (1984–89). It seems he chanced upon the method and it caught his personal attention. Today the system continues but in a routine manner, with rather little input from headquarters. As long as resources are not tied into it, the plan lacks teeth, and tying resources involves sizable devolution of financial authority that most foreign ministries in developing countries are, as yet, unwilling to undertake.

OTHER METHODS

Singapore, a city-state that has developed cutting edge administrative concepts and has been an innovator in many fields, uses an interesting 'Monthly Performance Report' to supervise missions, and to improve efficiency. Each month, missions report headquarters on the main tasks performed, the dispatches sent by each official, and details of the new contacts established. This is an effective continuous monitoring device. (Performance bonuses are given to senior officials, even to ministers, ranging from one to three months emoluments.) This method is worthy of emulation by other countries.

Germany is currently experimenting with a system of cost-effectiveness control, mainly covering services, administration and logistics, but also intended to extend to substantive work areas. With typical thoroughness, some 400 parameters have been established covering a range of activities. Others in the EU and elsewhere will surely watch with interest the first application taking place currently.

The assessment of the performance of individuals is another field that is susceptible to contemporary management technique. The enforcement of objectivity, standardization and motivation all belong to the broad arena of human resource (HR) management, where many diplomatic services have not moved beyond routine or conventional methods. Improved performance appraisal for collective entities like the mission presupposes and requires better, transparent measurement of individual performance as well. But that takes us into other sectors of HR management that is a vast field in its own right, and one where diplomatic systems generally have much to learn from business management methodology.

MFA PERFORMANCE

UK's Foreign and Commonwealth Office has developed a remarkable system of public transparency in setting out a series of foreign policy 'objectives'. Thereafter, the performance of the entire diplomatic system is closely measured, in achieving the objectives. This is done through analyzing the extent to which 'public service agreement' (PSA) targets have been met. The narration provided in a recent public document (see Bibliography), of concrete targets, in terms of additional exports generated, savings made, 'customer satisfaction' achieved, and capacity added to missions, is quite revealing.

In many countries, an account of the performance of the foreign ministry and the entire diplomatic system is provided in an annual public document that is presented to the national parliament, part of a system that applies to all ministries. The style in such documents is descriptive, supported by selected statistics on the budget, the personnel and some other indicators. As countries move towards more open governance, and stronger public accountability, the kind of self-assessment provided in the UK document offers one interesting model for setting out national foreign policy goals, and the extent to which the diplomatic system has delivered on its targets and expectations.[3] Everywhere, parliaments, the media and opinion leaders in democratic countries have the responsibility for close scrutiny of the performance of ministries and of the government in general. Unfortunately this does not happen with sufficient rigor in many countries around the world, especially in the developing world, even while all the instruments for accountability and good governance exist on paper.

Some other instances in this mainly uncharted territory are given below:

- In the US, the 'mission program plans' are collated together to produce a plan for the territorial bureau that has relevant jurisdiction, and the system goes on cumulatively up the hierarchy, to produce also in theory an evaluation of the entire State Department. In practice this does not work well.
- In UK, the PSA target method applies to the subsidiaries of the Foreign and Commonwealth Office, like the 'commands' and lower bodies, and since it is a system that applies to all the departments (ministries), it has a degree of refinement. But at the end of the day, if we try and assess the foreign ministry as a whole, it is hardly comparable with another ministry, except in terms of some very general yardsticks.
- In Singapore the performance of all ministries is evaluated in terms of set administrative standards and budget performance.
- This is the point where the utility of benchmarking against other

MFAs becomes attractive. It has probably been attempted within the European Union, but the only concrete instance of deliberate comparison with other foreign ministries has been in Australia, as noted in the Introduction. More such actions are needed.

- Another way in which performance enhancement is indirectly tackled is via reform of the ministry. A study of the Italian Ministry of Foreign Affairs that is under publication in its English translation[4] notes that of the 18 countries studied, 16 have carried out changes in their organizational structure since 1991, and that for some it has meant altering the old model entirely.

Apart from the above, the methods of performance evaluation that are applied to embassies are not widely extended to the parent ministry. We may see in this the typical headquarters–subsidiary syndrome, that is, unwillingness of the ministry to turn the mirror on oneself, save when it happens as part of a system for the entire administrative machine in the country.

Developing countries have been slow in adapting some of the techniques covered above, which is a pity because this is one area of activity where it is possible to emulate others at minimal inconvenience, and to narrow the gap with other systems. Improved diplomacy management is a relatively 'low cost' activity, in money and other resource terms. It also offers an effective way for stronger international performance, reducing some of the North–South disparity. But in doing this one also has to move from a system of individuals and of personalized decisions to a rule of systems and regulations. And the will to make the shift is often lacking.

The deeper objective of mission and ministry performance enhancement is the optimization of the system, to encourage emulation of what the business world calls 'best practices', and to harness better the energy and initiative of all, the star performers and those at average levels. The challenge is to apply contemporary management techniques to the task of bilateral relationship building, and to diplomacy as a whole.

A final word. The end objective of performance appraisal in diplomacy is not primarily the measurement of efficiency or output of individuals, though that may well appear as the first result. Individual performance is addressed via methods of good human resource management, and that is a vast topic in its own right. Mission or unit performance measures should integrate well with individual assessment systems, in a manner that finds a correct balance between reward and sanction for the individual. In diplomatic services, junior officials face a relative scarcity of material reward, and much of the professional satisfaction too comes at a later stage of service. This makes it essential to build morale with a correct policy that identifies the individual's achievement, and encourages good unit performance as well.

QUESTIONS

1. Why is the performance appraisal important? What results can it produce optimally?
2. As a 'Foreign Service Inspector' what would you look for on an inspection visit?
3. What issues should be covered in the instructions given to an ambassador going out to take up a new assignment?
4. What would be the main points you would cover in a mission's annual plan that you may prepare for the foreign ministry?

REFERENCES

1. UK Foreign and Commonwealth Office, *FCO: Department Report on the Government Expenditure Plans 2000–01 to 2001–02.*
2. Rana, Kishan S., *Inside Diplomacy* (Manas Publications, New Delhi, 2000), Chapter 3, pp. 73–89, Chapter 19, pp. 342–50.
3 Andrea Cascone, Italian Ministry of Foreign Affairs, *Us and Them—The Ministries of Foreign Affairs of EU and G8 Member States: Comparing Structures* (DiploFoundation, Malta, 2001, under publication).

NOTES

1. The French Secretary General is unique. He rarely travels abroad, and his principal task is the management of the diplomatic system. His British counterpart, the FCO Permanent Under Secretary works in a like manner, as the Chairman of the Management Board. Other systems burden the top civil servant with a multitude of political tasks. The Indian Foreign Secretary is the reporting head of several functional divisions and also the senior official in charge of relations with some 10 key countries, the major powers and principal neighbors. This makes it impossible for him to engage in intensive management tasks. The US uses another method, entrusting foreign service management responsibility to a specially designated 'Director General of the Foreign Service'.
2. There was initial resistance by some ambassadors to accepting the system. They felt it gave them too much responsibility!
3. During a survey of diplomatic practices it was learnt that some other EU countries are now experimenting with ways to apply the British system of setting out goals for the foreign ministry, and giving a detailed public account of performance.
4. Andrea Cascone, Italian Ministry of Foreign Affairs, *Us and Them—The Ministries of Foreign Affairs of EU and G8 Member States: Comparing Structures* (DiploFoundation, Malta, 2001, under publication).

CONCLUSION

16

Future Trends

In the post-Cold War world building bilateral relationships is more important than ever before. Former Israeli Foreign Minister Abba Eban wrote some years back: 'For the rest of the 1990s and beyond, the diplomatic scene will be marked by tension, complexity and paradox.'[1] Is the matrix of power now permanently one-superpower dominated, with even Russia co-opting itself into NATO, as Presidents George W. Bush and Vladimir Putin seem to promise? Can a proud Russia with its history, accept such tutelage as a long-term condition? In economic and technological terms, will not the European Union, Japan, and even Russia and China demonstrate their own capacity as independent players? Will India be a hard outsider, or spoiler, against the cozy and overlapping P-5 and G-8 groups?

Whatever one's prognosis of the future world power structure, for most countries, building cooperative foreign relations around the world is crucial. This is motivated by economics, as well as the need for stability and security. On the one hand, regional free trade areas coexist with the global free trading system—despite some contradiction with WTO principles. Across the world we see a resurgence of regional diplomacy, driven by economic logic. On the other hand, regions and continents make a strong push for cooperative links across geographic limits, with states searching for sustainable anchors that may embed relationships firmly, creating networks for pursuing mutual advantage. This is the setting for a renaissance of bilateral diplomacy.

It is universally recognized that a country's diplomacy should directly serve national interest. Even rhetorically, ideology has faded from the jargon of international exchanges. Some wonder if the old instruments of diplomacy are relevant any longer, particularly the resident mission, headed by the ambassador in all his formal trappings, accompanied by a phalanx of officials in elaborate hierarchical order. Many also ask: does even the foreign ministry have a substantive or policy-shaping role at a time when heads of state and government carry out their own direct foreign contacts, sometimes without reference to the diplomatic apparatus? To compound matters, different ministries and official agencies are equally engaged in their own external relationships. Has this made the entire system of diplomacy irrelevant? We might look at Europe where unification among the 15 members has created the most advanced political integration that the world has seen.

THE EUROPEAN UNION

The progressive pooling of sovereignty that has been taking place over the past three decades in the EU encompasses foreign affairs. For students of diplomacy, the EU offers a unique laboratory for observation. What shape do the Europeans expect for the diplomatic apparatus in their dealings with each other? Are EU embassies needed any more? A facile prediction was made some years back that the bilateral embassies of the EU member states, in each other's capitals, would be reduced to the role of hotel-arrangers and airport greeters. What is the reality?

- Some of the functions of embassies have indeed withered away, principally to negotiate agreements among member-states. That task is performed in Brussels, since such accords now cover all the EU members, and becomes the responsibility of the European Commission and the EU Council of Ministers, working directly with foreign ministries and other ministries, via the permanent missions in Brussels.

- Sometimes the embassies in member capitals are even bypassed by home-based MFA officials engaging themselves in direct dialogue with the local foreign ministry and the offices of the heads of state and government. In practice, this happens as a matter of convenience or urgency, and not out of deliberate intent to leave out the embassy. But despite such aberration, the embassy remains at the heart of the management of country relationships. The best information source on the country is one's embassy in that capital, offering 'real time' data, plus a comprehensive overview of the total scene.
- The typical EU embassy remains actively engaged in economic promotion, especially exports and the mobilization of investments for the home country. The emergence of regions as active sub-national and even trans-national investment destinations complicates the task, and gives even greater coordination responsibility to the embassy. As long as the nation-state remains the EU base unit, these economic imperatives require an implementing field agency, i.e. the resident embassy.
- The embassy has its fingers on the pulse of the host country, using its intensive knowledge of local constituencies, official and non-official. No one at home has the same capacity to act as the 'relationship manager' for that particular country.
- The embassy is particularly valuable in identifying for the home capital the second echelon of leadership, and guiding political and other contacts to be cultivated for the future.

In 2000, the German Foreign Office commissioned a senior diplomat to study the role of the EU embassy and the resulting 'Paschke Report' is now a public document,[2] undergoing debate in the government and the German parliament. It is also under close study in other capitals. Paschke's conclusions are summarized in the above listing of points, that there will remain a need for the embassy in the foreseeable future, but its tasks have both expanded and changed.

Thus within and outside the EU, the bilateral embassy remains a vigorous institution. It appears that for the present, 'Common Foreign and Security Policy' (CFSP) works well only on matters of relatively secondary interest, and on issues of principle where there is unanimity of view, because achieving consensus on these is relatively less complicated. An expanded EU, in which as many as ten or twelve new members from central, east and southern Europe, with strong cultural differences, will surely find it even harder to a reach common agreement on external issues.

The EU's organizational moves to establish a CFSP have expanded in pragmatic fashion. An elaborate mechanism for consultation among members, encompassing the foreign ministers, the permanent or state secretaries, the political directors, and even the heads of the territorial directorates has long existed, each of whom meet at least once a month at their separate levels. For the past ten years there has also been a system of rapid consultation via secure fax and intranet links, for decision on foreign affairs issues, called the 'Coreper' process. In the capitals of non-member states, the EU ambassadors act collectively on an expanding range of issues. They even write joint reports addressed to the foreign ministries in different EU capitals. Efforts to establish 'joint' embassies have so far floundered in the absence of an enabling legal mechanism, but Germany has moved ahead with legislation that would permit this, and others will follow shortly. In the meantime, the formula of 'co-location' of embassies is being followed at several places, for groups of EU embassies to share a common diplomatic compound or building, and share in the services.[3]

Some would argue that despite CFSP goals, major and minor EU members are unlikely to give away rights to independent judgment on important external issues. The designation in 2000 of an 'EU Foreign Policy Chief', former NATO Secretary General Javier Solana, is another joint step forward in a practical way. The title is clumsy and there is overlap with the European Commission's Commissioner for External Affairs (currently the dynamic Chris Patten). Nor have EU foreign ministries shown a willingness to relinquish their authority to these EU agencies. But despite this, the envelope of joint action is expanding, as for example, in the successor states to former Yugoslavia.

THE RESIDENT EMBASSY

In the case of countries around the world that have no plans for unification of the kind undertaken by the EU, the case for the resident embassy is as strong, even if not all of them have fully exploited the potential for using the resident embassy for bilateral relationship building. In sum, the embassy is vital because:

a) Only the resident mission can carry out the work of promotion and outreach to the fullest extent. A detailed narration of these major responsibilities has been given earlier.
b) Building personal trust with individuals who are important in relation building is not possible through any method other than direct and sustained cultivation. This is one serious limitation of the method of the 'non-resident' envoy that some countries use, as well as the technique of 'concurrent accreditation' (where the embassy covers one or more neighboring countries from one capital). The same is true of the notion of the 'virtual' embassy, which exists as a concept, but has not yet been put into practice anywhere. These techniques are supplementary methods, used when it is not possible to have a resident embassy, often for financial reasons.
c) A resident embassy is able to identify upcoming personalities and build relationships with them, using such windows of opportunity that may come up. This kind of 'talent-spotting' and contact building with the second echelon of leadership is realistically possible only by the resident mission.

d) Diplomacy is often a matter of making connections, between what may appear to be unconnected issues in foreign relationships. These are also called 'trade-offs'—doing one thing on the condition that the other side will do something else that is on one's own wish list. The breadth and complexity of issues that are handled today by diplomats increases the potential for such interconnections. While the resident embassy is not the only agency that can identify or pursue such interconnections, being on the spot focuses the diplomat much better in handling this work.

e) For any country, the nearest approximation of the total picture of the relationship with any country is visible only from the resident embassy. The main reason for this is the multiplicity of home-based actors. Unlike the old days when the foreign ministry exclusively handled external contacts, today an array of state agencies (ministries and other official agencies), and non-state entities (apex chambers of commerce, universities and think tanks, and even the media) are engaged in direct contact with foreign counterparts. No foreign ministry, even with an array of desk-officers concentrating exclusively on a single country, can match the embassy in its perspective, knowledge and understanding on all that is going on. There may be things that escape even a vigilant embassy, but usually not for long. And since in practice the hard-pressed desk-officer at headquarters has usually more than the tracking of a single country on his mind, he does not compete with the embassy in following local developments in the particular foreign country.

A consequence is that there has been a *de facto* empowerment of the embassy, as the 'relationship manager' for the country of location. Obviously this does not give it more power than headquarters, or any form of 'independence' of action. But it gains in responsibility for keeping under scrutiny the totality of the relationship with the country of assignment, and alerting headquarters to any impending problems or opportunities. Further, the same modern and instant communications that place it under the full direction of headquarters, also give it the real capacity to advise the headquarters on a constant basis on what needs to be done, and in effect write, or at least draft, its own instructions. When the pressure of international events demand, it also has a latent power to act on its own authority, while simultaneously informing headquarters of this action and seeking further instructions. All this places the embassy in the cockpit, handling the controls directly.

Are diplomatic systems willing to accept this larger role for the bilateral embassy, and give it the support it needs to perform at its full capacity? One does not know, because evolving concepts have first to be digested. High performers, ambassadors and others, will always give their best and do well regardless of systems. The diplomatic machinery faces the challenge of adapting systems in the situation described above, in a way that gets the maximum number of its personnel to perform to the available capacity. That is to say, optimization of the entire system is the requirement in each country.

MULTILATERAL AND REGIONAL DIPLOMACY

Countries engage intensely in multilateral diplomacy, because of a proliferation in the subjects in international dialogue, which is one feature of the globalization process. With enhanced interdependence among countries, it is natural that there should be accelerated consultation, and efforts to find joint solutions. One example is the world financial system, which almost has a life of its own, and is even beyond the capacity of the richest nations to fully control. For smaller countries, external currency fluctuations represent events that they cannot influence. The institution of summitry has also grown, with heads of state and government traveling abroad as never before, to regional, inter-regional, global and ad hoc gatherings. Not all of the summits are productive. A case in point was the Millennium Summit held at the UN Headquarters from September 6 to 8, 2000. That unprecedented assembly of heads, also used an occasion for numerous bilateral and group encounters, adopted a 'Millennium Declaration', aimed at infusing new impetus into international cooperation for resolving issues, ranging from UN reform to poverty eradication across the globe. But for all the rhetoric and good intentions, it would be hard to argue that it produced any lasting impact.

It is no one's case that multilateral diplomacy is irrelevant. There are galaxies of issues that can be tackled only through that medium. But realism demands that we understand both the promise and the limits of multilateralism. It is also evident that regional cooperation is the building block for strong multilateral action.

Regional diplomacy has a demonstrated track record. Clusters of neighbors, within sub-regions and regions have come together today for active relationship building. Besides the EU, there are ASEAN and MERCOSUR, in South-East Asia and Latin America respectively, that have emerged as successful groups attracting new membership, and tackling deep pockets of opportunity for joint benefit. NAFTA and APEC are other good models, the latter especially important as it traverses several regions to create novel cooperative alliances. There are other regional projects whose promise is as yet unrealized, like the Indian Ocean group IOR-ARC that encompasses some 15 littoral countries in an arc stretching from South Africa to Australia, and BIMST-EC that covers Bangladesh, India, Myanmar, Sri Lanka and Thailand. (In South Asia, SAARC is an example of a regional group that is unable to move forward because of internal tension.) Then there are the 'growth triangles' and 'quadrangles' that aim at cooperation among sub-national entities of large countries. Examples: the growth clusters of Singapore, and parts of neighboring Indonesia, Brunei and Malaysia, and the one covering the Yunnan region of China, Laos and Thailand. In all these different groups, the driving force is the economic advantage that accrues to all participants on a 'non zero-sum' basis. SADC in southern Africa is more ambitious and holds out the promise of economic integration, even if initial performance has fallen short of expectation.

Good bilateral relationships are the building blocks of regional and multilateral diplomacy. Of course, they are not a precondition. Nations that do not have much direct interaction can still cooperate at multilateral conferences and within regional bodies. There are also good instances where regional groups have facilitated bridge building among rival countries. (Example: At its foundation in 1967, the first task of ASEAN was to ease bilateral tension and territorial disputes among members; today it seems inconceivable that such problems can recur among them.) Invariably, good bilateral links serve as a solid foundation for the other forms of cooperation. Further, diversified bilateral cooperation in concrete areas like trade, also creates a mutual obligation to work together at international levels.

GLOBALIZATION

Globalization can be defined as an accelerated process of interdependence that the world has witnessed in the past decade, as a result of the complex and interlocking interaction of economic, financial, technological and other factors that have impacted on most countries around the world. It is an autonomous process that has offered opportunity as well as created new threats. Rich countries have derived considerable advantage from it, through expansion in trade, international investments and the opening up of many economies to liberal market forces. Developing nations have felt an adverse impact in exports and market access, financial flows, plus technology handicaps. Globalization has widened disparities between the rich and the poor, but small and mid-sized countries that are alert and innovative, and have put in place the right policies, have been able to take advantage of the opportunities that it has thrown up. Example: The Asian tiger economies that have overcome the turmoil of the 1997–98 crisis and moved back to high growth.

The World Trade Organization (WTO) has become a symbol of the globalization process in trade and in related economic areas. The vast majority of countries support the principle of relatively free trade that is at the foundation of WTO, though each country has its own definition of the areas where it wants to retain national economic controls. Developing countries feel threatened by the wide agenda of WTO to issues like investment conditions, intellectual property rights and environmental standards, particularly because they have seen little benefit from global economic expansion so far. Added to that there is the new worry that the world may be moving towards recession, jeopardizing further even the notional gains.

Diplomacy cannot directly mitigate the harmful consequences of globalization on developing countries, many of which face harsh competition, difficulties in foreign markets, and unbalanced terms of trade. But diplomacy can act to support sound policies at home with stronger effort to assist domestic exporters in reaching out to new markets, and in mobilizing FDI through innovative marketing. At the end of the day, it is the product that sells, and no amount of savvy country promotion, or cultural diplomacy, can overcome defects that are inherent in the product itself. Thus it is for the country, large or small, to get its act together and to reach out to an incessantly globalizing world with improved competitiveness at home. Equally vital is the role of the government in positioning the economy in the best way, through domestic regulations that optimize the nation's assets, and implement sound socio-economic policies such as improved funding for education, human resource development, infrastructure investments and the like.

The foreign affairs establishment also has the task to portray the external scene in realistic terms, looking to threats as well as opportunities. Given the involvement of non-state constituents in this sector, one may view this role as that of honest domestic advocacy, and of public diplomacy in the wider sense of the term.

INTERNATIONAL LAW AND SOVEREIGNTY

International law has moved to the center stage in foreign affairs, particularly after the end of the Cold War. A number of new international covenants have been signed that range from restricting the use of mines in warfare, to the banning of torture methods, to the cooperative international action against money laundering. The UN now has a Commissioner for Human Rights. Actions interpreted by external powers as 'war crimes' in the conflict in former Yugoslavia, are under criminal juridical investigation and legal cases by a UN War Crimes Tribunal at The Hague. The establishment of an international criminal court, an initiative undertaken by Canada, seemed closer to reality. In the final year of the Clinton administration, the US dropped its earlier objections and joined the move, but after taking office in January 2001, the Bush administration has gone back and signaled its reservations. This expansion in international law enhances the engagement among nations, and the role of diplomacy.

Following its egregious attack on Kuwait in 1990, Iraq faced the widest UN-sponsored coalition that the world has seen, and in 1991 suffered a crushing defeat under a multinational force that included some 540,000 US troops. But subsequent conflicts, including the 1998 Kosovo War against Serbia showed that UN backing for peace-making is not easy to achieve, and the US-led NATO coalition in this war was obliged to act outside the UN mandate. Several other international incidents have also shown the fragility of the will of the international community when it comes to peace-making activities, mainly because countries have divergent interests and expectations.

Where does this leave the nation-state? The UN Charter is ambivalent. It sets out high moral standards of a universal character, but also pays lip service to state sovereignty. Article 2 Section 7 reads:

> Nothing contained in the present Charter shall authorize the UN to intervene in matters that are entirely within the domestic jurisdiction of any state or shall require Members to submit such matters to settlement under the present Charter.

This provision has been overwhelmed by the evolution of events. The concept of absolute national sovereignty no longer exists, and the range of issues on which an amorphous 'international community' can interfere in what would have earlier been regarded as the internal affairs of a country, is wider than ever before. Human rights, treatment of minorities, religious and other freedoms are just some of the subjects on which nations face external demands, within the UN, and from coalitions of countries such as the EU, as well as individual nations. There are also the increasingly active NGOs that create their own coalitions and exert pressure on governments and international agencies. Limitation on sovereignty also comes from international accords under which countries have willingly transferred some authority to collective entities, be it to regional organizations or to world bodies like WTO. The key issue is not that sovereignty is being 'lost' to other states. Rather, on an expanding range of issues, nations cannot determine action on their own and must bargain with one another. There remain many gray areas where states and the non-state actors contest jurisdiction. An example: at the UN conference on racism held in Durban in August 2001, a number of Indian activists and NGOs argued that continuing caste discrimination (despite strong constitutional and legal provisions outlawing it, and long-standing policies of affirmative action), amounted to a form of racial discrimination. The Indian government opposed this, and was eventually able to get the conference to exclude such references, but there was sharp debate within India over whether this had been the correct approach to a real problem. The incident showed how it is no longer possible to argue that internal issues should not be subject to international scrutiny.[4]

There are other dimensions to the debate. After the end of the Cold War, democracy, good governance, and even the market economy system, are presented as absolute universal values. They are used as yardsticks—primarily by Western countries—for extending political support, bilateral economic assistance, trade concessions, and other facilities. But for all the posturing by the West on these themes, the application of these standards is selective and subjective. Countries such as the US that publish annual global reviews of human rights, and of religious freedoms, would deny this strenuously. Non-Western countries find their internal actions under greater scrutiny than ever before. These trends also enhance the importance of building and maintaining good bilateral relationships around the world, as a kind of safety net or support web of international friendships.

After the September 2001 terrorist outrages, an international coalition led by the US, against all forms of terrorism has apparently imposed its will in Afghanistan. Already there are signs that this will re-prioritize the other international concerns. Ruthless terrorism is amorphous and hydra-headed. Very rightly, the US President warns against an excess of elation over the first gains in ousting the Taliban from Kabul, and warns repeatedly of a long struggle against terrorism. But in addition to economic aid for and the rebuilding of Afghanistan, there is the wider issue of the physical and political conditions that breed terrorism. India's experience with its internal fight against terrorism has been that the problem has to be 'internalized' and turned from armed battle to political struggle. Among other things, the counter to Islamic fundamentalism is an improvement of the situation in West Asia, and moving the Palestinians from a sense of hopelessness to a participation in the political process.

DEVELOPING COUNTRIES

We need to reshape international relations, moving the North and the South from the confrontation of the past, and the benign neglect that is the hallmark of the present time. New working formulas are required, founded on real mutual understanding and acknowledgement by each side of the responsibility that falls on itself. Developing countries are increasingly differentiated among themselves, and some question if the concept of the South is valid any longer. Despite large variation in rates of economic growth, technology mastery and deployment of human resource talent between the 120 plus countries that fall in this category, they retain common characteristics. Many of them are setting their own houses in order; the realization has dawned that the era of free lunch handouts is over. Some of them need to move from past notions of the over-extended state and socialism, to pragmatic policies that develop own human resources to the fullest. Developing countries also need to refocus the state system to create the regulatory framework and public policy that is best suited to the circumstances of each, while permitting the flowering of individual and social initiative and entrepreneurship. Rich states have self-interest in helping them to higher prosperity, the best guarantee for both peace and security.

In their external relations, diplomacy is one field where countries of the South can level the playing field through autonomous action, carrying out rectification of own machinery as well as optimization, creating rational systems that deliver results. This would sharpen the instruments with which foreign policy is implemented and delivered. It would also constitute an act of improving the governance process.

Justin Robertson's study *Foreign Ministries in Developing Countries and Emerging Market Economies* notes that in most of the states examined, the challenge of integrating economic work with diplomacy had been well met, and that the MFA was also adapting to more collegial relations with other ministries and agencies. In order to handle the challenges outlined above, the MFA and its diplomatic system are called upon to adapt much further and faster. I have argued that improved mastery of the techniques of bilateral diplomacy leads directly to more effective projection of the country's external interests.

Bilateral diplomacy offers greater potential and is more necessary than ever before. It has evolved, as all things change and adapt to the times and circumstances. In an interdependent world, nations need one another as never before. All are subject to external forces. The threats faced are less direct and tangible than in the past.

Economic security, currency stability, external environmental hazard, and technology independence are real new issues that affect external relationships. There are also opportunities and gains to be made from stronger external cooperation. This calls for greater attention to the techniques for building bilateral relationships, which are the basic unit in external affairs.

One scholar, Richard Langhorne has written: 'Diplomacy has become a much more public, complicated and fascinating piece of kinetic art'. The situation demands that the methods of diplomacy, as also the training of diplomats, adapt to the needs and opportunities of the time.

QUESTIONS

1. How has diplomacy changed in the post-Cold War era?
2. What are the typical functions of an EU embassy in the capital of another EU country?
3. Why is the resident embassy relevant even in the current age?
4. What changes have taken place in the concept of sovereignty in current times?
5. Why do non-state entities and public opinion now play a greater role in international affairs?

REFERENCES

1. Eban, Abba, *Diplomacy for the New Century* (Yale University Press, New Haven, 1998).
2. Hocking, Brian, *Catalytic Diplomacy* (article in *Innovation in Diplomacy*, ed. Jan Mellissen), (Macmillan, London, 1999).

NOTES

1. Abba Eban, *Diplomacy for the New Century* (Yale University Press, New Haven, 1998).
2. The full text of the 32-page Paschke Report, in German is available

on the website of the German Foreign Office (www.auswaertiges-amt.de).

3. There has been difficulty, for instance, in establishing a unified chancery base in Abuja, the new Nigerian capital, and some half of the EU embassies that considered joining this initiative have elected for their own premises. At the end of 2001, Germany is the only EU member that has a legal authority for joint embassies in the full sense of the word; the others are working on the legal and constitutional issues.
4. In the end, the Indian delegation was able to avoid direct reference to the caste issue in the conference declaration, where this issue was overwhelmed by the much sharper debate over the Zionism issue.

Abbreviations

APEC	Asia Pacific Economic Cooperation Forum
ARF	ASEAN Regional Forum
ASEAN	Association of South East Asian Nations
B2B	business to business
BATNA	best alternative to a negotiated solution
BIMST-EC	Bangladesh-India-Myanmar-Sri Lanka-Thailand Economic Cooperation
CEO	Chief Executive Officer
CFSP	Common Foreign and Security Policy (of EU)
CIA	Central Intelligence Agency
CTBT	Comprehensive Test Ban Treaty
DCM	Deputy Chief of Mission
DRC	Democratic Republic of Congo
ECOWAS	Economic Organization of West African States
EU	European Union
FDI	Foreign Direct Investment
G-77	Group of 77 (grouping of developing countries)

G-8	Group of 8 (group of the rich states, earlier G-7, plus Russia)
HOM	Head of Mission
HR	human resources
IAEA	International Atomic Energy Agency
IMF	International Monetary Fund
IOR–ARC	Indian Ocean Rim Association for Regional Cooperation
MERCOSUR	Mercado Común del Sur (a common market covering Argentina, Brazil, Paraguay and Uruguay, plus Bolivia and Chile as associate members)
JC	Joint Commissions
MFA	Ministry of Foreign Affairs
NAFTA	North American Free Trade Area
NATO	North Atlantic Treaty Organization
NGOs	Non-Governmental Organizations
NPT	Non Proliferation Treaty
OAU	Organization of African Unity (renamed in 2001 as the 'African Union', AU, though the term has yet to gain wide currency)
ODA	official development aid
P-5	the five permanent members of the UN Security Council
PB	positional bargaining
PN	principled negotiation
SAARC	South Asian Association of Regional Cooperation
SADC	Southern Africa Development Cooperation
UN	United Nations
UNIDO	United Nations Industrial Development Organization
USP	unique selling proposition

Select Bibliography

Barston, R.P., *Modern Diplomacy*, 2nd edition, (Longman, London, 1997).

Berridge, G.R., *Diplomacy: Theory and Practice*, 2nd edition, (Palgrave, London, 2002).

Berridge, G.R. and James, Alan, *A Dictionary of Diplomacy* (Palgrave, London, 2001).

Cahill, Kevin M., *Preventive Diplomacy: Stopping Wars Before they Start* (Routledge, New York, 2000).

Cascone, Andrea, Italian Ministry of Foreign Affairs, *Comparing Diplomatic Services: Structures, Networks and Resources of the Ministries of Foreign Affairs of EU and G8 Member States: Comparing Structures* (DiploFoundation, Malta, 2001, under publication).

Cohen, Raymond, *The Theater of Power: The Art of Diplomatic Signaling* (Longman, London, 1987).

______, *Negotiating Across Cultures* (US Institute of Peace, Washington DC, 1991).

Cooper, Andrew F, ed., *Niche Diplomacy: Middle Powers After the Cold War* (Macmillan, Basingstoke, 1997).

Craig, Gordon A, and George, Alexander L, *Force and Statecraft: Diplomatic Problems of Our Times*, 3rd edition, (Oxford University, New York, 1995).

Denza, Eileen, *Diplomatic Law: A Commentary on the Vienna Convention on Diplomatic Relations* (Clarendon Press, Oxford, 1998).

Eban, Abba, *The New Diplomacy* (Weidenfeld and Nicolson, London, 1988).

———, *Diplomacy for the New Century* (New Haven, Yale University Press, 1998).

Evans, Peter B., Jacobson, Harold K., Putnam, and Robert D., eds, *Double-Edged Diplomacy* (University of California Press, Berkeley, 1993).

FCO—*Department Report on the Government Expenditure Plans, 2000–01 to 2001–01* (HM Stationery Office, London, April 2000).

Fisher, Roger, *Beyond Machiavelli: Tools For Coping With Conflict* (Penguin, London, 1996).

Fisher, Roger and Ury, William, *Getting to Yes: Negotiating Agreements Without Giving In* (Hutchinson, London, 1981).

Gotlieb, Alan, *I'll be with you in a Minute Mr. Ambassador: The Education of a Canadian Diplomat in Washington* (London, Routledge, 1995).

Haass, Richard and O'Sullivan, Meghan, *Honey and Vinegar: Incentives, Sanctions and Foreign Policy* (Brookings Institution, Washington DC, 2000).

Hamilton, Keith and Langhorne, Robert, *The Practice of Diplomacy: Its Evolution, Theory and Administration* (London, Routledge, 1995).

Herz, Martin F., ed., *The Modern Ambassador: The Challenge and the Search* (Institute for the Study of Diplomacy, Georgetown University, Washington DC, 1983).

Hocking, Brian, ed., *Foreign Ministries: Change and Adaptation* (Macmillan, London, 1999).

———, *Diplomacy of Image and Memory: Swiss Bankers and Nazi Gold* (Diplomatic Studies Program Discussion Paper No. 64, University of Leicester, April 2000).

Kurbalija, Jovan, *Knowledge and Diplomacy* (Mediterranean Academy of Diplomatic Studies, Malta, 1999).

Marshall, Peter, *Positive Diplomacy* (Macmillan, Basingstoke, 1997).

Melissen, Jan, ed., *Innovation in Diplomatic Practice* (Macmillan, London, 1999).

Rana, Kishan S., *Inside Diplomacy* (Manas, New Delhi, 2000).

Robertson, Justin, ed., *Foreign Ministries in Developing Countries and Emerging Market Economies* (Halifax, International Insights: Dalhousie Journal of International Affairs, Volume 14, Summer, 1998).

Sharp, Paul, *Making Sense of Citizen Diplomats* (Center for the Study of Diplomacy, Leicester, 2001).

Ure, John, *Diplomatic Bag* (London, John Murray, 1994).

Index